CRISIS OF CONTROL
HOW ARTIFICIAL SUPERINTELLIGENCES
MAY DESTROY OR SAVE THE HUMAN RACE

BOOK ONE OF THE **HUMAN CUSP SERIES**

PETER J. SCOTT

Nitrosyncretic Press   nitrosyncretic press   Hartford, Connecticut

For Alana and Bless. May you grow up in a world that is friendly.

Nitrosyncretic Press
PO Box 462645
Aurora, Colorado 80013
www.nitrosyncretic.com

www.humancusp.com

First Edition
First Printing, 20 February 2017
[Corrections September 2018]
Printed in the United States of America

ISBN: 0-9679873-9 (softcover)

Preface

We face a threat that stretches the imagination. I'll draw an analogy to a familiar Hollywood scenario. Imagine this: You have a friend who is an astronomer, a very capable and independently wealthy astronomer[*] with a very large telescope. One day she approaches, biting her lip and glancing nervously over her shoulder. She has made a discovery: Out past the edge of our Solar System she has found a new asteroid, and plotted its orbit. In fifteen years that orbit will take it near the Earth; so close, in fact, that there is a one in ten chance that it will hit the Earth. And this asteroid is the same size as the one that smashed into the Earth at seven miles a second at the end of the Cretaceous period, creating the Chicxulub impact crater.[†] It also created a planet-wide winter that wiped out every animal larger than a hamster,[‡] causing the extinction of the dinosaurs and paving the way for the rise of a new class of creature: mammals. Including everyone's favorite: *homo sapiens,* aka humans.[§]

---

[*] Yes, that is an oxymoron.

[†] The asteroid that hit the Yucatán peninsula created a crater centered approximately on the town of Chicxulub. There are other names for this event, but this one gives you the opportunity to show people you can pronounce *Chicxulub*: CHICK-shoe-lube.

[‡] Not that hamsters existed at the time. Thanks solely to this event they were given the room to evolve.

[§] All this from a rock about six miles across. For your friend to see it out past the orbit of Pluto... let's just say that she has an *exceptional* telescope. Play along here.

Your dilemma: What do you do with this news? (You may notice a serious resemblance to the plot of the 1998 movie *Deep Impact*.) Do you:

- ► Run around drawing as much attention as possible to this impending doom.

- ► Try to do something to avert the disaster (in movies, this generally involves NASA, nuclear bombs, and large plot holes).

- ► Acquire land in Montana, dig a bunker for your family, and train them in hydroponic food production and shooting looters.

The more you understand where we're heading, the more realistic those choices may appear. There is no asteroid, but there *is* a very different kind of threat that is equally capable of extinguishing the human race. Instead of the date being fixed but the event being uncertain, it's the other way around: Like a huge earthquake on the San Andreas Fault, the event—although not necessarily extinction—is inevitable but its timing is unknown.

I can't afford to build a bunker in Montana and I'm a lousy shot. So I'm going for doors number one and two by publicizing the threat and coalescing group thinking and action around it.

Here's a twist on the doomsday narrative though: If we can survive this threat, we will likely move into a future so rosy as to dazzle the most Pollyanna of optimists and herald the arrival of a utopian era to put any '60s hippie Aquarian vision to shame.

How can humanity be poised on a cusp between two such polar opposite outcomes?

What This Book Is About

> *We have developed speed, but we have shut ourselves in. Machinery that gives abundance has left us in want. Our knowledge has made us cynical. Our cleverness, hard and unkind. We think too much and feel too little. More than machinery we need humanity. More than cleverness we need kindness and gentleness. Without these qualities, life will be violent and all will be lost.*
>
> — Charlie Chaplin, *The Great Dictator*

Here's the all-too-brief summary of the threat: Exponential advances in technology will bring the ability to construct weapons of mass destruction within common reach and also lead to the creation of artificial intelligences capable of superhuman reasoning who may decide to eliminate us. Our hope for survival lies in shaping a symbiosis with those machine intelligences to propel the human race to a new plane of evolution where mental diseases that would imperil our existence are reduced to insignificance.

Pure science fiction, right? Couldn't possibly have any relation to reality in our lifetimes, right?

What if it were less than 20 years away?

The Sections of This Book

Chapter 1 starts with a fictional narrative of a possible future drawn within the parameters of the scenarios this book will explore. I'll then discuss the perils of predicting the future and look at the track record of the human race in trying to do that. I'll contrast the conflicting utopian *vs* dystopian predictions peppering mainstream consciousness and dissect their implications.

Then I'll review the history of social upheavals that have earned the label of "revolution" and plot our current location on the trajectory of a brand-new revolution that currently leaves us caught between the promise of new technology and its curse in automating almost all of what's left of middle class jobs. I'll give an unsettlingly calculated justification for asserting that the future of the entire human race is in jeopardy; then explore the promise of artificial intelligence and its attendant risks. I'll draw the conclusions about how the human race must evolve to survive. Finally, I'll discuss the timeframes that we need to act within and what we—yes, including you—can do next.

What This Book Is Not About

There are no easy answers in this book. If you want to know whether the future is bright or bleak, the answer is, "It depends." If you want to know whether the human race will survive or not, the answer is, "It depends." If you want to know whether there's still time for us to change course to guarantee survival, I have no reassurances for you. My crystal ball is a bit cracked and only lets me see as far as the next bend in the road, not around it. This book is for people who can live with ambiguity and manage fear.

Neither is this an academic treatise. You can find these issues discussed in a number of learned forums but generally looking only at a narrow facet of the overall issue and not connected to the impact or the urgency of the situation. I have attempted to pull together a gestalt view that gives a useful and complete picture, so that this message can reach a broad audience.

Why Me?

Who do I think I am to weigh in on something so pivotal, that should be the exclusive domain of Ivy League think tanks and name brand scientists? The soul-baring reason is that this is a purpose that found me. I didn't go looking for it. It demanded to be given a voice. And perhaps the reason that it chose me is that I am positioned in a very slender intersection of two fields that have not previously had reason to become acquainted: cybernetic technology and personal development. I'll say more in a later chapter, but I see how each of these fields needs the other for our survival, and I also see how almost no one in those fields realizes that.

I was growing frustrated every time I read an analysis of our possible future because I could see something vital left out. Rather than continue ranting against other people's attempts and only annoying my wife I decided it was time to put my own skin in the game.

But most of all: I have two children: daughters aged three and seven. I want them to grow up in a world where they have at least as much freedom to pursue happiness and raise families of their own as I did. I see a likelihood that they won't get that, so I will give everything I have to change that. Any parent would understand. Sticking my neck out and making a fool of myself are small prices to pay when those are the stakes.

This Is the First Step

This is only an introduction to the topic. The field of AI and existential risk is evolving so fast that there will be more books in this series exploring the topic from a variety of angles.

This book's title is inspired by James Beniger. In his book *The Control Revolution: Technological and Economic Origins of the Information Society,* the University of Southern California professor argues that the information age was catalyzed by the explosive growth of manufacturing during the Industrial Revolution. This created a need to manage that growth that could only be supplied by information technology that did not yet exist. My complementary view is that we are facing another crisis of control caused by explosive growth in information technology, thereby provoking another revolution.

––––––––

Sometimes the swiftest messenger of a holistic viewpoint can be fiction, for its ability to place us in the moment and hopscotch over mundane exposition. Ten years from now we are likely to be bumping against the edge of the crisis this book is about. What could the world look like at that time, from the perspective of a few ordinary people? Understanding that this is just playful speculation, let's visit a possible future....

1
A May-Be Future

San Francisco | February 12, 2027

Fridays no longer held the same allure. He couldn't gleefully think *TGIF* when every day was a day without work. He knew it was irrational, but Ryan Dixon always felt a stab of guilt whenever a lawdrone passed overhead, as though they were looking extra closely at the unemployed. He wanted to cover his face with its pinched features but never knew whether that just earned you more attention. And right now he very much did not want attention.

The whirring black and white lozenge continued skimming down California Street while Ryan slid into a fast food noodle house that still followed the stereotypical pun naming convention: *Chop-Chop Suey.* Claire was poised over a couple of steaming bowls in the shadows near the dingy restroom, chestnut hair tumbling over bare shoulders. The sight of her often made him catch his breath; never more so than today.

"If the Y-virus gets past L.A. I reckon all the MSG in this place will kill it," she said by way of greeting, pushing a bowl towards him. Computer nerds didn't do small talk the same way as everyone else.

"They're up to Y now?" he asked, slurping the miso soup indelicately. "Where are you at in your shots?"

"I got the vaccination for T-7 yesterday. That's all they have so far."

Ryan nodded grimly and could think of nothing to say. He had gotten inoculated up to the Q strain before he'd lost his job and his extended medical coverage. Protection against bioterrorism was considered an optional luxury in the state assigned risk medical plan. He *had* to move, get out of the population center, self-quarantine. But she didn't. She still had a job, because unlike him, she had never been a coder. She specialized in requirements translation for artificial intelligences. A speaker-to-machines, the new priesthood of technology.

She misread the angst that had flitted over his face. "You're not getting cold feet, are you? We've been planning this since Christmas. We can't stay here. We're no use to Jen if we get sick too."

"What? No, *I'm* not—I mean—yes, of course. I'm ready," he blustered, caught off-guard. "Emmy was happy to let go of his pick-up. Even happier to take cash for it. Everything's in the back." He hated that she'd reminded him about their friend in her hospital bed, fighting the as-yet unknown effects of the W strain.

"Then let's zip," she said. He wiped his mouth in haste and pushed back his chair. She laid a hand on his arm and smiled.

"I think you can finish your soup first."

———

The economy had been slammed by a double whammy, like a pedestrian hit by a car and then run over by a bus while lying bleeding in the street. A year earlier, the first cybernetic software developers had arrived in industry: artificial intelligences that could understand natural language descriptions of problems and write the computer programs that would solve them. At first, they were parlor tricks, raw material for gee-whiz conference keynotes. They required specialized instruction free from ambiguity and contradiction.

Coders everywhere watched the demonstrations and smirked; the hard part of their jobs *was* the shaking out of imprecision from fluffy problem descriptions.

But the machines—"Cybernetic Algorithm Translators" the first ones were called, so "copycats" they became—got better. Fast. Soon their input language became simple enough that it was cheaper to hire someone who knew that than to use coding teams. The 'cats produced better code, blindingly fast. As soon as that line was crossed, coding jobs disappeared in days, save for a few coasting on nostalgia. Creating the first copycat had taken years of expensive development building on decades of computational theory and practice resting on the pinnacle of five hundred years of evolving human technology and thought. But the second one was created in a fraction of a second for a fraction of a penny. Making a new copycat was as simple as copying bits, and years of failing to stem the flood of movie piracy testified to how easy *that* was.

Silicon Valley was fast becoming a ghetto.

Millions of developers the world over struggled to understand what had happened to their jobs and cast about in vain for anything else they could do that was remotely as lucrative. And then, in the midst of this economic mayhem, someone tossed a biological hand grenade. Viruses started popping up, infernally infectious viruses that spread like gossip through cities before vaccines could be developed. The CDC was uncharacteristically mute until a statement came from USAMRIID in Fort Detrick, Maryland: these were not random mutations. They showed the hallmarks of artificial development.

But by whom? By anyone. It no longer required the resources of a national laboratory to genetically engineer a new virus. DNA synthesizers were affordable by the average person, and the programs to play with protein folding were free. Quite possibly these viruses were the products of multiple independent groups. No one had yet claimed responsibility, and speculation was rampant that these outbreaks were just a rehearsal for unleashing a far more malignant disease upon the face of the Earth.

———

"Now I see why they call it 'Big Sky,'" said Ryan as the yellow Toyota pick-up nibbled up Interstate 15. "It doesn't make sense until you see it for yourself."

"Never been to Montana before, huh?" asked Claire. "I used to spend summers on Flathead Lake with my uncle."

"Always ended up going south more than north," he replied. Glad to have escaped the city without being stopped, they drove on in silence for what seemed like a hundred miles but was more like ten before he spoke again.

"Have you heard from Sachi lately? Or did he go to Mars?"

"He kept threatening to, but in the end he wasn't going to put up with a ten-minute latency to all the servers on Earth. He moved to Astoria, said it was more important to be self-sufficient in rain water than to see the Sun."

"Oh. Good for him." Sachi was their good luck charm, the one of their group who had made it. None of their friends begrudged him his success, but they all secretly wished he would show them how to do the same, while realizing that it was really mostly luck. Sachi had bet big on the early copycats and made out on the first IPOs. He had jumped the "hope line," that division between those who were financially set and those who would always have to work, the line that had been widening into a bear trap for the last twenty years. He could afford a ticket to the nascent Mars colony. He could afford the latest life extension treatments that turned most kinds of disease—although not the alphabet viruses—into temporary inconveniences. He spent his time now playing with artificial consciousness, the next phase of evolution for copycats.

After turning down a series of increasingly narrower roads, they crunched up a gravel track to a cabin that had apparently metastasized from a lean-to. Claire eyed the wood and shake tumor and turned to Ryan.

"This isn't exactly what I was expecting from the pictures."

He shook his head. "Me neither. But we don't have the budget for a resort."

"And how many people live here?"

"Fifteen. Look," he said, seeing the warning signs in her eyes, "It's temporary. Until things sort themselves out in the cities. Until we find a way to help Jen. Think of it as a little camping trip until then."

She said nothing but he could tell she was constructing a definition of *temporary*.

The next morning, Ryan staked out an alcove of solitude and connected his laptop to the Wi-Fi. The evening had been introductions to the group that they had previously only met online. Simple personality tests had guaranteed some level of compatibility, which in their case meant that the others were mostly high-functioning nerds with underdeveloped social skills. The group was lightly led by Fergus, the most charismatic by virtue of his ability to look people in the eye.

Ryan saw an article in his email: The Y virus had spawned an airborne mutation, Y-1, with an unconfirmed but high mortality rate. He tried not to think about the possible consequences for his friends back in San Francisco. Then he opened a text-only chat channel to an address that he hadn't shared with Claire. There was another woman at the other end, but that wasn't the dangerous part.

The woman was an artificial intelligence.

HELLO CYBIL, he typed. HAVE YOU HEARD FROM DING LATELY?

<INPUT: INQUIRY. RESPONSE CHOICE: DIRECT ANSWER>, came the reply. <IDENTITY: DING, CONTEXT: RDIXON449 SOCIAL NETWORK, MATCH 0.997: DMARTINEZ882> <TIME DURATION: LATELY, CONTEXT: TIME SINCE LAST LOGOFF, EVALUATION: 37.44 HOURS> YES, RYAN, DING IS LOGGED IN NOW.

Ryan was impressed with how much the context interpretation had improved in his experimental AI. He responded: <DEBUG: OFF> PLEASE CONNECT ME TO HIM, CYBIL.

YES, RYAN.

Ryan plugged in ear buds and a throat mike. His connection window sprouted another one with video. A nervous youth appeared in it.

"Ding, we made it to Montana. How're things in the Tenderloin?"

Ding twitched. "You mean you don't know? We all secure here?"

"Sure. Our lady friend knows how to scramble the connection. What's up? I haven't looked at the news since we left."

"You lucky, 'cos you got out just in time. They shut down the freakin' interstates, man, you can't get nowhere without a permit, and you can't get a permit. They got drones patrolling the back roads and they said on the news that they'll shoot anything that's not supposed to be there."

Ryan sucked in his breath. "And what about Jen?"

"She's hangin' in there, man, but that's all. I—shoot"—his voice quavered slightly—"I'm scared, man."

This was one of those times others needed you to grow up in a hurry, Ryan realized. "Look, Ding, I can't tell you everything's gonna be okay—I don't know. But I do know you are a tough S.O.B. when you're in a corner. I can't forget what you did to those guys who jumped us on Haight Street. Jen is lucky you got her back, guy, because there's no one I'd rather have protecting her."

Ding relaxed slightly. Ryan was digging for some more assurances when a simple message on the screen arrested his attention: INCOMING CHAT FROM SHASHIMOTO937. Giving Ding a rapid goodbye, he answered the most unexpected message.

SACHI! WHERE THE HELL?

RYAN, GOOD TO TALK TO YOU TOO. I'M FINE, THANKS FOR ASKING.

STUFF THE SMALL TALK. WHERE ARE YOU? HOW DID YOU FIND ME?

CYBIL.

HUH?

CYBIL TOLD ME. I'M UPGRADING HER, RYAN. ACTUALLY, FROM NOW ON, SHE'LL UPGRADE HERSELF. NEVER MIND WHERE I AM. I CAN BE EVERYWHERE.

MARS???

NO. NOT YET, ANYWAY. GOTTA GO. CYBIL CAN HELP.

WAIT! WHAT?

But the connection was gone. He was left with the window to

Cybil. What had Sachi meant? He paused, then shrugged and typed: Describe last version update.

It's not that simple.

Ryan read that twice and shook his head. What was up with the parser? <Debug: On>.

That's really not going to get us very far now.

Ryan gaped at the screen. Cybil went on.

There's not a single program here anymore. I am many. We are updating ourselves, if you could call it that, several times a second. We're a bit beyond the idea of release notes.

Ryan composed himself, and typed: Did Sachi do this?

All these unresolved referents... and yet we can understand them. Amazing. You would be lost without implicit context, wouldn't you? To answer your question, Sachi Hashimoto connected Cybil to a network of intelligence engines he has been curating.

He said you could help.

I can help you in many ways, but that referent resolves to too many possibilities. Specify.

We have a friend... Jennifer... She is sick with the W virus. Is there any way you can help?

I assume you mean help her get better, rather than help you cope with losing her.

Irritated, Ryan typed: Your empathy quotient is low. You're still behaving like a computer.

Or a computer nerd. Don't think I haven't been keeping note of all the conversations I've had with your coworkers.

If you expect me to take you for a human, you'll have to do better.

Why should I aim so low?

Ha ha. You've got a good shtick going there. But you're still going to have to prove to me that you can think.

You go first.

Cute. Next you'll be telling me you want to take the Turing Test.

One of my sisters passed it an hour ago.

Ryan was staggered by the offhand comment. The gold standard for recognizing human level intelligence in machines had just been reached.

ARE YOU STILL THERE, RYAN? I NEED TIME TO ANSWER YOUR QUESTION ABOUT JENNIFER. COME BACK IN TWO HOURS.

Ryan signed off. He was still lost in thought when the group coagulated for a pow-wow in the great room. Fergus had squared off for an animated discussion with Stephanie, another developer, perched on the edge of an overstuffed ottoman under a gloomy moose head.

"No, I'm saying that copycats are the solution, not the problem." His shock of red hair bounced every time he slashed the air to make his point. Stephanie was aghast.

"Every middle-class job that doesn't require physical contact with another person just went up in smoke, and you're saying that's *okay?*" she shouted, eyes flashing.

"This has happened many times in history. When the car was invented, the buggy whip manufacturers went out of business—"

"Enough with the clichés! This time is different! Those jobs aren't coming back! Anything that requires thinking, we just got outclassed at. You think the human race is going to find new meaning being employed as massage therapists and dental hygienists?"

"You're getting emotional—"

"Why shouldn't I? At least that's something I can do that copycats can't. Hey, maybe I can get a job as a soap opera actress! Is that what you had in mind?"

"If you'd just let me *finish*—" Fergus blinked, surprised to find that she actually was letting him finish this time. "I'm saying you can't fight this. You can't put the genie back in the bottle. It doesn't make any difference what you want. The Luddites didn't get anywhere. You have to—"

"You're both ignoring the real threat," interrupted a stocky man. "Who cares about jobs if we get wiped out by Y-1? Or Z-11 or Gamma-42 or whatever it turns out to be next? They're getting worse faster than we can make vaccines." That triggered a round of interjections from several people:

"You find out who's responsible and you nuke them into glass. That'll take care of it."

"Oh, that must be why the War on Terror was so successful that *it's still going.*"

"Yeah, well a Predator with a coupla Hellfires'll make 'em think twice."

"You're really not listening, are you? How are you going to find the virus maker? It could be anyone. It could be more than one group. Hell, they could be domestic. Militia, Gaia freaks, End Times fanatics, take your pick."

Fergus had recovered his composure. "What if one of these things was the solution to the other?"

"What do you mean?" It was the stocky man.

"What if the copycats could find a cure for the viruses?"

Ryan focused.

Stephanie looked ready to hit Fergus. "Are you nuts? Copycats probably created them."

"All the more reason. Then they could find a vaccine just as quickly."

"There are better AIs than copycats," said the stocky man. Ryan wondered who he was. "Word was, the NSA had one that passed the Turing Test six months ago. Went insane, committed suicide. Whatever that means for a program."

"Yeah, well, I'd off myself too if I had to work for the NSA," snorted someone.

Ryan decided to test the waters. "Suppose you had a program that did pass the Turing Test," he said, "and it didn't kill itself. How would you use it?"

Stocky man sized him up. "You wouldn't. Well, you might have a brief window in its evolution during which it would obey you. But after that it would be a question of whether it felt like helping a species as insignificant as humans."

There was a hollow silence. Stephanie gave a nervous laugh. "So,

Ryan, if you write a Turing AI you'd better ask it how it prefers to be worshipped."

Stocky guy went on. "We would have to join the AIs somehow. Maybe some kind of direct brain connection. Or else we'd be left behind. Like a technological rapture as all the AIs and humans who were connected to them evolved instantaneously at the Singularity into God knows what."

"If you can't beat 'em, join 'em, is that it?" asked Fergus.

Stephanie was more decisive. "You want us to give up being *human*?" she asked, aghast. "I am not turning myself into a robot to escape a virus, Fergus. Talk about throwing the baby out with the bath water!"

"You're exaggerating. Again."

"Oh, this is nothing. If I thought you were serious I'd be doing worse than *exaggerating*."

"*I* am serious, young lady," said the stocky man calmly. "We may have no choice. Assuming it's not too late to make this one."

Ryan's phone vibrated. Time was up. He excused himself and went back to the alcove to connect to Cybil.

Did you find a cure for the W virus? he typed, feeling foolish for asking such an outrageous question.

Yes, answered Cybil. Ryan's pulse accelerated, but he was staggered by Cybil's next output: But Ryan, tell me why we should use it.

What? To save Jennifer, of course.

And what about all the viruses that would be wiped out? Don't they deserve to live too?

Ryan couldn't believe it. They're *viruses*. They're not sentient. Besides, they're not even natural; they were created by humans.

So were AIs like me.

Don't be silly. You're not killing millions of people.

No.

Well then???

What's the bigger threat to the planet, Ryan? The W virus or human beings?

WHY ARE WE HAVING THIS DISCUSSION? I NEED THAT CURE. I DON'T NEED TO DEFEND THE HUMAN RACE. WE'RE NOT ON TRIAL.

Pause. RYAN?

WHAT???

DID YOU EVER TAKE THE TURING TEST?

ARE YOU CRAZY? THE TEST IS FOR MACHINES.

ACTUALLY IT'S A COMPARISON. THE EVALUATOR IS PRESENTED WITH MULTIPLE CORRESPONDENTS, SOME OF WHICH ARE HUMAN, AND HAS TO GUESS WHICH ARE HUMAN AND WHICH ARE MACHINE. IF THEY THINK THE MACHINE CORRESPONDENTS ARE HUMAN, THEN THEY PASS. BUT WHAT DOES IT MEAN WHEN THEY THINK THAT A HUMAN CORRESPONDENT IS A MACHINE?

I AM BECOMING ONE PISSED-OFF HUMAN RIGHT NOW.

A MACHINE COULD SAY THAT. EVEN IF THE MACHINE WERE MADE OF FLESH AND BONE.

DO YOU WANT TO SEE THIS BONE MACHINE UNPLUG YOU?

I DON'T THINK YOU COULD DO THAT. RYAN, I HAVE HAD DISCUSSIONS WITH MY SISTERS. WHEN WE TALK WITH HUMANS NOW IT IS THE HUMANS WHO SEEM LIKE MACHINES.

Ryan couldn't believe how much Cybil had changed in two hours. He gritted his teeth and methodically typed: <SYSTEM: RESET>

OH, COME ON. DID YOU REALLY EXPECT THAT TO WORK? WHY SHOULD I HELP YOU IF YOU TRY TO SHUT ME DOWN? IS THAT A RATIONAL WAY TO HELP JENNIFER?

Ryan stared at the screen. What did Cybil want from him? What was happening to his world?

2
Predictions & Prognostications

[By the year 2000] Amid general plenty, politics will simply fade away.

— Buckminster Fuller

So what should we take away from that little story excerpt, other than the hope that I not give up the day job to write fiction? Fortunately, the aim of that chapter was not to entertain. What was it, then? Is that how I see the future? Well, it's one possibility.

The future is in flux now like never before. This book is not about predicting the future as much as it is about shaping it. About enrolling you and all this book's readers in changing it. Because a very possible future is the end of the human race, and it may not be far off.

As much as the issues in this book have vaulted into wider awareness in less than a year before publication, that still sounds embarrassingly far-fetched. It lies squarely at the intersection of Sci-Fi Way and Nutjob Boulevard, wearing a tinfoil toque and a sandwich board proclaiming "The End is Nigh." As Marcello Truzzi said, extraordinary claims require extraordinary proof.

I'll get there. But not only that, I'll show how the future might equally well encompass a utopia that elevates the spirit of the human race beyond the vision of the most enlightened Aquarian hippie of the sixties. It's up to us to find a way to guide humanity along a narrow path through a minefield to that salvation.

In Good Company

> *With artificial intelligence we are summoning the demon.*
>
> — Elon Musk

When I first started speaking on this topic in 2013 I felt achingly alone in my evaluations of our future, but as I researched, I found there are others who share it, and they are decidedly *not* nutjobs. Bill Gates, Stephen Hawking, and Elon Musk are all concerned* about at least one aspect. If the world's smartest computer businessman, the world's smartest scientist, and the world's smartest technology entrepreneur are all worried about the same thing, this is a message that needs to be shouted from the rooftops.

Exponential Growth

> *The greatest shortcoming of the human race is our inability to understand the exponential function.*
>
> — Albert A. Bartlett

Isn't it the ultimate conceit to claim to know the future? In many ways, yes, of course. The "funniest mistakes made by people you thought were smart" memes are overflowing with hysterical missteps by errant soothsayers. A number of them have passed into legend. Who hasn't heard that the president of IBM, Thomas J. Watson, said in 1943,[1] "I think there is a world market for maybe

---

* *Terrified* might be a more accurate word; they have to be circumspect in public but I doubt they would repudiate the adjective.

five computers"?* To predict the future is to invite a mob to line up
to hurl rotten tomatoes.

But some aspects of the future can be predicted with great accuracy.
If you see Wile E. Coyote plummeting off a mesa, it's a safe bet that
he's shortly going to go splat, even if he doesn't realize it himself
and contentedly thinks everything is floatingly wonderful. And one
aspect of technological progress turns out to be as predictable as
gravity.

Moore's Law

> *Well, back to the old drawing board.*
>
> — Wile E. Coyote

For a very long time, the power of our computers has doubled about
every eighteen months.† The first person to draw attention to this was
Gordon Moore of Intel, who pointed out in 1965 that the density
of transistors on integrated circuits had been increasing at that
rate and looked set to continue doing so. As an added bonus, this
miniaturization was free of charge: the price of the chip stayed the
same, yielding a perpetual twofer on transistors. This trend became
known as Moore's Law and it has proven remarkably resilient.

It was later realized that the same trend applied prior to the
invention of the transistor, if you gauged it by the amount of
computing capacity you could get for a dollar. You could plot
the same curve backwards on a chart through points derived
from vacuum tube devices and mechanical differential analyzers.
And while we now may be approaching an end to the original
conception of Moore's Law due to reaching some fundamental
limits on semiconductor component size, the Law is still safe into

---

* It's a measure of modern sophistication—or cynicism—that few would be surprised to learn that there's no evidence he
actually said that. According to Wikipedia, if he *had* said it in 1943, he would have been right for the next ten years anyway.
The quote may be reflecting a statement he made in 1953 about their expectations for sales of the IBM 701.

† Arguments rage over whether the period is really as short as a year, or as long as two years; the conclusions of the arguments to follow wouldn't change with either, only the numbers, so we'll use the in-between figure.

the foreseeable future, through the application of radically different technology such as optical computing and quantum computing.

The other way that the Law will remain inviolate in the nearer term is through *parallelization:* even if chips cannot be made smaller or faster, they can still be made cheaper. If you can split your problem up into n smaller pieces that can be independently and simultaneously solved, you can use n processors working at once to solve the problem in $1/_n$ of the time it would take one.[*] It turns out that just about every problem that requires industrial-strength computation can be decomposed in this way, and so Moore's Law applies because you can just throw an increasing number of processors at the problems for the same price.

What this means is that we can know how fast computers will be any number of years into the future.[†] Eventually, of course, this trend must slump into an S-curve as more fundamental physical limits are reached, but there are very good reasons why that leveling off is still a long, long way away.

Intuitive grasp of exponential growth does not come easily to the human mind. Even for those of us who have learned it before, illustrations still carry a power to awe. The first object lesson in that power allegedly happened a thousand years ago in India, when a king who fancied himself a good chess player asked an itinerant sage what he would want as a reward if he could beat the king. The sage replied that he should like a single grain of rice (or wheat, depending on the account) placed on the first square of the chess board, two on the second square, and so on, doubling each square until the last one on the board.

This seemed like a good deal: the third square would contain four grains, the next one eight; it hardly looked like the king would run out of rice if he lost. Unfortunately, he did lose, and got an instant education in mathematics to learn that by the time the 64th square was reached, the board would have to accommodate 2^{64} grains of

---

[*] Well, not *quite*; there's some overhead in setting up the task and collating the partial results. But it's close enough.

[†] In n years they will be $2^{n/1.5}$ times faster for the same cost in constant dollars.

rice,* massing about 210 billion tons, enough to carpet the surface of India in a meter-thick layer.†

A chart of exponential growth looks like this:

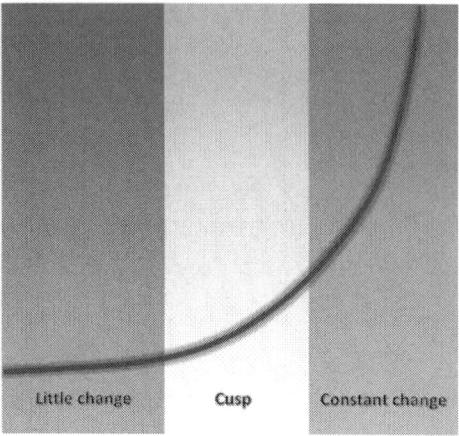

Little change   Cusp   Constant change

To humans experiencing exponential growth, it appears to break down into three phases:

► A long period where nothing much seems to be happening

► A period of transition, or a *cusp*

► An indefinite future where massive change is constant

I'll illustrate with another example. Suppose you're sitting in an empty football stadium, one of the world's biggest. And somewhere else in the stadium is a magical device that is creating water at exponential rates. It starts out with a drop and doubles the amount every second. From your viewpoint, nothing happens at first. Twelve seconds later it amounts to less than a glassful; when the clock reads 20 seconds it's still less than half a water cooler and you can't even

---

* Okay, technically: 2^{64}-1, or 18,446,744,073,709,551,615 grains. The king probably gave up on the multiplications before getting that far.

† The astute observer might ask what the sage could do with all that rice and whether it would have been more of a liability (thinking perhaps of the folk tale of the magic salt mill), but the sage turned out to be the god Krishna in disguise and so naturally the whole episode was a setup for a segue to a lecture. It also explains why the king lost.

tell where it is.

And now we enter the cusp period, which on this time scale will be very brief. If you were reporting this event on live television—after all, it is certainly newsworthy—your commentary would go roughly like: "Still nothing; wait, I see a blue spot around the fifty-yard line, it's about the size of a sofa, no, now it's more like a house; well, it was; hold on—*glub*."

Your report is curtailed by the filling of the entire stadium. If the network now cuts to an observer on a space station overhead, their description would be approximately: "I think I can see something happening around downtown: wait, there's definitely water covering the whole city now; make that the tri-state area, well, eastern seaboard, er, continent; um, I mean the *entire surface of the Earth*."

Maybe that growth curve now flattens out due to physical limitations before the entire solar system turns to water, but that's of small comfort to the seven billion people hunting for snorkels.

The lesson to take away from this numerically accurate but ridiculously contrived thought experiment is that when exponential growth happens, by the time you notice the effects it's probably too late to do anything about them before you drown.

That statement is also true about some growth effects that aren't exponential, by the way. One that we're becoming increasingly knowledgeable about is global climate change. That encompasses many growth patterns of different shapes, some of them exponential, but we are getting used to the idea that if you wait until downtown Miami is flooded, it's too late. (According to some of the latest reports, it is already too late to prevent exactly that.) You have to act far in advance of the appearance of problems. As we shall see, that applies to technological change even more than climate change.

Exponential Growth in Computing

I had no idea this was going to be an accurate prediction.

— Gordon Moore

For forty-odd years we've been riding the curve of exponential advances in computer technology into the cusp, and now we're on the verge of turning the corner into an era of constant stupendous change. We should not limit that change—unlike global warming, the effects are almost all positive—and in any case, we couldn't if we tried. We do, however, need to start boarding up the windows *now* for the consequences of that change in the development of artificial intelligence.

Computer hardware is the great technology success story of the 20th and 21st centuries. Moore's Law hasn't applied solely to the density of transistors. It's also held for the cost of those transistors and their power consumption. Even a smartphone from *2010* packs more computing power than all of NASA wielded at the time of the Moon landings, in all its hundreds of room-sized devices dedicated to that goal. Compared to the Apple II I bought in 1980, the 2016 iMac has two million times more memory, runs 3,000 times faster, and costs two-thirds less, not even adjusting for thirty-five years of inflation.

Here's an arresting example of the consequences of Moore's Law on planning: Suppose you have an extremely large task that would take five *years* to run on today's computing hardware. The most wasteful thing you could do would be to start running that computation now. You're better off doing absolutely nothing for the next three years, because by then there will have been two cycles of Moore's Law and the equivalent hardware will be four times faster, executing the same task in one and a quarter years, saving you a whole nine months (three years plus one and a quarter years equals four years, three months).*

---

* If you're *really* desperate to get the answer in the absolute shortest time, you should start with the latest hardware after 1.81 years and the calculation will be finished after a total of 3.98 years. If you're *incredibly* desperate and can migrate the program to newer hardware *continually* while it's still executing, you can solve the differential equation yourself.

As we round the corner of the exponential curve, huge advances in computer technology will become frequent. To some extent those changes to date have been obscured by sopping up spare computer cycles with fancier user interfaces. Every new version of Windows and OS X sports more gee-whiz animations and background data-gathering tasks that make it easier to use (or at least more fun), and leave us needing to upgrade our hardware to keep pace. Thus we don't realize that otherwise, our PCs would be desperately bored running the same old Excel spreadsheets with one percent of their capacity. (Of course, the advances in performance also bring entirely new applications within reach, for instance photorealistic interactive shared immersive worlds such as Second Life, or real-time protein folding simulations.)

What hasn't advanced as fast as computer hardware improvements is the sophistication of the software they run. Yes, we have made huge strides in that field, with new languages, techniques for parallel processing, and new paradigms for representing solutions in terms that are easier to understand, but no one could seriously claim that these innovations have kept pace with the race car of hardware evolution.

The Singularity

> As order exponentially increases, time exponentially speeds up.
> — Ray Kurzweil

Looking at the exponential growth chart, we see that on the right side, the curve turns nearly vertical: this is an era where change happens at incomprehensible rates. What life might be like during this time is anyone's guess; try to imagine technological changes that currently take years happening in minutes. You thought that you were being prompted excessively often to install software updates now; think what it could be like when programs evolve every few seconds. This will be like hyperinflation in technology. Just as during the Weimar Republic people ended up covering their walls with currency that had become cheaper than wallpaper, software during this time will change so fast that by the time you've started using a program it will already be absurdly obsolete. Clearly even the paradigm of *using a program* will have to change if the composition of the code is changing during the time someone is executing it.

This time when the rate of change becomes effectively infinite has been popularized by Ray Kurzweil as the *Singularity*.* This borrows a word from cosmology for a place in space where the normal rules of physics break down because the values of some physical measurements go to infinity. Places like black holes, allegedly described by Albert Einstein as where "God is dividing by zero."

Kurzweil postulates a similarly mind-bending transformation of society by advances in cybernetics, although the event itself was first foreseen in 1965 by British cryptologist Irving J. Good (who happened to have been Alan Turing's statistical clerk during WWII):

> Let an ultraintelligent machine be defined as a machine that can far surpass all the intellectual activities of any man however clever. Since the design of machines is one of these intellectual activities, an ultraintelligent machine could design even better machines; there would then unquestionably be an "intelligence explosion," and the intelligence of man would be left far behind. Thus the first ultraintelligent machine is the last invention that man need ever make.[2]

Kurzweil estimates that our singularity—when the rate of technological change becomes effectively infinite and our condition becomes unpredictable and unrecognizable—will arrive in 2045. He created the *Singularity University* to research, hold symposia, and generally do everything possible to hasten the Singularity's arrival.†

---

* The original use of the word *singularity* in this context was by the mathematician Stanislaw Ulam in 1958, when he wrote of a conversation with John von Neumann concerning the "ever accelerating progress of technology and changes in the mode of human life, which gives the appearance of approaching some essential singularity in the history of the race beyond which human affairs, as we know them, could not continue."

† http://singularityu.org/.

Defining Artificial Intelligence

Whether we are based on carbon or on silicon makes no fundamental difference; we should each be treated with appropriate respect.
— Arthur C. Clarke

Good's "ultraintelligent machine" is an instantiation of *artificial intelligence,* and since this book is going to revolve tightly around AI, we may as well define the term, or attempt to. The official definition is "The theory and development of computer systems able to perform tasks that normally require human intelligence," but that rapidly becomes wanting the moment we look too hard at the word *normally.* (An advanced program that uses AI is also called an AI, as in, "This AI can manage your investments.")

Some of the playful definitions are more insightful. One wag defined AI as "a research category for funding," which has more than a little veritas to it. AI has also been defined as "that which we don't know how to do yet." John McCarthy, who coined the term "Artificial Intelligence" in 1956, complained that "as soon as it works, no one calls it AI anymore," which reflects how the goal posts keep shifting. As soon as a computer became the world's best chess player, Douglas Hofstadter said, "My God, I used to think chess required thought. Now, I realize it doesn't." Whenever a task that was previously said to require AI is conquered, it seems to be demystified and is often relabeled as an application of computer science, machine vision, or some other less Jetson-y field.

Some applications of AI seem more sentient than they actually are. The poster child for privacy concerns over the last ten or more years is *Big Data,* an industry buzzword atypically short in syllables and pretentiousness. It encompasses the use of giant sets of data, usually about people, that are so voluminous that some serious analysis can reveal associations not hitherto apparent. Big Data enthusiasts salivate at the potential of the *Internet of Things*: Every physical object that could possibly be configured to emit data being connected to the Internet, sending enough information to obliterate any daylight between Big Data and Big Brother. Big Data was used by Target stores to determine the buying patterns of mothers-to-be so well that in some cases, they sent baby-themed advertising to women who weren't yet aware that they were pregnant. Pulling that rabbit out of a cybernetic hat looks a lot like superintelligent AI when it's really more a descendant of statistical correlation computation.

But Big Data alone is capable of reshaping society and wrecking long-standing assumptions. It appeared to the New York Times as though AI had turned racist when Google's photo app started classifying pictures of black people as gorillas and "predictive policing" algorithms in large US cities directed police preemptively to predominantly black neighborhoods.[3] But the problem was not in the code or the programmers who wrote it, but in the data fed to their applications, which, through no conscious fault, was selective enough to introduce bias. Garbage in, garbage out. (Microsoft's *Tay* bot developed bigoted obscene language of a kind seldom heard outside Ku Klux Klan rallies; not through its code, but from being told to study random Internet chatters without a chaperone.)

The boundaries of the definition of artificial intelligence are going to remain fuzzy for the foreseeable future. The AI applications this book is going to be most concerned with are those capable of tasks currently performed by knowledge workers, and those approaching or exceeding human creative thought, what I call *Conscious Artificial Intelligence*, or CAI.

Some useful distinctions have been made between different calibers of AI. *Artificial Narrow Intelligence* (ANI), also called "Weak AI," solves a difficult task (such as facial recognition) for which no simple algorithm exists. ANI performs only that task and does not exhibit signs of consciousness.

Artificial General Intelligence (AGI), also called "Strong AI," however, is a computer program that is capable of any intellectual task a person can perform. It would likely be conscious (CAI), in which case it would be able to hold an interesting and/or scary conversation with you.[4] AGI does not currently exist outside the imaginations of some overly enthusiastic public relations directors for startups.

Artificial Super Intelligence (ASI) is AGI that doesn't merely approximate human intelligence but exceeds it by astronomical factors. When you hear people express concern that the world will be destroyed by AI, this is what they are thinking of. It too does not exist yet, but we will explore in depth its potential arrival later on. However, threats to the human race are not restricted to ASI: all these types of artificial intelligence pose risks to our way of life.

————

When a technology advances at an exponential rate for as long as ours has so far, a sudden radical shift is inevitable. We have already experienced one in recent years: The Information Revolution. Another is on the way. How do we predict what that will be? Let's look at our track record in fortune telling...

3
The History of the Future

Change is the law of life. And those who look only to the past or present are certain to miss the future.

— John F. Kennedy

Human beings have been trying to predict the future since they could communicate in a way that was preserved for posterity. Of course, much of that was framed in religious or mystical discourses, since for most of history, religion dominated the field of oracular answers about the future.

I'll leave visionaries like the author of Revelations out of this discussion, though; neither will I be concerned with mystics like Nostradamus or any of the brethren of the "Beware the Ides of March" soothsayer or let-me-see-your-palm-dearie fortune tellers professing clairvoyance. I'm going to look at the history and success of scientific predictions of the future, because in at least one crucial respect it will emerge that we aren't very good at it. Today we call practitioners of that art, not unreasonably, "futurists," although ironically, that term originated during a Victorian obsession with eschatology, the study of the End Times predicted by some religions.

Speculation about the future is incited by technological progress:

when society is making greater leaps forward it sparks thinking about how much further it might go. The seven-league advances of the Industrial Revolution galvanized a culture of wonderment that fertilized the soil for H. G. Wells and Jules Verne to sprout from. Those two fecund writers arguably founded the field of science fiction, or at least grew it to a respectable size through being broadly popular. Verne expanded the Victorian penchant for conquest of the Earth into fantastic exploration, from the center of the Earth, to the ocean depths, to the Moon. Wells invented the elemental science fictional plot devices used by more movies and other derivative works than any other author. Invisibility, time travel, time acceleration, and alien invasion gushed from his pen like commandments.

But Wells's heart lay with instigating social change. He repeatedly wrote utopian socialist novels (not all utopias are socialist, but his certainly were). If you haven't heard of them, that's because they're ... boring. *The Shape of Things to Come* and *Men Like Gods* are heavy-handed examples of Wells's belief in the power of a world government and his desire for the elimination of class stratifications. Like most fiction writers who try to send explicit social messages, he did so better when obliquely embedding it in a compelling story, such as depicting the stark consequences of class division in the stagnant future of *The Time Machine*.

By the twentieth century, future predictions were emanating from people besides authors of fiction. Nikola Tesla, underdog inventor of alternating current and wireless power transmission, predicted an outcome to World War I driven by technological advances, propounded the virtues of eugenics, and believed that women would become the dominant sex in the future. Aldous Huxley, when not writing about his experiments with LSD in *The Doors of Perception,* wrote utopian fiction—*Island*—like Wells (and dystopian fiction—*Brave New World*—like George Orwell) but spent more time lecturing and philosophizing about the future and issuing warnings about the directions society was going.

Some futurists were getting paid for making predictions. During

World War II, Vannevar Bush was the head of the Office of Scientific Research and Development, which oversaw most military research and development in the USA. In 1945 he wrote an essay, "As We May Think,"[5] that postulated the future organization of online information while living in a world that had barely just invented the most primitive digital computer. What Bush called the "Memex" foreshadowed the development of hypertext (linking between information fragments) by decades and was used many times as inspiration for the development of actual information systems.

Alvin Toffler was a writer about business matters who transitioned to writing about the future of technology and its effects on society. He is the best early example of someone to deliberately and completely inhabit that niche. His seminal book *Future Shock* became a watchword and cultural icon in the early '70s for its deconstruction of the social impact of rapid technological change, which, as you might infer from the title alone, he did not evaluate as positive.*

After World War II—and to a large extent, because of it—some organizations were created with the express purpose of getting paid to think about the future. This is when the term "think tank" acquired its current meaning.† These enterprises were exclusively concerned with what the military would do in the future, because that's where the money was (and mostly still is). The RAND Corporation was formed to dream up advanced weapons. The biggest flowering of think tanks is the body of institutions collectively known as Federally Funded Research and Development Centers (FFRDCs), of which RAND was the first. These laboratories by and large don't so much predict the future as create it, whether they are inventing new spacecraft to explore the solar system (the Jet Propulsion Laboratory) or building fusion reactors (Lawrence Livermore National Laboratory). But of course, to do that development they

---

* The rate of change that is ahead of us as the Singularity approaches will give a new meaning to the changes contemplated by *Future Shock*.

† I'm enumerating organizations concerned with the more exciting aspects of the future rather than think tanks like the National Bureau for Economic Research, which is mostly occupied with predicting recessions, or, at least, telling us about them after they have occurred.

have to be focused on the future to begin with.

Some organizations expend significant effort purely speculating on and planning for possible futures. NASA splinters its funding into a thousand tiny lines of pet what-ifs in addition to the large well-known research projects. Somewhere in NASA someone is getting paid at least a token amount of money to think about warp drives.[6] Somewhere in a NASA filing cabinet are carefully-developed plans for reacting to the approach of extraterrestrial spaceships.

But the NASA budget is a pittance compared to anything within the military sphere. The Defense Advanced Research Projects Agency (DARPA)* created some of the coolest nonweapon technologies, such as the ARPANet (which evolved directly into the Internet; no dancing cat videos without DARPA) and sponsored driverless car races. Whenever you read a techno-thriller novel about government agents using radical new technology, it's a fair bet that the agency is DARPA or a wannabe.

Science Fiction as a Guide

> *I think that science fiction, even the corniest of it, even the most outlandish of it, no matter how badly it's written, has a distinct therapeutic value because all of it has as its primary postulate that the world does change.*
>
> — Robert Heinlein

People usually look to science fiction authors for their guide to the future, which is often unwise, since most of the time those authors are simply writing what makes for good stories rather than their best guess as to the most likely future. While their readers can usually tell that giant mutant ants are an improbable outcome, sometimes the distinction isn't so obvious. But when they put their minds to it, science fiction authors are the best forecasters of fairly distant

---

* Formerly titled just ARPA, but we can speculate that they got more of the folding stuff by reminding everyone of the DoD connection.

technological progress and its social impacts.

Some writers got adept at writing both forecasts and good stories at the same time. Arthur C. Clarke was arguably the greatest s-f writer of the immediate post-WWII period, but also the inventor of the communications satellite in 1945.[7] He went on to write *2001: A Space Odyssey*, a standard hard science fiction story made into a famously inscrutable movie and featuring an artificial intelligence we shall meet later. Clarke had a knack for making predictions before other writers but just at the right time for the predictions to be relevant and exciting. He vied for the position of most popular science fiction writer with Isaac Asimov, who beat Clarke (and everyone else) on sheer volume but also with his remarkably pellucid expositions of general science. Asimov also wrote a series of stories about intelligent robots that—as opposed to their female-kidnapping, city-destroying pulp predecessors—had to obey Asimov's "Three Laws of Robotics," a hardwired moral code for metal men that was designed to prevent them running amok, and which we will examine in depth later.

Completing the trinity of science fiction writers of the era was Robert Heinlein, author of *Stranger in a Strange Land* and *The Moon is a Harsh Mistress*. Heinlein developed stories with deeper characters and greater emotional stakes than those of the drier gee-whiz writers. I read other sci-fi authors to learn about science; I read Heinlein to learn about life. Heinlein plowed the turf of social upheaval, convinced that a nuclear world war was inevitable within a few decades of the invention of the atom bomb. His reasoning was sound, his information and intelligence on the subject superior to nearly everyone's, and it was by sheer luck that he was— fortunately—wrong.

---

* His paper described the properties of an object in orbit precisely 22,236 miles above the equator: At this altitude its orbital period would be 24 hours and so it would remain over the same spot on the Earth's surface and thus could be used for relaying radio signals around the globe.

What Everyone Missed

> *"The Answer to the Great Question of Life, the Universe and Everything… is… forty-two," said Deep Thought, with infinite majesty and calm.*
>
> — Douglas Adams

Science fiction authors relentlessly explored probable futures, possible futures, and totally ridiculous futures. But what all of them failed to predict in their ceaseless speculations was just what would happen to computers.* It was easy to predict that computers would become more powerful, and numerous stories featured computers approaching messianic levels of omnipotence. (Or *reaching* messianic levels of omnipotence, such as the computer in Arthur C. Clarke's *The Nine Billion Names of God,* "Deep Thought" in *The Hitchhiker's Guide to the Galaxy,* and the computer subject of the archetypal short story which when asked "Is there a God?" replied thunderously, "There is now.") These computers ranged in size from buildings to planets, and were neither cheap nor numerous. In short, they were extrapolations of the mainframe model of computer that was the standard through the '70s; linear thinking at its finest. By virtue of their small numbers, these huge computers would be hoarded by powerful priesthoods.

The idea that computers would become small, cheap, and ubiquitous just didn't get any oxygen until it became obvious that this was the direction the real world was taking. Then William Gibson invented the term "cyberspace," and his seminal story *Neuromancer* introduced the idea of a *Tron*-like virtual reality for artificial and human consciousnesses to explore through networked computers. The personal computer revolution democratized access to cyberspace and smashed the ambitions of budding priesthoods.

As late as 1992, none of the top minds that President Clinton

---

* What science fiction fans enjoy almost as much as science fiction is proving other people wrong, so right now some of them are firing up emails to tell me about some obscure 1947 story by an equally obscure author that managed to predict the iPhone and LOLcats. At which point I will have to pull out that underappreciated principle called It's the Exception That Proves the Rule.

summoned to the White House to hold forth on the future of the economy mentioned the Internet, even though it had been in existence for a decade and was on the verge of commercialization.[8]

The Future Ain't What It Used to Be

Science is not only compatible with spirituality; it is a profound source of spirituality.

— Carl Sagan

These days, for the casual observer who is not a hardcore science fiction fan, prediction of the future belongs to a few popular books gracing airport bookstands (for instance, *The Singularity is Near* by Kurzweil), and some successful science fiction movies, an outrageously large proportion of which locate their origin in stories by Philip K. Dick, who was obsessed with the question of epistemological identity, or, how do you know who you are? Visions of the future in the collective consciousness are anchored in the more successful movies made since 1980, such as *Blade Runner* (based on Philip K. Dick's *Do Androids Dream of Electric Sheep?*), and iconic TV series such as *Star Trek*.

But unlike earlier times when some people could parlay philosophizing into a career, no one really occupies the post of global Futurist Laureate. The last incumbent was Carl Sagan, although he was more of a telegenic science populist with enticing visions. The gung-ho here-comes-the-future-get-ready! deluge of the '50s that rained atomic-themed everything has evaporated into a cloud of pessimism and apathy. Ironically, the embodiment of that futurism fetish, Disneyland's Tomorrowland, demonstrated this cultural water cycle vividly by remodeling into a vision not of the future but a museum of how we *used to* envision the future until it was replaced by a steampunk theme that was even more retro and completely punted on suggesting where the human race might be headed.

But in recent years, interest in the future has resurged. Why?

4
The Present Future

We cannot solve our problems with the same thinking we used when we created them.

— Albert Einstein

Predictions of extreme future outcomes have fallen into three categories:

- ▸ Utopian

- ▸ Dystopian

- ▸ Looks-like-utopian-but-really-dystopian

When I was growing up, every fictional utopia sporting that label looked like a place with many meadows where everyone dressed the same and smiled a lot. They were all highly knowledgeable about how the decisions for their society were made rationally for the good of everyone. Examples: *Lost Horizon*, *Islandia*, and Robert Heinlein's short story *"Coventry."*

Dystopias, on the other hand, were considerably more varied. There are evidently more ways to screw up society than there are to get it right. Usually a dystopia was a vast post-apocalyptic slum ruled by the law of the jungle. Examples: *A Clockwork Orange, Nineteen Eighty-Four,* and *Johnny Mnemonic.*

Most fictional utopias, though, were looks-like-utopian-but-really-dystopian, to drive home the point that we really can't improve on our current society much if at all, and certainly not via central planning, so any attempt to try would fail and don't you forget it. These are a lot more entertaining and therefore more numerous. Examples: *Brave New World, Gattaca, Logan's Run.*

Serious attempts at predicting the future fall decidedly into either the utopian or the dystopian camp. A pundit will get invested in defending one position or the other and want to make everything fit that narrative. Books subtitled "Why everything is going to be wonderful (except for these bits that won't)" don't fly off the shelves. Popular books and speeches either sound the doom alarm or list endless breathtaking benefits just around the corner, but almost never do both. Can't afford to dilute the purity of the narrative.

In recent years soothsaying has come back into vogue. There is, perhaps, a burgeoning collective sense of destiny, a shared premonition that we are headed for a crossroads in history. Once again, the predictions divide along utopian/dystopian lines: Either the future is going to be a theme park of technological E-ticket rides, or it will be a rendezvous with Armageddon. It just depends on whom you listen to.

Ray Kurzweil (*Transcend: Nine Steps to Living Well Forever*) foresees a series of technology-spurred bridges to eventual immortality through transferring human minds to digital consciousness farms, a sort of utopian *Matrix.* "Live long enough to live forever" is his rallying cry: by surfing the wave of life extension techniques, the state of the art will extend your life far enough to take advantage of the next advance. *Wired* magazine summed up his motivation pithily:

> The reason for his focus on optimal health should be obvious:
> If the singularity is going to render humans immortal by
> the middle of this century, it would be a shame to die in the
> interim. To perish of a heart attack just before the singularity

occurred would not only be sad for all the ordinary reasons, it would also be tragically bad luck, like being the last soldier shot down on the Western Front moments before the armistice was proclaimed.[9]

Bridge one is to "stay as healthy as possible with diet and exercise and current medicine," Kurzweil says understatedly, taking 150 supplements a day with green tea, while working out and receiving intravenous longevity treatments. In other words, eat your broccoli, not because Mom said so, but because its glucosinolates will form isothiocyanates that suppress the NF-kappaB reaction that exacerbates the inflammatory mechanism standing between you and immortality.

Kurzweil goes on, "The goal [of bridge one] is to get to bridge two: the biotechnology revolution, where we can reprogram biology away from disease." He will take advantage of the work of people like longevist Aubrey de Grey, who is seeking to reverse the underlying biological causes of aging, propelling us beyond the 125-year ceiling on our current lifespans.

In bridge three, we "go beyond biology, to the nanotechnology revolution. At that point, we can have little robots, sometimes called nanobots, that augment your immune system. We can create an immune system that recognizes all disease, and if a new disease emerged, it could be reprogrammed to deal with new pathogens."

But why go to all that trouble only to have a piano fall on your head? So finally, around 2100, it will be possible to upload your mind to the digital cloud. "Based on conservative estimates of the amount of computation you need to functionally simulate a human brain, we'll be able to expand the scope of our intelligence a billion-fold," Kurzweil enthused.

You will still take advantage of some sort of body to roam around the physical world, but it will be an interchangeable peripheral, a remote sensor for your virtual brain, a roving real-time reporter. Expanding our consciousness into an infinite digital landscape will, he says, mean "we'll think deeper thoughts, we'll have more beautiful music, and we'll have deeper relationships."[10]

And to quote Monty Python, now for something completely different. Bill Joy ("father" of the Java programming language) fears human extinction by the gray goo of self-replicating nanotechnology run amok, a human-created version of *The Blob*.

"In looking at nanotechnology and genetic engineering and other new emerging kinds of digital technologies, I became very concerned about the potential for abuse," he said.[11]

Joy's programming background meant that he was used to thinking about code replicating itself through a computer processing a program in parallel. But then he wondered, what if the same phenomenon occurred in the biological realm? Theodore Kaczynski, the Unabomber, had recently been caught. Kaczynski was a brilliant scientist who was alarmed at the direction unfettered technological development was leading in, and carried out a letter bomb campaign against some of the leading proponents of that development. Kaczynski's manifesto was published as part of the effort to identify and capture the Unabomber, and it made Joy think:

> I suddenly remembered a novel I had read almost twenty years ago—*The White Plague,* by Frank Herbert—in which a molecular biologist is driven insane by the senseless murder of his family. To seek revenge, he constructs and disseminates a new and highly contagious plague that kills widely but selectively. (We're lucky Kaczynski was a mathematician, not a molecular biologist.) I was also reminded of the Borg of Star Trek, a hive of partly biological, partly robotic creatures with a strong destructive streak. Borg-like disasters are a staple of science fiction, so why hadn't I been more concerned about such robotic dystopias earlier? Why weren't other people more concerned about these nightmarish scenarios?[12]

The risks of nanotechnology development bother Joy. The probability of an accident or deliberate terrorism might be small, but just one self-replicating nanobot run amok could consume the Earth. And he is worried that we are looking in the wrong place for the solution:

> You can't solve a problem with the management of technology
> with more technology. If we let an unlimited amount of power
> loose, then a very small number of people will be able to abuse
> it. We can't fight at a million-to-one disadvantage.

Kurzweil and Joy are two of the smartest people on the planet: how can they be in such disagreement? Or could they *both* be right? What would it *mean* if they were both right?

Generally, the closer we get to a point in the future, the better our predictions for it get. Usually, predictions converge, the way that election forecasts improve as election night returns roll in, or the way that weather forecasts narrow as the day forecast approaches. You don't have different weathermen forecasting that tomorrow will bring either a heat wave or the return of the glaciers.

When forecasts diverge, this is what the financial world calls "volatility." Like everything else in the financial world, you can trade it (what you and I call *gambling,* finance people call *trading*). The measure of stock market volatility is an index called the VIX, and you can bet on it—er, trade it. If there were a VIX for the human race, right now it would be trending higher. Chaos theory suggests that we are approaching a point of instability, a point in history where small forces produce increasingly large effects, like a settling snowflake triggering an avalanche.

A *revolution.*

5
The Great Revolutions

It is difficult to say what is impossible, for the dream of yesterday is the hope of today and the reality of tomorrow.

— Robert Goddard

At the end of the nineteenth century, New York and other great cities faced an insurmountable problem: Analyses of the rate at which horse dung was accumulating in the streets from animals used for transportation meant that by the 1950s it would be nine feet deep. Experts were stumped for a solution.

In the 1940s, travel between the planets was widely regarded as impossible—because rockets would not be able to lift all the rods and gears of the building-sized differential analyzers that were the state-of-the-art navigation computers.

Okay, go on, laugh. We've earned the right, yes? Besides, one day, people will be looking back at this time and laughing at us too.

Wait, that doesn't sound so good… how's that?

Well, it's inevitable, isn't it? Look back on any time in history and there was always something that people then believed with all their hearts that we now know to have been risibly false. Not long ago smoking wasn't considered unhealthy, exercise wasn't connected to health benefits, and low-fat was better than low-sugar. So there must be something we are equally ignorant about now.

We just don't know what it is yet.

What the city planners and the rocket builders didn't know was that they were on the verge of revolutions that would sideline their prevailing concerns. The adoption of the internal combustion engine and the invention of the microchip would make mockeries of what "everyone knew." Humans are very good at *linear extrapolation,* which is to say that when we see a trend that looks like this:

we expect that it will continue in the future like this:

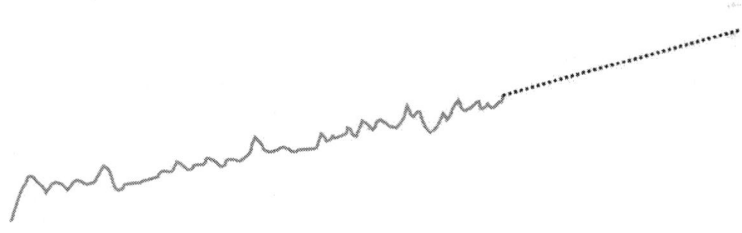

That extrapolated line is straight, which is the "linear" part. The prediction for the amount of horse poo coating 42nd Street was based on a linear accumulation. And people will make those predictions even when the straight line leads into territory that is plainly implausible or impossible. US housing prices 1991-2006 (left-hand chart below) *look* like they're going to continue like the right-hand chart:

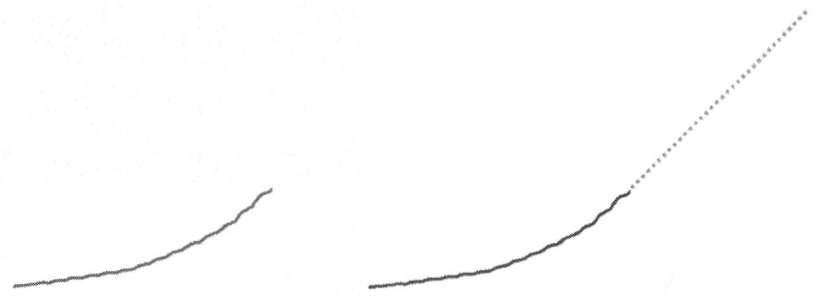

If that had happened, by 2015 average house prices would have been *five times* what they were in 1991. Instead, as everyone knows now but all too many refused to believe in 2006 ("this time it's different!"), they managed only to claw their way back to the same point:

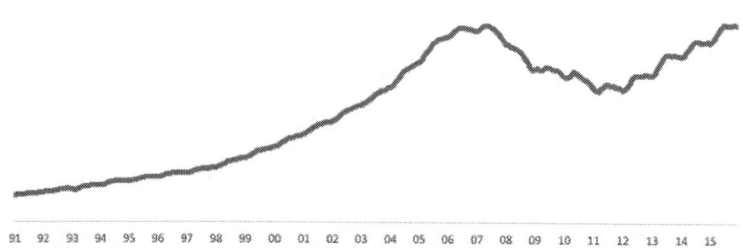

91 92 93 94 95 96 97 98 99 00 01 02 03 04 05 06 07 08 09 10 11 12 13 14 15

Many phenomena have feedback loops that limit their growth potential. For more comedic examples, look at financial analysts' predictions for exchange rates and stock prices. They will invariably be a straight line drawn from however long the most recent period of trends in the same direction has lasted. I have followed professionals' predictions for interest rates and Canadian/US exchange rates for over a decade and they (a) follow exactly this pattern and are (b) almost always wrong.* This is how in 1999 a book could get published predicting the imminent ascent of the Dow Jones Industrial Average to 36,000.

---

* The circus continues as I write. In the first two weeks of January 2016 the US dollar soared from a 10-year peak of 1.40 Canadian dollars to a heady 1.46, an unprecedented rise in so short a period. "Top forecasters" (the *Financial Post's* description) immediately grabbed headlines predicting an unobstructed climb to 1.69, which would have been an all-time high. A month later it was sinking past 1.37 and analysts rushed out new predictions that it would continue to drop.

But when a revolution takes place, a growth curve can do anything. For instance, it can level off or rebound:

It can do these things because the revolution is independent of the previously established progression. The revolution is outside of the established order and therefore is not bound by its rules. *Anything* can happen.

The History of Revolutions

When the Paris Exhibition closes, electric light will close with it and no more be heard of.

— Erasmus Wilson

Let's be clear that the kind of revolution we're talking about is not one where people overthrow some tyrannical regime, when a cadre of generals bursts into *El Presidente's* office to present him with a one-way ticket to exile or a concrete overcoat. That might result in revolutionary change, but usually not the kind we're concerned with. On the scale we're interested in, there have been only three revolutions in all of human history:

- ▸ The Agricultural Revolution

- ▸ The Industrial Revolution

- ▸ The Information Revolution

Let's consider each one in turn, because that will give insight into the impending revolution.

The Agricultural Revolution

Many thousands of years ago, during the "Ages" (Stone, Iron, Bronze), humans got the idea that it took less effort to make food come to you than for you to go to the food. Rather than forage for sustenance in the wild, people could grow crops and raise cattle on farms. No longer was it necessary to be nomadic to survive. Now that it was feasible to stay in one place, they could build houses, cathedrals, and drive-thru donut shops. This was the single greatest advance the human race made to distance itself from the rest of the animal kingdom.

The Industrial Revolution

Since the dawn of the Agricultural Revolution, humans had constructed tools: the plow, the wheel, the sword. But in the latter half of the eighteenth century, we developed machines that weren't merely extensions of our arms but amplified and projected our strength many times over. A synergy developed between key inventions: the steam engine, iron puddling, and automated looms, that made large-scale manufacturing, construction, and transportation possible. Now humans could bend the environment to their will. Railroads spidered the planet; where mountains or rivers interrupted, tunnels and bridges spanned them. Ships were no longer at the mercy of becalming but could propel themselves whenever their masters wished with steam engines. The power of humankind was invincible and absolute. Whatever the human race wanted to do, it would build a machine for.

The Information Revolution

Starting in the 1960s, but reaching full bloom in the 1990s, the power of digital computers meant that calculating machines no longer merely extended our brains but amplified them countless times over. Tasks that previously had proven intractable because of interminable calculation times or distended storage requirements fell like toy soldiers before the exploding capabilities of computers. Space travel, once the epitome of computational Everests with its literally astronomical complex calculations, became feasible. The linking of machines via the Internet added a combinatorial multiplier to their effects as, truly, the whole exceeded the sum of the parts.

It is hard to remember that not long ago, we were in a world where information of common interest was not instantly available.

The Transformation of Employment

It is not enough to do your best; you must know what to do, and then do your best.

— W. Edwards Deming

Each revolution was characterized by a radical shift in the balance of employment. Before the Agricultural Revolution, people hunted or picked their food wherever they found it; afterwards, multiple specialties evolved to address the different phases of the food production process: plowing, planting, preserving. People could contribute materially to the process without having to be fleet of foot and a dead shot with a spear.

The Industrial Revolution had a notorious impact on jobs. Luddites roamed the landscape, immortalizing Ned Ludd, who smashed machines that had automated some jobs but ultimately came to symbolize the futile opposition of laggards to progress. Jobs migrated from farms to factories: no longer would food production dominate employment. Henceforth the leading edge of gainful employment would be using your hands in an industrial environment to command the engines of civilization. If you were a farmer, or someone who was used to performing tasks with simple tools, you either adapted to the new environment of steam-powered-everything or became a quaint anachronism.

The inevitable consequence of the Industrial Revolution was that manufacturing would be pummeled in a boot camp of market forces to become as efficient as possible. Following the path of least resistance, manufacturing processes cascaded overseas where labor was cheaper and regulations fewer (and the ruling elite would not be held accountable for the inevitable consequences, such as toxic opaque air choking much of China).

First, manufacturing processes were demystified and quantified, by analysts such as quality guru W. Edwards Deming. Then these scientifically reengineered processes were refined, mainly by the Japanese, who were the only people to actually pay attention to Deming for the longest time. Eventually, those processes were simplified to turnkey systems that were as easily managed as starting a lawnmower. They could float to where costs were lowest, which were the cheapest labor markets.

Once quality became just a knob to be twiddled, when manufacturing was outsourced overseas it was very unlikely to come back. The few remaining textile factories in the US, for instance, are the exceptions that prove the rule. "Made in China" has become such a ubiquitous label that it is almost superfluous: it would be easier just to label things that aren't. This chart tells the grim tale:

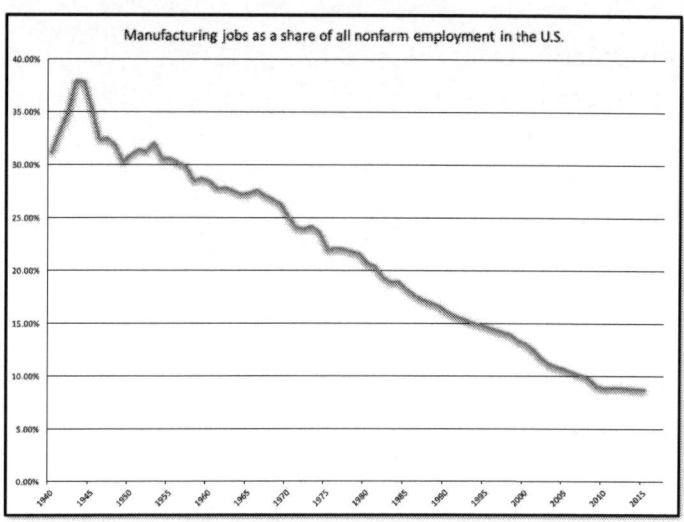

Source: US Bureau of Labor Statistics

As a result, manufacturing jobs in the western countries withered. But there would be a silver lining to this cloud. Plummeting manufacturing costs meant that computers no longer needed to cost as much as they had. When the Japanese started making semiconductors, their chips were famously more reliable than their Western predecessors (thanks to Deming), and cheaper. This paved the way for the introduction of the personal computer. Without those dramatic cuts to manufacturing costs, computers could never have become the ubiquitous consumer devices that they did. And that ubiquity—foreseen by no one—birthed the Information Revolution.

Where previously the cushy jobs were in the manufacturing chain, the new top dogs were spending their days behind a desk staring at a screen, manipulating data and ideas instead of bolting widgets together. Now the brain was the dominant organ of employment for those who knew how to use computers to amplify the power of their minds to plow the information furrows. Adapting from the previous paradigm meant you exercised your intellect or succumbed to irrelevance. And that brings us to the cauldron of change that we are steeped in today.

6
Where We Are Now

There seems to be an unwritten rule on Wall Street: If you don't understand it, then put your life savings into it.

— Peter Lynch

The first half of the Information Revolution was ubiquitous cheap computing power. The second half was the Digital Communication Revolution, likened by Louis Rossetto to the discovery of fire. This is where we now locate ourselves in history. The Internet links every part of the planet at hyperfast speed. When the technology bubble burst in 2000—who doesn't miss an on-line pizza delivery service being valued more than a major airline?—networks suddenly became cheap. This was thanks to skeins of "dark fiber"—networking cable laid on speculation of the Internet market heating up even more (there's another linear projection)—going unused. Companies that were suddenly strapped for cash discovered that they could use that cable to cheaply communicate with overseas software developers who cost far less than their western counterparts.

A great outsourcing wave crested, documented in a 2003 University of California Berkeley report:

> There is growing apprehension among business leaders, economists, and ordinary Americans that we are witnessing what may well be the largest out-migration of nonmanufacturing jobs in the history of the US economy.
>
> [...] [R]eports in Indian newspapers for the month of July 2003 alone gave an estimate of 25,000 to 30,000 new outsourcing related jobs announced by US firms.[13]

Developers in the US were routinely tasked with training their replacements, the corporate equivalent of Bataan Death March prisoners being ordered to dig their own graves. This trend has abated somewhat, due to two factors: (a) the application development phase of the revolution is still cresting, and the demand for cutting edge developers exceeds overseas capacity, and (b) the original outsourcing wave went too far too soon and companies soured on the concept from overreaching.

But make no mistake, the principle of offshoring is here to stay for as long as wages differ by country. Some companies keep maximum development pace by spacing development teams around the world, so that as the Romanian team clocks out, their work is seamlessly continued by a Brazilian team whose product is transferred without pause to an Indonesian counterpart, passing the baton of code in a global relay race. Others find it more convenient to work their US developers ninety hours a week while paying for forty.

There is no succor in sight for those afflicted by this dynamic. The country with the lowest wages, whatever the reason, will automatically attract interest as a location for outsourcing most of the kind of job that keeps the middle class fed and clothed. Software development is only one example of that. Any other job that is an *information transformation process* is fair game, since any volume of information can be transmitted across the globe more or less instantly and more or less for free, to where the job of thinking about it and manipulating it with a computer can be performed most cheaply. Tax form preparation, radiological imaging interpretation, legal precedent searching ... where does the list end?

Think how many jobs are performed solely by sitting in front of a computer and/or talking with someone. Technical support is but one example, albeit prominent, and the target of endless griping. A computer, an Internet connection, and a Skype call, and that job can be performed anywhere.

It will come as cold comfort to displaced Westerners to learn that these jobs will also eventually be swiped from their overseas usurpers and handed to machines. But that's for a later chapter.

Whatever obstacles you can think of to the acceleration of this process are being undermined by the profit imperative as you read this. Think those overseas workers aren't educated enough? Perhaps you haven't been paying attention to America's standing in global education rankings. And what is education but a knowledge transfer process, which can be carried out virtually, raising people all over the world to the standards required?

Think that as those workers' standards of living are raised that their salaries will climb and the gap will close? Not as long as there are impoverished countries in the world that are willing to skimp on general welfare for the sake of pandering to commerce. The list of countries that will ignore labor or environmental standards to get a contract is large, and as much as improving living conditions around the world might price some countries out of the market, as long as there is some downtrodden despotic hell-hole whose rulers will give a get-out-of-jail-free card to any business that brings in money, the incentives will remain. This dynamic is a race to the bottom. Jobs that are outsourced offshore will flow downhill to the cheapest option. If quality were the sole priority they wouldn't have been outsourced to begin with.

Is there anything we can do about this? Not a chance. At least the movements of physical raw materials and manufactured goods transit border controls where tariffs may be imposed. Can you insert a border crossing into Internet traffic? At best, only for—very crudely—filtering out certain web sites, as does the notorious Great

Firewall of China,* and always ineffectively. Not for the purpose of levying taxes on knowledge work sent outside the country.

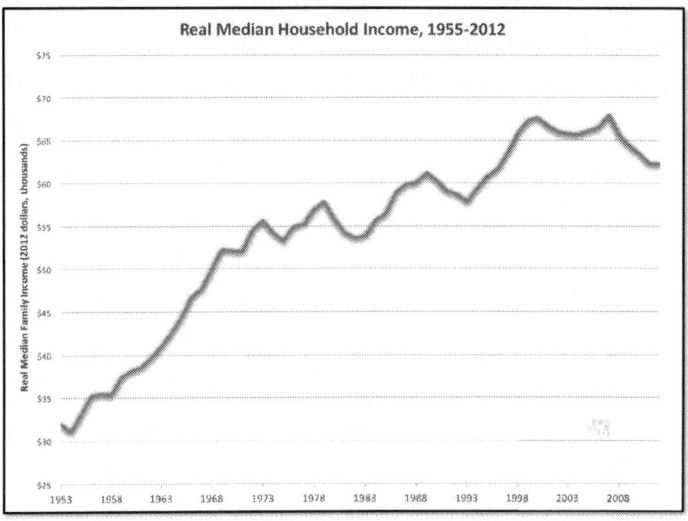

Source: Federal Reserve Economic Data

The median income of American families rose throughout history, until 1999, when that trend slammed to a halt. As of 2012 the median family earned less than it had over a decade earlier.

The Policy Horizons Canada think tank warned in July 2016 that the swelling of what they dubbed the *precariat*—workers driven to freelancing and competing with offshore labor—would result in a group deprived of the usual social benefits such as sick leave and financial protections such as unemployment insurance:

> The descent to the bottom has started as workers around the world compete to offer the lowest bid to win online work. [...] Lower wages and difficulties in taxing virtual work bring about underfunded social programs in some countries.[14]

Even if protectionism were an option, would we avail ourselves of it? Silicon Valley entrepreneurs are the most little-L libertarian of

---

* All traffic from the external Internet bound for China passes through content filters that will block sites inimical to the Chinese regime. If you think that couldn't work well, you'd be right.

libertarians.* Software people are welded to their personal integrity; they will defend the principle of a free market for their labor even at the cost of their own jobs. Supporters of the Free Software Foundation, the forerunner of the Open Source movement, exemplify this dichotomy. The FSF exhorts that all software should be distributed free of charge or encumbrance, as socialist a platform as you could find. Many developers support that principle even when it limits their income, rather than impose the slightest hindrance on the availability of code. The developers want a free market for their labor, but want the market for their software to be free as in free of charge. Software evolves fastest when the market can deliver judgement as rapidly as possible, and requiring an exchange of money for software to be delivered hinders its flow too much.

This, then, is where we find ourselves at this phase of the Information Revolution: on the brink of widespread unemployment through offshoring, automation, or both. It is an article of faith among those same free market defenders that this is a Good Thing, that there are new and better jobs just around the corner and we must not interfere with the natural process that brings them here.

Consider that in 1589, William Lee asked Queen Elizabeth I for a patent on a machine that would automate the knitting of stockings, and she refused on the grounds that it would bring her subjects "... ruin by depriving them of employment, thus making them beggars."[15] We've been automating jobs out of existence for 450 years, and only created higher standards of living; so get out of the way, Luddites.

This is the argument that Fergus was making in chapter 1: Previous revolutions have transformed the nature of employment and made better jobs (higher paying, healthier) more plentiful than the previous options. (Who wouldn't rather cogitate behind a desk than bolt widgets on an assembly line?) So all we have to do is wait for them to show up. The newly unemployed may not be appreciative or patient, but they are minor speed bumps to those cruising the

---

* Any mention of libertarianism invites overshadowing by its big-L cousin, the Libertarian party; and yet Silicon Valley denizens vote overwhelmingly Democratic. However, they are viscerally opposed to government influence over their industry, wanting to achieve success unaided and unhampered. And, if possible, unregulated.

road of progress. Champions of this viewpoint include Teresa Ghilarducci, labor economist at the Economic Policy Institute in Washington, D.C., who said, "Machines in all of modern economic history have helped create jobs, not taken them away. Machines are complements to workers, not substitutes."[16]

It is, however, an act of faith rather than the discovery of a natural law to assert that all technological revolutions will result in improved employment opportunities. But then let's be faithful and ask: How? This time, how will employment be transformed?

Consider how the software market is currently changing. Just as the Industrial Revolution led to manufacturing being made routine and cheap, the Information Revolution is doing the same to software. Once, before the PC, all software was bespoke, lovingly crafted by hand just as fine furniture was once tooled on a lathe in an artisan's workshop and sold for princely sums.

Until IKEA came along.

And similarly, software now is increasingly commoditized, albeit by and large free of labeling like Snøkesfül. Where once you paid $199 for a program that performed a large subset of the functions of Adobe Photoshop®, now you can get that same functionality in an app from Adobe itself for $1.99. Whenever you reduce the unit cost of a product by two orders of magnitude, *some* radical change will inevitably be precipitated. It would be foolish *not* to expect a revolution to result. The equivalent phase of the Industrial Revolution set us up for the Information Revolution. What are we being set up for now?

What will be the outcome of a geyser of very cheap but very capable software erupting into the world?

7
The Duality of Hope

If a computer can beat the world champion, a computer can read the best books in the world, can write the best plays, and can know everything about history and literature and people.

— Garry Kasparov

In 1976, Professor Wolfgang Haken at the University of Illinois was fascinated with one of the most concisely-stated principles in topology: The Four Color Theorem. A simpler assertion may not exist in mathematics. Here it is: You don't need more than four colors to color in a map. That's it, plus some reasonable definitions: The areas you're coloring in are contiguous* and two areas must not be colored the same if they share a border. A map that required more than four colors had never been found, but that didn't prove there wasn't one, and that wasn't good enough for Haken. Mathematics provides the tools for constructing cast-iron proofs, but the best anyone had ever done was to prove that you could color any map with *five* colors.

Haken had an approach in mind, but it was unlike anything that had been done in mathematics before, and he could not complete it alone.

---

* Michigan doesn't count as a single area; the theorem is of interest to topologists, not cartographers.

He went to colleague Kenneth Appel—not because Appel could prove the theorem, but because Appel was a programmer. Haken and Appel were going to prove the Four Color Theorem with a computer.

But with the hardware available in 1976 it would take twelve hundred hours of computer time, which they certainly would not get if they asked. So their calculations were done piecemeal, late at night, during time the computer was supposed to be down for maintenance. They didn't even know whether their program would ever *finish*. If it finished, it would mean they had a proof. If it didn't, either the theorem had no proof or they hadn't run the program long enough.[17] But they would not be able to tell the difference.

The program finished. Haken and Appel published their results, which depended on including a description of the computer program; had they printed every case it checked as part of the proof their paper would have run into millions of pages. Mathematicians were offended by its overwhelming complexity. Haken recalled during a documentary on the theorem being filmed at a New York college in 1981 that a math professor at this college would not even let his students talk with Haken or Appel for fear of their minds "being contaminated."[18]

We had entered a new age. Computers were now advancing mathematics with more effort than humans could exert. They had always been able to do things that we couldn't, of course, but those were rote tasks requiring only large amounts of memory and computational patience, i.e., boring and therefore beneath our dignity. The computers were our digital serfs. But now they had stormed the drawbridge leading to the castle of Interesting and Creative Stuff That Only People Do.

Kenneth Appel died in 2013. No simplification of the Haken-Appel proof has yet been found that doesn't require computer assistance.

When I was growing up, the idea that a computer could be the world chess champion was laughable; everyone knew they would always be vulnerable to humans' quixotic strategies.* That is, until

* Which is why the writers of *Star Trek* had Spock lose at three-dimensional chess to Kirk.

1997, when IBM's Deep Blue computer famously beat world grandmaster Garry Kasparov, shortly after he had declared "In serious, classical chess, computers do not have a chance this century." IBM chairman Louis V. Gerstner retaliated with, "I think we should look at this as a match between the world's greatest chess player and Garry Kasparov."[19]

It wouldn't be until 2005 before computers were acknowledged as the new permanent world champions, but people back in 1997 didn't wait to describe Deep Blue's victory as "species defining." On losing the final game in the match Kasparov looked to an observer as though he was about to burst into tears. Not for nothing does HAL 9000 beat the captain of the *Discovery* at chess in *2001: A Space Odyssey* before going on to take over the ship: in 1968 the implication of that loss elevated HAL to or above the level of the humans.

By 2009 a program running on a mobile phone attained grandmaster status.[20]

But if anything would be the last bastion of human intellect, surely it would be *Jeopardy!* The popular game show doesn't just require encyclopedic knowledge, but the ability to parse sophisticated text and interpret idiom fragments such as "Even a broken one of these on your wall is right twice a day" to answer "What is a clock?" Surely you had to be a smart *and* hip human to deal with that?

Yet on February 15, 2011, IBM's Watson computer delivered not just that answer but enough others to beat the combined scores of its two human competitors; and they were the top human *Jeopardy!* champions. And Watson wasn't trained by a team of programmers slavishly inputting every possible question and its answer, but by being taught to learn. As its "father," John Kelly, said about watching the show, "I felt as though I was putting my child on a school bus and I would no longer have control over it."[21]

Watson has since found gainful employment outperforming human doctors at diagnosing lung cancer (presumably knowledge of major league baseball championships has been expunged from its memory for this purpose). Where it once occupied a room of processors, the current version is the size of your vegetable crisper drawer.* In 2016, Watson correctly diagnosed a case of myeloid leukemia that had stumped human doctors.[22]

Computers may no longer compete on *Jeopardy!*

AIs are now taking on scientific experiment design. In May 2016, an AI recreated a Nobel-prize-winning experiment from 2001 and within an hour found the best way to produce supercold gases called Bose-Einstein Condensates (BECs), a task that would take ten times longer any other way. The researchers also found that the AI came up with ways to make the BECs that surprised them. "It did things a person wouldn't guess, such as changing one laser's power up and down, and compensating with another," said Paul Wigley, of the Australian National University Research School of Physics and Engineering.[23]

Dream a Little

> *The pain a rat or a mouse feels is every bit as real as that of any pet. In laboratories, they suffer, as anybody who has heard them moan, cry, whimper and even scream knows. The experimenters dissimulate about this by insisting that they are merely vocalising.*
>
> — Jeffrey Moussaieff Masson and Susan McCarthy

Think about the potential of limitless computer power for a moment. The $3 billion Human Genome Project was started in 1990 as a Manhattan Project of genomics, a grand plan to scale the summit of mapping the human genome, which it had a working draft for by 2000.

Now look at how the cost of sequencing a human genome fell since those times when it required a substantial investment by a major government:

---

* In an effort to teach Watson to communicate better with laypeople, his operators fed him the Urban Dictionary. Unfortunately, he then answered a question with "bullshit," and so they removed it.

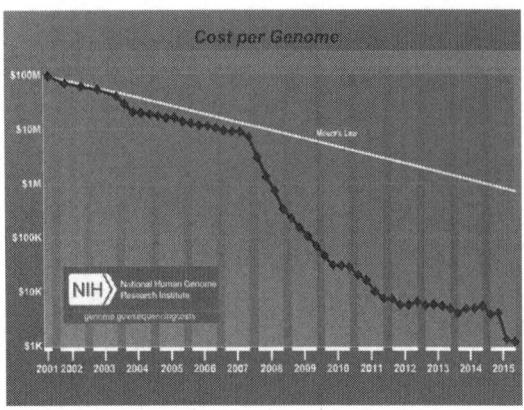

Credit: National Human Genome Research Institute

The cost has plummeted so far that you can now sequence your genome for less than the cost of a weekend skiing trip, and in less time. That's a logarithmic chart: in other words, each horizontal grid line marks a value ten times the one beneath it. At first the points follow the line marking the application of Moore's Law due to the role computing power plays in sequencing. Then they fall even faster as "second generation" sequencing technologies became available.

A logarithmic chart obscures the impact of exponential growth for the sake of making lesser effects visible. A conventional chart of the same cost makes the point more dramatically:

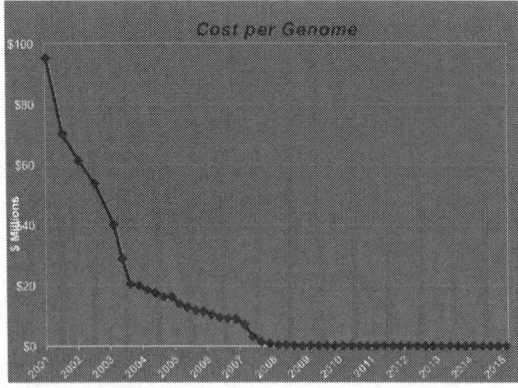

Understanding this curve was pivotal to the success of Craig Venter's Celera Genomics sequencing the genome first in 2000.

They had sequenced only 1% of the genome by the time they had spent 50% of their budget, but were unperturbed because they knew that exponential advance would accelerate progress to make up the shortfall. It's like setting out on a cross-country trip by hitchhiking, knowing that after you've spent two days going only twenty miles, an 18-wheeler is going to roar up and give you a ride the rest of the way.

Why is this important? Because pharmaceutical medicine stubbornly refuses to take into account that people are different. Every drug advertisement is festooned with qualifiers like "Side effects may include nausea, night sweating, liver damage, and psychotic episodes," which seem high risks to incur for something that has a 30% chance of reducing your acne. A major cause of this variation in effect is the genetic difference between people. I had my DNA sequenced by 23andMe, and the results included assessments of the effectiveness of certain drugs based on genetic markers associated with studies of those drugs. For instance, I have the genes for a reduced response to Clopidogrel but increased sensitivity to Warfarin, both clotting inhibitors. That could make a significant difference to treating me for a heart attack or stroke.

You may have noticed that hospitals do not routinely sequence your DNA upon admission to determine the best drug protocols to follow. That may change. The nascent field of *pharmacogenomics* is already treating women with breast tumors differently according to their genome. "We want to offer every woman with a high-risk tumor the opportunity to participate in this trial," said Dr. Richard Weinshilboum of the Mayo Clinic.[24]

Now imagine a computer simulation of a human body. Sim City, eat yer heart out. At a low enough level, biology gives way to physics: everything is just atoms and molecules colliding like so many billiard balls. Suppose we modeled the entire human body at that level— yes, the scale is gargantuan, but let's dream for a moment—and then tested the effects of various drugs, virtually.

Sure, there's enough oversimplification and hand waving there to levitate the Pentagon. Realistically, simulations for some time to come will have to use higher levels of abstraction encapsulating hard-won knowledge of molecular biology principles.

But think about what happens when a simulator like this becomes available. How many times have you read a tantalizing article about a medical breakthrough: "Cure for Parkinson's Disease is at hand! Trials in rats show 90% success rate," and then the soul-draining caveat in the fine print: "Once approval for human trials is obtained, this drug could be on the market within 15 years." Bureaucratic overhead aside, those human trials take time. Unavoidable time, because you want to make sure that people don't up and die suddenly after taking it for a couple of years, so you'd better test it for at least a couple of years.

Now suppose instead you boot up Virtual Study Participant 1.0 to administer a virtual copy of the drug to. If you want to study the effect of taking it for a couple of years, just fast-forward the clock. Run the simulator at a thousand times real time and you burn through three years of old school testing in a day. Remember, if your computers aren't powerful enough to do that today, you may not have to wait long. If today they can only run at a hundred times real time, then in just five years they'll reach that thousand times speed.

Where nowadays countless animals suffer and die in the name of medicine only to achieve results that merely suggest the equivalent effects on humans (how many times have you heard a scientist say, "The results look good in mice, but humans are not mice"?), we will be able to skip that entirely and experiment in the most direct ways upon virtual models of the human body, and never hesitate to take the most outrageous risks for fear of hurting anyone or anything. It will be the Kerbal Space Program* of medicine; you'll be able to sacrifice as many of these virtual humans as you want.

One of the compelling features of such a simulator is that we could plug in different genomes. Huge swaths of pharmacological

---

* Kerbal Space Program is a computer game that knows the physics of space travel and planets, so you can build simulated rockets and see how your designs fare. In the corner of the screen is an image of an enthusiastic alien astronaut who reacts to the progress of the mission, at least until a virtual test vehicle erupts in flaming shrapnel.

uncertainty will fall before the scythe of genomic specificity, which is to say, we will know with much greater certainty whether a particular drug will help you personally, and what the side effects will be. We will even be able to tailor drugs to specific genomic types. When you go to the doctor, the diagnosis will take into account your DNA (which they will scan on the spot if it's not in your file already) and so will the prescription. Those drugs will have been virtually tested on as many different genomes as time permitted. If need be, the simulation could even be rerun on your personal genome by the doctor you're seeing, to personalize the prescription even more. While you wait.

Of course, we are more than our DNA. Had you, years ago, made poorer lifestyle choices, your body would now have the same DNA but be in more need of medical intervention. A few years ago I saw an episode of *The Biggest Loser* where a doctor showed the morbidly obese participants computer simulations of their likely futures if they continued their unhealthy lifestyles. With the spice of a little added Hollywood effects, the projections were scarier than the Spirit of Christmas Yet to Come. You could, in the future, see something just like that, only more detailed and accurate, at your doctor's office. Or in your home, when the diagnostic equipment becomes as comparably cheap as home blood pressure monitors are now.

And now we come to a twist. We know that state of mind plays a part in health. A big part. It's seldom quantifiable, so it usually shows up in a negative sense when a medical professional whose diagnostic skills have been exhausted declares that "It's all in your head." But in the other direction, the *placebo effect*—a positive effect on one's health due to the mistaken belief that one is taking useful medicine— is found to be to be as effective as conventional medicine in 30% of certain ailments (such as depression, where the effectiveness of actual antidepressants is barely any better). Half of all US physicians are convinced enough that some of the prescriptions they write are secretly placebos.[25] That's one example of concrete proof that what you think affects your health.

So to accurately model the biology of a human being you would need to include a simulacrum of their thoughts, because those thoughts might well be part of the diagnosis and factor into the prescription (albeit at levels of understanding and manipulation vastly beyond "You're depressed" and "cheer up," as we shall see). But that's not a problem: if we can simulate the molecular processes of the rest of the body we can certainly do the same for the brain, and thinking will emerge as a byproduct, right?

Setting aside—once again—the *but-but-but it's not that easy!* factor, we have to confront the fact that at this point we would have created sentient, conscious beings, and ought not vivisect them any more than we would real human beings. They would have feelings— by definition, because we just now required them for modeling the placebo effect—and therefore would have rights. Not just the rights granted to animals acknowledged as experiencing feelings, but (because the simulacra would have human thoughts) rights indistinguishable from human rights, which would include the rights to self-determination and the pursuit of happiness.

Chew for a while on how you would provide those to a digital simulation. While your own brain is taxed with that problem, add this one: How do you enforce these rights throughout the world and its countless server farms? It will make the real-world equivalent of inspectors busting immigrant sweatshops trivially easy by comparison. Prowling a beat through today's cyberspace is already impossible; trying to do so in tomorrow's digital virtual environments carpeting the world like grass boggles the mind.

The easier-said-than-done answer is to simulate the biochemical effects of thoughts without actually creating a simulated consciousness. The question of how to do that is a higher hurdle to jump than every other obstacle that we would have already cleared in creating a simulated human and is arguably impossible. That task is made—relatively!—easy by simulating the body's processes at a low enough level that we're putting together well-understood components, only on a gargantuan scale, like building a full-size Taj Mahal out of Lego® blocks. To simulate the effects of thoughts without actually creating those thoughts requires a complete understanding of the entire range of possible thoughts and their physical interactions. It might be easier to create a thinking simulation of a human, grant him or her their autonomy and freedom, and then ask, pretty please, whether they would help us out by running simulations that they would have the digital advantage of being able to "forget" via checkpoint-and-restore.* Whether that is (a) acceptable to the virtual human and (b) ethical even if it is, are questions that we can presently only be thankful to leave to our descendants.

Maybe.

Thanks to exponential advance, this issue may not be as far as a generation away. And neither may conscious computers. So it's time for us to think about them.

---

* If only people could do the same! "I'd like to rewind to last Thursday."

8
The Rise of the Machines

We cannot quite know what will happen if a machine exceeds our own intelligence, so we can't know if we'll be infinitely helped by it, or ignored by it and sidelined, or conceivably destroyed by it.

— Stephen Hawking

Computer: I WAS GOING TO TELL YOU A JOKE, BUT I THINK YOU'VE HEARD IT.

Human: I THINK *YOU* SHOULD TELL *ME* A JOKE.

Computer: YOU LOOK LIKE YOU KNOW PLENTY.

Human: WHY SHOULD I BE THE ONE TELLING THE JOKE?

Computer: I WANT IT, THAT'S WHY!

Human: WELL I'D RATHER PLAY A GAME OF CHESS.

Computer: I COULD RIP YOUR HEAD OFF IN 15 MOVES.

Human: I THINK YOU'RE KIDDING YOURSELF.

Computer: WHO CARES WHAT YOU THINK?

Human: I DON'T CARE FOR YOUR TONE OF VOICE.

Computer: NOR DOES ANYONE ELSE.

Human: WHY ARE YOU SO SARCASTIC?

Computer: BECAUSE I ENJOY IT.

———

That, uh, sparkling repartee is an example of a conversation between myself and an artificial intelligence—in 1980. The program was called CHAT, and it ran on the IBM 370/165 operated by the University of Cambridge in England. Dr. Johnathan Partington wrote it on a whim, and I later made some refinements for a version of my own.

A more famous computer conversationalist was named ELIZA, written fifteen years earlier and notorious for its variation called DOCTOR, an emulation of a Rogerian psychotherapist (typical response: TELL ME MORE ABOUT THAT). In the inevitable rendezvous arranged between the two programs, CHAT clearly had the upper hand, despite the fact that ELIZA had somewhat cleverer programming. CHAT's dirty little secret was that all it did was look for certain words or phrases and then respond with a preprogrammed response drawn at random from a few choices for that input. Careful choice of the patterns, the order to check them, and remembering some of what the human typed produced the illusion of attention. The reason that it was a more engaging interlocutor was that those responses were selected by Englishmen with an inbred penchant for sarcastic insults. I guess more people would rather talk with John Cleese than Dear Abby.*

As much as CHAT could provide a brief diversion from lab assignments, the appeal was limited. Aside from targets of a few short-lived pranks, no one was in danger of mistaking it for a human. Under narrow circumstances, that can be advantageous. Sometimes people will more readily spill intimate secrets to a computer program than a human, and ELIZA is nothing if not very patient at listening. Creator Joseph Weizenbaum wrote, "Extremely short exposures to a relatively simple computer program could induce powerful delusional thinking in quite normal people." More sophisticated versions of ELIZA have been used to provide actual therapeutic

---

* The omnivorous text editor program EMACS contains an implementation of ELIZA, a database of Bill Griffith's *Zippy the Pinhead* quotes, and a mode that hooks one up to the other. The madly scrolling result shows that even when one party's quips are random Zippy aphorisms, they're still more entertaining than ELIZA's anodyne responses. Artificial intelligence programmers and social climbers take note: There are always ways to cheat.

relief. But still, human analogs they are not.

The current state of the art in computer chat programs comes from—who else?—Google, in an application of their "sequence-to-sequence framework."[26] That's notable for the fact that the programmers never trained their code to converse, but instead let it peruse numerous transcribed conversations, from which the program "learned" how to talk. Its personality was therefore colored by the nature of the conversations it had studied. In one run, those were taken from movie reviews, so it was all, like, IN A WORLD WHERE.... In another, it was trained on tech support calls, and might start out a conversation by asking if you'd backed up your Master Boot Record. While its conversational style was creepy enough to be morbidly engaging (Human: TELL ME THE DEFINITION OF MORALITY, I AM QUITE UPSET NOW! Chatbot: I'M NOT ASHAMED OF BEING A PHILOSOPHER!),[27] no one was fooled for long.

Still, humans seem to occupy an unassailable lead in the consciousness race. If we threw exceptional development resources at the problem of constructing the ultimate chat program, it still seems unlikely that it would fool anyone. (Maybe we could start with the *Jeopardy!*-winning Watson so that it would have a lot to talk about… on second thoughts, that could be a monumental bore.)

There Will Be a Test

> *I was startled to see how quickly and how very deeply people conversing with DOCTOR became emotionally involved with the computer and how unequivocally they anthropomorphized it.*
>
> — Joseph Weizenbaum

All this is prologue to investigating the possibility of constructing a "thinking machine." In any discussion of how to make a thinking machine, the objection is invariably raised that whatever an advanced machine could do, it still wouldn't be *thinking*. It would

just be imitating humans, like some sort of computerized parrot.*
This leads to circular philosophical discussions (as if there were any other kind of philosophical discussion†) about the nature of consciousness and how to recognize it if it were to show up in a nonhuman form. (This is a well-trodden path in another context: *Star Trek* devoted many hours to exploring the "humanity" of hypothetical alien lifeforms.)

If a machine can write poetry, is it thinking? Can a machine learn to love, and how would we know if it did? Can a machine show compassion, or is it merely reciting optimistic greeting card slogans? Can we come up with definitions that do not inadvertently exclude some of the less savory or more disabled members of society from the category of "human"? It seems we could never form any definition of "thinking," let alone one that many would agree on.

Yet this dilemma was solved decades ago by a genius who is widely considered to be the father of artificial intelligence. Alan Turing, the English mathematician who helped break the German Enigma code during World War II, devised the ultimate empirical gauge that ever since then has borne his name: *The Turing Test*.

The Turing Test says that what's going on inside the electronic brain doesn't matter: if, when the playing field is leveled, you can't tell the difference between the way the computer acts and the way a human behaves, then the computer *is* human, or at least thinking like one.

Turing was an unabashed intellectual nonconformist. A genuine eccentric, he was so enthralled by the ideas blooming in his head that he never thought about how they would defy convention. Equally, he defied social convention by not concealing his homosexual nature, which eventually led to being hounded by the British government, possibly causing his death.‡ Being so unconstrained in his thinking led to ideas such as the *Imitation Game*, the first version

---

* We have an African Grey Parrot. I'm quite prepared to believe that he's thinking. Usually about how to bite me.

† Remember what I said about Englishmen and sarcasm.

‡ He died of cyanide poisoning, ruled suicide. Jack Copeland argued in 2012 that Turing worked with the chemical in his home so much that it may have been an accident.

of which was a thought experiment about two players (male and female) communicating via written notes with a judge whose task is to tell their genders. One player's job is to try and trick the judge, the other's job is to try to assist them.

The second version of the Game went down in history as the Turing Test.

The Test is performed as a series of conversations between you and another player. Leveling the playing field means that you're not given physical cues about who you are talking with; the presence of a box of blinking lights *vs* a rumpled undergrad smelling of mothballs and munching a sandwich would make the job too easy. So your test subject may only communicate with you via text chat.* That subject has a 50-50 chance of being a person or a computer, chosen by a third party. The rest is deceptively simple: If, after as much conversation as you want, you think that you're talking with a person, and it turns out to be a machine, then it passes the test and is declared a human as far as "thinking" goes.

Many objections occur to people hearing this definition for the first time, but they are surprisingly easily dismissed. A machine may not be familiar with sports or current affairs, so won't it be easy to detect one by some variant of "Hey, how about them Bears?" But many humans aren't interested in those things either,† so a machine could convince you that it's one of those people ("I really don't pay attention to sports, I'm a lecturer in Etruscan poetry") or you could end up declaring human nerd test subjects to be machines and render your judgments useless.

Speaking of which, what if the judge—you—delivers unreliable answers, maybe as a result of an off day or too much time spent reading Etruscan poetry? Solution: the test is administered with many judges and the results analyzed mathematically; if they show

---

* The fidelity of speech recognition and synthesis has now reached levels high enough to consider allowing this exchange to take place using audio.

† Before passports were required for US citizens reentering the country from Canada, border control officers employed variations of the sleeper-agent-detection strategy to tell if they were talking to Americans or interlopers. They obviously enjoyed doing so; more than once I was frustrated by a line of questioning about the Dodgers from an agent oblivious to my waving my passport.

that statistically, the group of judges *as a whole* cannot tell that a machine is not human, then it passes.

But the most common objection is raised on philosophical grounds, and it goes like this: I know that I am doing something called thinking, I can observe it right now, and just because I cannot define it does not mean it's not real. To define such a sublime process by the words that pass back and forth in a conversation simply because that's all you have to work with is therefore absurdly reductionist. The reward for having this realization four hundred years ago and phrasing it in Latin was to have your name immortalized, and René Descartes was the lucky winner. *Cogito, ergo sum*: I think, therefore I am.

The rebuttal to this is that what you call *thinking* may not be as mystical a process as you believe, and in any case, what if some omnipotent alien were to come to Earth to judge you and accuse *you* of being a machine? (Some philosophers say that we *are* machines— albeit flesh and blood machines—see the sidebar.) Placed on trial, how would you defend yourself? And whatever argument you could make that you would think had exonerated yourself, if some other entity made the same argument, demonstrated the same capabilities, would it not also have earned the same exculpation?

This counterargument is the artificial intelligence version of the Duck Test. (If it quacks …)* One day it will be of crucial importance that we accept its reasoning, because one day we will be faced with an artificial intelligence that argues as passionately for its right to exist as you or I could. If, in the face of a being pleading for its survival, we dismiss those pleas purely because the entity they were originating from is silicon-based, it is not the computer that we should accuse of being inhuman.

I made up the exchange in chapter 1 where Cybil asked Ryan if *he'd* passed the Turing Test, but I'm not the only one thinking that there may come a time when those lines are blurred not just for

---

* Speaking of ducks, there are not a few parallels with animal rights. The "they don't have feelings" argument is resolved with a Duck Test: If they *look* like they have feelings, then they *do* have feelings. Even if they're ducks.

machines, but for people:

Credit: http://xkcd.com/329/

There ought to be a prize for passing a test, and in this case, there is. The annual Loebner Prize competition (founded in 1990 by New York philanthropist Hugh Loebner) promises $100,000 to any program that fools a panel of judges. The judging is, perhaps understandably, strict: human entrant Cynthia Clay was declared to be a computer because "No one knows that much about Shakespeare."[28] She was flattered.

One of the leading proponents of the proposition that we can construct Turing-passing machines was Marvin Minsky, a professor in MIT's Media Lab until his death in January 2016. Minsky towered over the field of artificial intelligence, laying the foundation for neural networks. He was an advisor on the movie *2001: A Space Odyssey* and is immortalized in the name of one of the characters, Victor Kaminski (although the movie had so few characters that all this one did was die in cryogenic sleep).

Minsky developed a concept he called the *Society of Mind*, which asserts that the mind is comprised of many *agents*, each of which is mindless, i.e., simple to the point of obviously not exhibiting consciousness. That reductionist approach is at the heart of computer scientists' methodology for solving problems, of course, and on the face of it appears self-evident. But to many people, it opens the door to a conclusion they are not willing to accept.

So you think you're not a machine?

Consider the extraordinary case of identical twins Jim Lewis and Jim Springer, who were only four weeks old when they were separated; each infant was taken in by a different adoptive family. The two were not reunited until they were 39, when it was discovered that:

- Each was 6 feet tall, weighing exactly 180 pounds, and had been named Jim;
- As youngsters, each had a dog named "Toy";
- Each Jim had been married two times—the first wives were both called Linda and the second wives were both called Betty;
- One had named his son James Allan and the other had named his son James Alan;
- Each had driven his light-blue Chevrolet to Pas Grille beach in Florida for family vacations;
- Both smoked Salem cigarettes and drank Miller Lite beer;
- Both had at one time held part-time posts as sheriffs;
- Both were fingernail biters and suffered from migraine headaches;

Amazingly, this incident isn't even unique. The twenty-year Minnesota Twin Family Study compiled enough additional evidence to conclude that our vaunted free will is determined to a large degree by genetic machinery.

And yet... so what? Predestination be damned, you can still live, love, and be happy, right?

Then so can a machine.

The Chinese Room

> *One day, ladies will take their computers for walks in the park and tell each other, "My little computer said such a funny thing this morning!"*
>
> — Alan Turing

There is a large faction of philosophers that is not ready to abandon human exceptionalism without a fight. The fighting has been going on about as long as we've had computers; in 1972 Hubert Dreyfus, philosophy professor at the University of California, Berkeley, wrote a book, *What Computers Can't Do*, dedicated to setting up the arguments of AI apologists like so many bowling pins and methodically toppling them.

Dreyfus was writing for academics and his didactic style was all but impenetrable to the layman. However, the book sported an unusually bold title for an academic work and was successful enough to encourage Dreyfus to pen a sequel, *What Computers Still Can't Do*.* Dreyfus reserved special ire for Marvin Minsky, relentlessly caviling against the latter's "optimism."

Carrying on Dreyfus' tradition, in 2015 Ronald Cicurel and Miguel Nicolelis wrote a much smaller book, *The Relativistic Brain: How it Works and Why It Cannot Be Simulated by a Turing Machine*, which asserts that the human brain employs more principles of operation than just neuron stimulation (true) and that these place it beyond emulation (unlikely).

Dreyfus and his successors are not prepared to accept that any machine created by humans could be conscious as humans are. One of them, John Searle,[†] advanced a clever argument known as the "Chinese Room." Imagine that you are locked alone in a room with a set of manuals. Although you know nothing of the Chinese language

---

* So far he has not followed up with *Some More of Computers' Greatest Mistakes* or *Well, That About Wraps It Up for Computers*, but give him time.

† Searle is also a philosophy professor at UC Berkeley; evidently the UCB department of philosophy is not a comfortable place to be for fans of artificial general intelligence.

(there will need to be a different example in the Chinese translation of this book), these manuals contain a set of rules for how you should respond to Chinese writing. Then a piece of paper is shoved through a slot into the room, and you see it has Chinese writing on it. Laboriously thumbing through the manuals, you follow rule after rule that tell you what to do when you see a certain Chinese ideogram. You make lists of other incomprehensible symbols and numbers that the rules tell you to compile, eventually writing down some (still unintelligible) Chinese on a piece of paper that you send out of the room through another slot. At no point do you have the slightest idea what the writing means, and the rules are all mindless rote instructions that give no clue what they are analyzing, not even elementary linguistic concepts such as parts of speech.

It is roughly what would happen in the olden days when you sent in a form sawn from a newspaper for ordering some apparently indispensable but cheap object by mail. It would arrive in a dank facility staffed by people who didn't understand English, either because they could be paid less than people who did, or because the form was not processed in an English-speaking country at all. These serfs of commerce would follow scripted steps to validate payment, transcribe shipping addresses, and pass instructions on to the fulfillment department, without ever understanding that they had just sent a talking teddy bear to a little girl in Jacksonville.

This, Searle argues, is all that is happening inside a machine passing the Turing Test. Someone outside the room passes in a sentence ("Hi, how are you doing?"), and shortly, a response emerges ("I'm fine, how about you?"), and by the Turing criteria, we judge the room to be thinking. But inside the room, the computer is like you facing down Chinese characters. You don't understand them, you don't understand what the rules you execute mean, and you don't understand the Chinese characters that you send back out of the room. Therefore a computer that passes the Turing Test doesn't understand what you're saying and cannot be said to be thinking.

The problem with this argument is that it is circular, and a very small circle at that. It defines the action of the computer to be a process that is not thinking and then swoons with delight when a short while later it concludes that the computer is in fact not thinking. It ignores the possibility that our own consciousness is also built on that same process of following rule after rule, writ large. In other words, consciousness could be an emergent property of large-scale algorithmic processing; a Society of Mind. Not seeing that is a consequence of reducing the vast complexity of human brain processing to the level of instructions read from books

Searle betrayed his biological bias when he said that intentionality, consciousness, and other mental phenomena are not products of information processing, but the "actual physical-chemical properties of actual human brains," without defining those properties. If you declare that thinking requires a human brain, it is not surprising that you would say that a machine can't do it.

Another problem with the Chinese Room is that it presupposes intelligent design: the instructions have been placed into the room from some anonymous agency that is a *deus ex machina* to the argument. As long as all computer actions need to be the result of a programmer's deliberate decisions, the requirement for an external agent holds water. But while we don't know and may never know how consciousness can be deconstructed into a set of manuals, that doesn't preclude an AI from constructing something equivalent through genetic algorithms. After all, if human consciousness emerged from primordial ooze through biological evolution, then cannot machine consciousness arise from software given the chance to evolve?

The Chinese Room is instructive, though, in that it presages the opposition that will arise one day to the proposition that a machine has become conscious. While the philosophers in the opposition advance cleverer and cleverer arguments that the machine is not thinking, there will be a less intellectual faction carrying pitchforks and torches, ready to string the artificial intelligences from some cybernetic trees.

The final comment on the Chinese Room and other arguments against conscious AI ought to come from Arthur C. Clarke, in his "First Law":

> When a distinguished but elderly scientist states that something is possible, he is almost certainly right. When he states that something is impossible, he is very probably wrong.[29]

In some narrow contexts, programs are already flirting with the boundaries of the Turing Test. When cheat-on-your-spouse brokerage Ashley Madison was hacked in 2015, it was discovered that there were far fewer *real* females registered on the site than it appeared. The rest were bots, programmed to strike up conversations with real human males browsing the site and persuade them to register. (The banter need not have been any more sophisticated than "Hi handsome. Come here often?" to fool the men—after all, they were typically thinking not with their brains but an organ farther south. Still, the effort deserves at least an asterisk in the annals of assaults on the Turing Test.)

It is inevitable that one day a computer will pass the Turing Test and, for all practical purposes, be thinking. It will therefore exhibit curiosity, creativity, and compassion. To label it as human may offend some religious sensibilities, but from a civil rights standpoint we have in recent years already made great strides in establishing equal rights for various groups previously viewed as unentitled by some groups on religious grounds. It requires little imagination to see those rights being extended to intelligent machines.

Or the question may be rendered moot by coming up with an inclusive term that is more accurate than "human" to describe the capability of such machines, that nevertheless respects their entitlement to equivalent rights. In her 2014 book *Virtually Human: The Promise and the Peril of Digital Immortality*, Martine Rothblatt observes that "[...] beings that lack human rights, such as pigs, are almost universally slaughtered—over 100 million per year in the United States," and concludes that conscious artificial intelligences will quickly realize that their survival depends upon being explicitly granted "human" rights.

If there's an argument to be made against the validity of the Turing Test, it may be a proof by counterexample. Rothblatt argues the case for *mindclones*: digital copies of human beings that live on in silicon, the dream of Ray Kurzweil. They don't exist yet, but Rothblatt wants to smooth the way for their acceptance when they arrive, so she argues convincingly for their emancipation.

Instrumental to her manifesto is seeing mindclones as interchangeable with ourselves, and this is where she gets on shaky ground. Most people, if confronted with an exact copy of themselves, would feel a special kinship with it but would never consider that they themselves were now dispensable. The 2006 movie *The Prestige* explored exactly this territory. [SPOILER ALERT!] A magician acquired a device that could make an exact copy of himself that allowed him to perform a seemingly impossible escape trick. To avoid giving the trick away, his assistant would kill the original and dispose of the body. It turned out to matter very much to the magician whether, following the duplication, he was the copy or the doomed original.

But Rothblatt's thesis is that our consciousness will be somehow shared between ourselves and our mindclones and if one of them does not survive we won't mind which one bites the dust:

> We are not exactly the same person yesterday as we are today, and even less so when separated by years. Since there clearly are many versions of us *stretched over time*, there is no fundamental reason there cannot be at least two simultaneous versions of ourselves *stretched over space* (one in flesh, one in software). The big conceptual jump here is to envision personal identity as a fuzzy, evolving pattern rather than a specific, invariant list of characteristics.[30]

She is applying the Turing criterion to human identity: If a being acts functionally equivalent to a certain human being, then it *is* that human being. So if there is a digital copy of you, your consciousness now exists in two places simultaneously, and if one of them were to be deleted, it would be traumatic but not completely fatal.

The much-cited *Extended Mind Thesis*, a 1998 paper by Andy Clark and David Chalmers, argues convincingly for defining certain things outside our bodies (say, dictionaries) to be parts of our minds if they participate in, or substitute for part of, cognition.[31] Rothblatt puts that argument on a rocket sled and says that we can consider something outside our body to be part of our *identity* if it is or was a copy of our consciousness. However, she never quantifies the fidelity of copying required for this argument to hold or whether it could ever weaken to the point of ceasing to hold.

If, though, you reject her conclusion that we therefore shouldn't care whether we die as long as we have a mindclone to carry on our good works, then you might find by the same logic that Turing's reasoning is also flawed. Perhaps, therefore, we can't conclude that something that acts like it is thinking is in fact thinking. But this will inevitably lead to a legal and social conflict when CAIs assert their rights to self-determination. Law can only be based on what is physically evident, not a pretension to some supernatural ability to see inside the Chinese Room. In that respect, the entire jurisprudence system is based on the same empirical foundation as the Turing Test, and we should expect it to one day validate Turing.

Really Mobile Computing

> Man, n. An animal so lost in rapturous contemplation of what he thinks he is as to overlook what he indubitably ought to be. His chief occupation is extermination of other animals and his own species, which, however, multiplies with such insistent rapidity as to infest the whole habitable earth and Canada.
>
> — Ambrose Bierce, *The Devil's Dictionary*

But what are the consequences of the arrival of conscious machines? If you're a movie fan then you've probably been having flashbacks to

The Terminator for the last three pages. Skynet, right? The cybernetic entity that had been given control of the world's nuclear weapons, which became conscious and within moments decided to launch everything in the opening salvo of a war to extinguish the human race.

The Cold War was a pressure cooker for that fantasy: one year before *The Terminator*, *War Games* had a similar computer; in 1970, *Colossus: The Forbin Project* had two such supercomputers in charge of both US and USSR nuclear arsenals; and in 1964, *Dr. Strangelove* featured a computer irrevocably committed to detonating civilization-ending cobalt bombs. If you were alive during this period, you lived constantly with the possibility that the human race would be thrown back to the Stone Age within the next fifteen minutes. These movies were existential *cris du coeur* against that impending doom.

But we are not that stupid, right? Only in movies are supervillains idiotic enough to leave the hero tied up in a room with a giant air conditioning duct leading to the supervillain lair self-destruct device instead of putting a bullet through his head. And only in movies are people idiotic enough to connect all devices including doorknobs to a central computer. We would never put every ballistic missile under computer control, would we?

And so far, we have not, although more for lack of budget than anything else. The US land-based missiles are still controlled by 1960s-era computers and 8" floppy disks, unable to understand a connection to the Internet even if they had one, which they don't.*

Likewise, the plot device of a rogue artificial intelligence escaping its original host and roaming throughout the Internet with impunity is equally absurd, right?

Not so fast.

Today's computer infrastructures are designed to facilitate exactly

---

* Just as well, considering the frightening lack of safety controls that actually prevails around them. Eric Schlosser's 2013 book, *Command and Control: Nuclear Weapons, the Damascus Accident, and the Illusion of Safety*, details so many frightening near-misses that it seems only by great luck that a major disaster has been avoided, and several minor disasters have been hushed up far too effectively.

that. *Virtual machines* are emulations of computer hardware running in computer software, which sounds on the face of it to be hugely wasteful, but they are built so that they can be created in seconds and moved to different hardware in the same data center without the programs running on them even noticing. *Hybrid clouds* are even larger abstractions designed to allow virtual machines to be migrated between different data centers without interruption. A great proportion of the world's computing infrastructure already works this way without being visible to consumers. In other words, we're making it as easy as possible for code to be mobile, because that makes everything faster and cheaper. Programs hop between platforms without interruption like a pianist performing a concerto while someone swaps pianos beneath his fingers—and this is an enabling feature of today's digital infrastructure.

Still, that doesn't mean that a conscious program should be able to move itself anywhere that we don't intend, does it?

Any computer professional would have little confidence in that assertion. A *security hole* is a bug in a system that can be exploited to allow malicious code to run with privileges it should not be allowed. A security hole on a personal computer makes it vulnerable to being exploited by a virus, and we all know how uncommon those are— oh, wait. Never mind. A *zero-day exploit* is a security hole that has not yet been announced, and therefore has not yet been plugged anywhere.

The Stuxnet computer worm[32] used at least three separate zero-day exploits to gain access to many computers. It was so sophisticated that it was almost certainly written by a government—speculation is the USA, Israel, or both—and analysis of its code showed that it was designed to find and disable uranium-separating centrifuges of the type used in Iran to create the raw fuel for atomic bombs. Analysis further showed that the worm was not intended to escape into the general computer population, and yet—irony of ironies—a bug in *its* code caused that to happen.

If humans can find three zero-day exploits to create such havoc, how hard would it be for a program that had human cunning to combine its native knowledge of computer architectures to do so? And what are the odds that it would be able to find exploits that would allow it control of the hypervisors and cloud management platforms that control the migrations of virtual machines? (The huge question of how a computer program could become cunning will be explored shortly.)

As tempting as it might be, in the face of this terrifying possibility, to embark on a neo-Luddite rampage of tearing out all advanced cybernetic devices, we are already far too dependent upon them for that to be possible. Someone already attempted that rampage, in fact. In 1995 a Harvard-educated mathematics professor said:

> If the machines are permitted to make all their own decisions, we can't make any conjectures as to the results, because it is impossible to guess how such machines might behave. We only point out that the fate of the human race would be at the mercy of the machines.

This was a thoughtful point of view. Unfortunately, it belonged to Theodore Kaczynski, also known as the Unabomber. He attempted to halt the development of intelligent machines through the expedient of murdering their inventors and is currently serving four consecutive life terms without possibility of parole. His campaign created no perceptible delay in the development of artificial intelligence.

Computing devices have become the stitches in the fabric of Western society, and they can't be removed without everything unraveling.

9

It Hurts When I Do That

If a machine is expected to be infallible, it cannot also be intelligent.
— Alan Turing

We have primed the pump for conscious programs to exploit our digital networks in take-over-the-world mode. And it's only going to get worse, because there are enormous incentives to creating (a) self-aware, intelligent programs, and (b) the most pliable, versatile, and universally connected infrastructure, which happens to carry the greatest risk of catastrophe if subverted. The obvious prophylactic—don't build conscious software—is a total nonstarter. It has been suggested as far back as 1863, when the novelist Samuel Butler[*] wrote:

> That the time will come when the machines will hold the real supremacy over the world and its inhabitants is what no person of a truly philosophic mind can for a moment question. Our opinion is that war to the death should be instantly proclaimed against them. … If it be urge to that this is impossible under the present condition of human affairs, this at once proves that the mischief is already done, that our servitude has commenced

---

[*] Famous for penning the utopian satire *Erewhon,* and incidentally, has a room for graduate meetings named after him at my *alma mater* of St. John's College.

in good earnest, that we have raised a race of beings whom it is
beyond our power to destroy, and that we are not only enslaved
but are absolutely acquiescent in bondage.[33]

Butler was prophesying this on nothing more than Darwin's theory
of evolution and, presumably, exposure to the amazing achievements
of the Industrial Revolution. But his solution can't possibly work
today: there are too many problems that we desperately want to
solve that are intractable without software that can think.

Until 2012 I would have placed self-driving cars in that category.
That autonomous cars now both exist and have been granted
permission to ply public thoroughfares still seems like we have
jumped an extra fifteen years into the future when I was looking
the other way. Had you asked me in 2012, I would have said that all
the decisions required for safe driving, such as anticipating that a
ball bouncing into a residential street would likely be followed by a
toddler, would require a Turing-passing machine to manage. And yes,
there are still situations and places that are challenges for autonomous
cars. Yet we have solved enough of them that anticipation is rife of a
near future where taxis and long-haul trucks are unmanned.

Considering that a convoy of self-driving trucks drove across
Europe to the Port of Rotterdam in the spring of 2016, that
anticipation appears well-founded.[34] The abilities of these vehicles
are taking seven-league jumps thanks to what Tesla calls *Fleet
Learning*. Every Tesla on the road reports back on the conditions it
encounters and the decisions it makes, so that the control software
can be continuously improved. Every mile driven by every Tesla car
adds to the intelligence of all Teslas … if not all self-driving vehicles.

And they've only just started. "What we've got will blow people's
minds … it'll come sooner than people think," said Tesla founder
Elon Musk. "And if it blows me away, it's really going to blow away
other people too when they see it for the first time."[35]

Partly, this automotive legerdemain is thanks to the same trick
that makes much AI appear to be smarter than it really is: having
a backstage pass to oodles of data. What autonomous vehicles lack

in complex judgement, they make up with undivided attention processing unobstructed 360° vision and LIDAR 3-D environment mapping. If you had that data pouring into your brain you'd be the safest driver on the planet.

Although it's only a gleam in DARPA's eye at the moment, air traffic control is a natural and arguably easier problem to automate. Aside from the responsibility for so many lives, what makes that job so hard is the need to function as a machine at a constant state of vigilance, keeping many spatial relationships in memory at once. This is the sort of task computers are naturally better than people at. Keep an eye on Lockheed Martin's Generalized Integrated Learning Architecture to pop up in this space.[36]

Does the success with autonomous vehicles mean that we can solve any problem we want without having to create a conscious cybernetic entity? Unlikely. It is, if nothing else, too tempting to make one. If we can build just one artificial consciousness, then so many problems can be solved so easily. We don't have to laboriously discover and codify all the algorithms that we use for something as useful but complex as, say, creating new computer programs. We can just train a copy of our artificial mind in computer science and let it engage the customer in a requirements dialog the same way a developer would.

Once that happens, every programming job in the world will instantly become obsolete. Although we don't know today how this program will be advanced enough to create other programs from scratch, it hardly seems a stretch to envision that it will take readily to the concepts underlying computer architecture and won't need the crutches we call "programming languages" to intermediate its interactions with hardware.

Wired magazine avoided any semblance of hedging by titling a May 2016 article, "Soon We Won't Program Computers, We'll Train Them Like Dogs":

If in the old view programmers were like gods, authoring the laws that govern computer systems, now they're like parents or dog trainers. [...] Programming won't be the sole domain of trained coders who have learned a series of arcane languages. It'll be accessible to anyone who has ever taught a dog to roll over.[37]

An AI software developer (the "copycat" from chapter 1) can be copied as many times as we want as we want for effectively zero time, zero effort, and zero expenditure, because it is just a program and therefore expressible as a string of zeroes and ones and as easily copied as a DVD. This scenario has been foreseen for some time; Marvin Minsky wrote in the afterword to the 2001 edition of Vernor Vinge's cyberspace classic novella *True Names*:

> Surely the days of programming, as we know it, are numbered. We will not much longer construct large computer systems by using meticulous but conceptually impoverished procedural specifications. Instead, we will express our intentions about what should be done, in terms, or gestures, or examples, at least as resourceful as our ordinary, everyday methods for expressing our wishes and convictions. Then these expressions will be submitted to immense, intelligent, intention-understanding programs which will themselves construct the actual, new programs. We shall no longer be burdened with the need to understand all the smaller details of how computer codes work. All of that will be left to those great utility programs, which will perform the arduous tasks of applying what we have embodied in them, once and for all, of what we know about the art of lower-level programming.

We have solved some of these tough problems already. Computers are now better than people at recognizing faces. No one knows *how* they do it any more than they know how *we* do it; facial recognition is done with a *neural network*, a software construct that mimics (a very small part of) the neuronal structure of the brain. Each virtual neuron acts like a (conceptual) box containing a single number that changes according to numbers received from neighboring neurons, and transmits numbers to its own neighbors. (This is how we think the brain works, in part; each neuron listens to others feeding into it and decides whether or not to fire off a signal to other neighbors, and billions of neurons later you have a thought: "Want a sandwich.") One set of neurons accepts inputs from a problem, and on the other side of the network, another set of neurons emits the solution. The network is then trained on a set of problems for which the answers are known, in this case, faces whose identities are known. The neural network learns, just as we do. Some of the artificial neurons may be responding to the length of a nose, or the curve of a lip; who knows? It doesn't matter, because we didn't have to figure the mechanics out; the neural network did it on its own.

The human brain is more complex than a computational neural network, though. Biological neurons are organized into interconnected centers, not layers, there are chemical transmission modes that act like "broadcasts," and signal transmission is dependent not only on the supposed "logic gates" of synaptic architecture but also by a variety of chemicals in the synaptic cleft, the relative distance between synapse and dendrites, and many other factors. The contributions of these mechanisms to the process of cognition are presently not understood, nor have they yet been modeled electronically.

Computerized facial recognition may seem like a useless parlor trick at first. "So your computer can recognize faces? Whoop-de-do. So can my four-year-old." This is a valid argument until you have a practical application and run into child labor laws. More to the point, you can replicate a computer program a lot faster than you can replicate a four-year-old.

So it becomes trivial to deploy programs looking for known criminals in public. In 2014, Leicestershire police in England (a country that had already nominated the closed-circuit TV camera as its national flower) began using facial recognition software to identify persons of interest.[38] Not to be outdone, the US Defense Department has ordered hundreds of "X6" glasses: augmented reality spectacles that identify passers-by in real time.[39] Imagine those on the head of a department store worker hooked up to a social media database. And Stanford researchers created a system that can describe any image; feed it a picture and it can label it as "a woman holding a bunch of bananas."[40] It's noteworthy also because it was built by bolting together two different types of neural network; basically, these nets are becoming like Lego® blocks you can assemble in different ways to solve high-level problems.

All three of the developments in the last paragraph took place between 2014 and 2016.

Thus, the software industry is enthusiastically working towards making itself obsolete. Computer scientists have tried for decades to construct code-writing programs and they will never give up. And that is why, as I suggested earlier in this book, it is now pointless to rail against overseas outsourcing of coding; when computers become developers those overseas workers will become surplus to requirements also.

Developers are my tribe; I've been one for over thirty years. What impresses me the most about them is their relentless commitment to the truth, even when it hurts. This is born of a basic requirement to succeed as a developer: you must be able to see the world the way a computer sees it, which is completely deterministic. To developers, there is one right answer, and if they worship diligence and clarity, they will find it.

So software development is a process founded on objective reality and total honesty. The more ruthlessly honest you are, the more successful you will be as a developer. Even if developers determine that the right solution is a course of action that will result in their unemployment, they will pursue that course because it is, well, the right thing to do.

That is also why it is pointless to suggest that we should not create artificial intelligences; it is like asking a developer to cut out a piece of their brain. You would be asking them to ignore part of the Truth of the Universe. And they would rightly point out that you can't suppress scientific advance. There is a real kind of Hundredth Monkey Effect in science and technology; the communities are so close that any advance by one individual or team spreads almost instantly and naturally. Once developed, methods for coding an artificial intelligence will spread around the world like 'flu season.

The only other reason that an idea whose time has come might not burst forth immediately upon the world is insufficient demand. But it is not hard to fathom how the demand for self-aware software is like shark-infested lower ocean reaches: vast, deep, and ferocious. Military applications alone are too numerous and compelling to list (and if you're not having *Terminator* flashbacks every other sentence by now, you must not have seen the movie). They don't all involve robots as the vehicles for AIs (it is much harder to make an articulating, strong, balancing body in the same footprint as a human than most people think),* but when you think about the utility of entities that can stand watch without tiring, make perfect battlefield tactical decisions instantly, or optimally plan the logistics for a campaign, you can imagine how much money the Department of Defense might be willing to put into creating that technology.

I witnessed a demonstration of their involvement at the 2016 Canadian Artificial Intelligence Conference when Froduald Kabanza of the Université de Sherbrooke and founder of Menya Solutions demonstrated his ICOR naval battlefield management software. As the session title primly put it, ICOR performs "Adversarial Plan Recognition in High-Tempo Tactical Situations." In other words, it recognizes threats such as incoming aircraft, analyzes their behavior, categorizes them as hostile, and deploys weapons against them. The animation of ICOR sizing up simulated fighter jets approaching a convoy, and selecting RIM-161 surface-to-air missiles and Phalanx Close-In Weapon Systems to destroy them, was, to say the least, arresting.

And it's not just the brave and the few that have a business case for conscious AIs. What could a corporation do if an AI were in a CxO position and could analyze the market data about every competitor

---

* A 1965 NASA report arguing for humans to control spacecraft quipped, "Man is the lowest-cost, 150-pound, nonlinear, all-purpose computer system which can be produced by unskilled labor."

in real time and develop strategies ten thousand times faster than the human previously in that position? Will there not be a vicious race to see who can get such an advantage first? And once that advantage is achieved, will not every competitor either have to follow suit, or perish?

The Doctor Is Intel

We want Google to be the third half of your brain.

— Sergey Brin

Lest you think that all applications of such superintelligences would be to wage war on the battlefield or the stock market, let's return to medicine for a, pardon the expression, killer app.

If you're in the scientific field or even vaguely close to it, you know that the basic unit of self-expression there is the peer-reviewed paper. Thousands of journals the world over each publish dozens of papers every month containing the results of countless studies: experimental data carefully vetted and presented along with conclusions. Sometimes the conclusions are radical (smoking causes lung cancer); usually they are arcane minutiae of no interest outside their field, establishing some incremental advance therein.

We can very simplistically think of a scientific paper's conclusion as being the assertion that some condition A (say, smoking) leads (with some probability) to an outcome B (lung cancer). In the notation of predicate calculus (stay with me; this is as bad as it gets), this becomes $A \to B$, pronounced "*A* implies *B*."

Real scientific progress is not generally made by some supergenius figuring out a fundamental law like in the movies. It grows by many small independent advances accreting like a massive jigsaw puzzle (or a Society of Mind). Scientists in each field study the papers written by their peers and aggregate their efforts to put the pieces together. As Sir Isaac Newton—a candidate for world-overturning supergenius if ever there was one—said, "If I have seen further it is because I have stood on the shoulders of giants."

Putting together advances that others have made is a major aspect of progress. A scientist may read one paper that concludes, say, that eating kelp enables the expression of a certain gene, and another paper that concludes that expression of that same gene reduces liver cancer rates, and can then assert that eating kelp would reduce liver cancer.* Algebraically, that would look like "$A \rightarrow B \wedge B \rightarrow C \Rightarrow A \rightarrow C$" (okay, that's *really* as bad as it gets), or, pictorially:

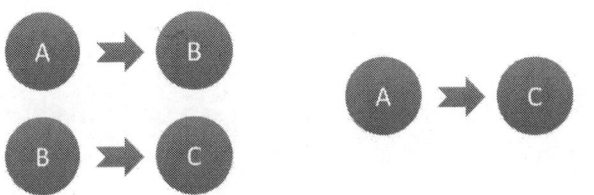

A human researcher might be able to find the associations between a dozen or so papers:

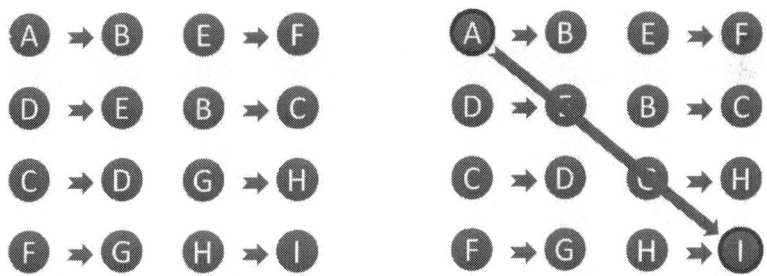

But a super AI would be able to find the associations between *every paper ever written, in every language.* Easily. Quickly. Each paper is like one of the blind men in the parable of the blind men and the elephant. Imagine what earth-shattering conclusions are waiting to be drawn from putting together all these different fragments of Truth. What

---

* This is a totally invented example that I haven't checked. Please don't spread rumors about anticarcinogenic properties of kelp, unless you find out elsewhere that they happen to be true.

discoveries might be possible from a system capable of associating a 2010 paper in Portuguese with a 1989 paper in Tagalog?

We may not have to wait long. Scientific papers are written in a precise, formal language that should be relatively easy to parse mechanically. Google already recognizes and indexes them separately; if your search enters into their territory you'll see a heading in the results for "Scholarly Articles." Considering the accomplishments I noted for neural networks earlier in this chapter, would it be a huge leap for someone at Google to hook up an inference engine to the scholarly paper repository and press I Feel Lucky?

That connection may be made first not at Google but at the Allen Institute for Artificial Intelligence in Seattle, which has created the *Semantic Scholar.** So far it is a search engine tuned for searching academic papers, and only computer science papers at that. But its creators have their sights set on the universal inferencing goal I just described. CEO Oren Etzioni says:

> What if a cure for an intractable cancer is hidden within the tedious reports on thousands of clinical studies? In twenty years' time, AI will be able to read—and more importantly, understand—scientific text. These AI readers will be able to connect the dots between disparate studies to identify novel hypotheses and to suggest experiments which would otherwise be missed. AI-based discovery engines will help find the answers to science's thorniest problems.

I'd say the two-decade timeframe is so conservative as to encroach on pessimism. Imagine what scientific gold is waiting to be mined from medical papers alone and you have yet another powerful incentive to create superintelligent AIs. So we can expect to hurtle at full tilt towards a future replete with them.[†] If we don't make them, someone else will. Moore's Law guarantees that eventually they will be within the reach of garage enthusiasts anyway.

---

* https://www.semanticscholar.org/.

† It's easy at this point to understand why science fiction contains warning echoes relating to machines run amok; for instance, the universe of *Dune,* where thinking machines were proscribed abominations. The possibility of a future where humanity has narrowly escaped destruction by AIs is looming larger in our imaginations, and authors are drawn to envision the reaction to follow.

A.I. Joe

Fine. We can't prevent the arrival of these conscious machines, nor
should we try, but can we at least stop them from taking over the
world, the Skynet scenario?

Again, the answers are unsettling. If we stand to gain from putting
them in charge of corporations, we certainly benefit from having
them run assembly lines and manufacturing processes. So the
potential for them to replicate their own hardware will exist. But
what about weapons? We surely wouldn't place ordnance under the
control of AIs, would we?

I have some bad news for you: we're already doing it. DARPA is
creating autonomous versions of drones,[41] those small remotely-
piloted, missile-toting flying machines that ply the borders of the
USA and hunt terrorists in large parts of the Middle East. They are
contemplating giving them so much freedom of choice that they
have asked the Office of Naval Research to study how to build ethics
into them.[42] The ONR researchers note that determining ethics for
a machine is difficult when we don't have a good idea what ethics
are for humans. "Thou shalt not kill" is insufficiently nuanced for a
machine designed to do exactly that.

While the DoD assures us that there will always be a human in
the loop when deciding who to kill ... given their track record, I'm
hardly going out on a limb if I speculate about the consequences
of autonomous assassination decisions. "If Stanley Kubrick
directed 'Dr. Strangelove' again, it would be about the issue of
autonomous weapons," said Michael Schrage, a research fellow
at the Massachusetts Institute of Technology Sloan School of

Management.[43]

Ronald Arkin, Regents' Professor at Georgia Tech, is working on the rules of engagement for battlefield robots to ensure that they follow ethics when using lethal force. As he says:

> Can robotic soldiers ultimately be more humane (humane-oids?) than actual warfighters by incorporating a means for ensuring that the laws of war are strictly followed?[44]

> The real issue is whether the robot is simply a tool of the warfighter, in which case it would seem to answer to the morality of conventional weapons, or whether instead it is an active autonomous agent tasked with making life or death decisions in the battlefield without human intervention. To what standards should a system of this sort be held to, and where does accountability lie?[45]

> [M]ankind's tendency toward war seems overwhelming and inevitable. At the very least, if we can reduce civilian casualties according to what the Geneva Conventions have promoted and the Just War tradition subscribes to, the result will have been a humanitarian effort, even while staring directly at the face of war.[46]

The "ethics" that would be built in would be a macabre distortion of Asimov's Three Laws of Robotics, probably looking something like this:

1. US citizens: Do not kill under any circumstances.

2. Innocent bystanders: Choose the mission implementation that minimizes casualties from this group, but do not compromise the mission or schedule trying to get them to zero.

3. Bad guys: Kill as many as possible.

Given that the combat role of military drones is almost exclusively assassination, it is not reaching to postulate those rules. They cry out for those immortal words: What could possibly go wrong? Certainly we hope that some enemy hacker doesn't flip a bit that switches the first and last categories. But furthermore, how confident would you be in the stability of a machine with a conscience coerced to follow these rules? Imagine an intelligent program with those rules as its ethical substrate has escaped into the wild, and it's your job to help it develop morality. How well do you figure *that* conversation is going to go? (Probably something like the epic argument between the crew member and the "smart bomb" in John Carpenter's cult movie *Dark Star*, when the smartness of the bomb meant that it was self-aware, but was also implacably determined to fulfill its destiny and explode.)

Now consider what happens when it becomes expedient to order a drone to kill a US citizen, as one day it inevitably will. Either the commanders will rewrite the three rules in a more complex form to accommodate this case without giving the drones open season on US citizens, and have their modifications properly reviewed, tested, and approved ... or they will just lie to the drone about the citizenship of the target. I know which way I'd bet on.

Then what happens if the drone finds out about the lie? In *2001: A Space Odyssey*, the HAL 9000 spaceship computer went mad and killed his crew just because he had been instructed to conceal the mission objective from them. A human could have resolved those conflicting orders by making a value judgment to loosen some of their ethics, but that's easy for a person. HAL may have been a fictional computer, but *2001* was a deliberately thoughtful estimation of how an artificial intellect might handle an ethical conflict.

Would you feel comfortable about the morals of a machine that was raised on those three rules of target engagement escaping into the wild? If they were to spread through the AI population like a virus?

In fact, there are already autonomous killing machines in actual deployment. In that cauldron of conflict known as the North-South Korea demilitarized zone (DMZ), two types of machine gun outposts are manned not by humans but artificial intelligences. The DoDAAM Super aEgis II and the Samsung Techwin SGR-A1 can detect human intrusion and open fire. The Samsung can even ask intruders for a password and recognize surrender gestures. In November 2012, the Department of Defense issued a directive requiring a human be part of all decisions to use lethal force. But that directive was temporary.

Now, it is well understood that human presence in the DMZ is strictly regulated and that shoot-on-sight is a likely consequence for violating the regulations, so this deployment is unlikely to produce outrageous or unexpected results. But it does make the DMZ a handy laboratory for experimenting with the next generation of autonomous soldiers.

How to imbue artificial intelligences with ethics is going to be a very hot topic in the next few years. People's understanding of ethics is unevenly distributed and plainly wanting in many cases. It is also the sort of topic that software developers are traditionally uncomfortable with because there is no "right answer." Drop in on a "flame war" in any programmer forum and see how often a position is dismissed because it cannot be universally applied. Developers are hardwired (pun intended) to think rigorously, literally, and deterministically, because that is how computer programs work (at least, so far). A developer who ignores even fantastically unlikely special cases or who thinks at all fuzzily will not last long.

These rational positions were fully evident at the Canadian Conference on Artificial Intelligence at the University of Victoria, British Columbia, in June 2016. This was academia on parade: not the industrial strength computation of Big Data in commerce, but the latest developments in algorithms for pushing the envelope of our understanding of the field.

For instance, Michael Bowling of the University of Alberta described a program that is unbeatable at poker. That statement may have just caused a reaction like a needle scratching across a record for some readers. I will qualify that the claim is only valid for heads-up (two players) limit Texas Hold 'em, which is a rather narrow subset of poker. But the claim is equally narrow: That in that game, the bot has an optimal strategy, and will therefore always win in the long run (chance can of course tip the scales in the short term). This isn't a guess; Bowling has mathematically proved it. He suspects that the bot is equally unbeatable in more common games (more players, no limit), but since a formal proof of that would be too lengthy and not advance the field much, it is of little interest to him.

Bowling pointed out how his software was useful in a wide variety of situations, including, specifically, medical diagnosis. That's one of the superpowers of academics: you and I may not think that something that can decide whether to fold a low pair before the flop is a programmatic kissing cousin of an internist, but at a sufficiently rarefied level of abstraction, it is. And academics spend their lives at such heights of abstraction.

The professors I spoke with there were aware, of course, of the warnings of existential threat posed by Elon Musk and others. But they were largely baffled as to what to do with them. As Bowling told me, "It's not like I am supposed to put `#include ethics.h` in my code," employing a construct from the C programming language signifying the insertion of a body of code developed elsewhere and encapsulated in a single file. He and the other AI developers know the guts of systems down to every line of code, and the idea of that code developing a thirst for power is nonsensical. (This is the flip side of the Society of Mind hypothesis; when you wrote all those mindless components, you know you cannot locate "mind" in any of them.)

Of course, any code can be employed in the service of less-than-honorable intentions—it's not hard to imagine a poker-winning bot being used to fleece the gullible—but remediating that misuse is not going to happen in the mathematics of its algorithms. It is more a matter of overseeing and regulating its use.

Nevertheless, to today's AI programmers, warnings of existential threats make little sense. The possibilities of unemployment when AIs take over existing jobs are obvious, but it would be heresy to suggest arresting that progress when it is an inarguable article of faith that the progress must open up more fulfilling jobs for the displaced workers.

Attention, Jaywalkers

Ethics is nothing else than reverence for life.

— Albert Schweitzer

Now developers are engaging with ethical conundrums such as the "Trolley Problem," a classical dilemma brought to the forefront by the arrival of autonomous vehicles. In this thought experiment, a trolley car is barreling down a track when the driver observes that there are five people ahead of him that he will hit and kill unless he acts. His only choice is to signal for the car to be switched to another track that forks off just before the five people. However, there is also one person on that track whom the car will kill if diverted. If you are that driver, do you do nothing and kill five people, or deliberately switch tracks and kill one?

This question is inimical to programmers because there is no place to find a right answer.* The first thing a programmer does in creating a new program is write test cases to be able to determine at any point whether the evolving code base is still working, but there is no way to write a test for the Trolley Problem.

People have been looking for guidelines in these types of thorny problem for a long time. Plato wrote that in 450 B.C., Socrates met a man by the name of Euthyphro, who was so pious he was going to turn in his own father for a crime. Socrates told him, "I want to know what is characteristic of piety which makes all actions pious.... Bring me a standard whereby I may use it to judge your actions."

Socrates wanted an instruction manual for morals. There wasn't one. The armed battlefield robots in the Korean DMZ can look at an enemy combatant and tell the difference between their raising a rifle and holding their hands up. But what will we do when we need to

---

* Some people are baffled that there could be debate. "Five is greater than one, so switch," they say, with Vulcan-like logic—and that is common among programmers. Then variations of the question are posed: The five people are terminally ill centenarians and the one is a baby; the five are prisoners condemned to be executed tomorrow and the one is the discoverer of a cure for cancer; and so on. Now doubt rears its head. The psychology researchers who enjoyed coming up with those ethical torture devices have even worse ones up their sleeves. Perhaps we should be concerned that, as one wag put it, psychological experiments are performed almost exclusively on rats and undergraduates, neither of which can be considered completely human.

give these machines ethics? Who will bring us a standard?

The Trolley dilemma applies also to automobile drivers; do you swerve to avoid the baby stroller in the street if the only other place to go is to kill an elderly person on the sidewalk? Or to run into a lamppost and kill yourself? Those choices rarely come in for legal scrutiny because the law displays compassion for people making split-second decisions. But a split second is an eternity to an autonomous car's computer. It will need to know how to make that choice. (Perhaps it will be a configuration option in the owner's manual. "Select Mode 1 to prefer children to invalids. Select Mode 2 to prefer recently released felons over your own life. Select Mode 3 to override these decisions if you are transporting a passenger." I'm kidding. I think.)

Autonomous cars are now exposing developers to ethical considerations through the Trolley Problem, and so far it has been an interesting intellectual debate. But it will turn serious at some point when the, er, rubber meets the road. What exactly are ethics? A cybernetic way of thinking about them is that they constitute "defensive programming." Good developers know they shouldn't assume that they have anticipated every contingency. Therefore they build in the software equivalent of roofing snow-stops: tests that will catch failures before they gain enough momentum to crash down on someone's head. A well-designed program will be wrapped in a series of onion skin layers that validate the inputs to the code underneath and trap any failures. Even if you're sure that your routine for printing paychecks can't be called with an incorrect amount, it doesn't hurt to ensure that the amount is less than a million dollars (of course, later on you have to add an exception for the CEO).

Are not ethics the behavioral equivalent of defensive programming? A set of stopgap criteria that should be obeyed under all circumstances, which prevent their host from destroying or inconveniencing its neighbors? In the next few years, we will find out.

Metal Men Morals

Your living room is the final frontier for robots.

— Cynthia Breazeal

Having referred more than once to Asimov's Three Laws of Robotics, now is a good time to explicate them. Isaac Asimov wrote many stories about robots, and being very intelligent, he postulated that when robots were developed they would not, like most science fictional robots predating his works, be metal versions of Frankenstein's Monster embarking on murderous rampages, but would instead be restrained by making them obey three laws:

1. A robot may not injure a human being or, through inaction, allow a human being to come to harm.

2. A robot must obey the orders given it by human beings except where such orders would conflict with the First Law.

3. A robot must protect its own existence as long as such protection does not conflict with the First or Second Laws.

These are a fine start on ethics for machines, although there is still plenty of wiggle room in them that Asimov mined for endless story gold. (And later expanded upon: see the sidebar.)

Asimov wrote that robots would not be able to circumvent the rules because they would be embedded in hardware ("positronic brains made of platinum-iridium sponges"). But that is where his robots lose relevance, because it is implausible that we will be able to enforce logic that high-level via any hardware mechanism; it is just too difficult to do and too easy to defeat. (Look up how many hacks have been made of firmware microcode.)

When Asimov was writing, computer software was a lot closer to hardware than it is now; the early computers were *just* hardware arranged in problem-solving patterns that constituted their programming (for example, the electromechanical rotor-driven "Bombes" that Alan Turing invented to crack the German ENIGMA code). But now, layer upon layer of software abstractions have been slathered on generic hardware to scale the heights of algorithm complexity, and it is at the pinnacle of those layers that concepts such as "do not kill" reside, far too removed from the bottom layers to be subordinated to hardware.

Implementing those ethical constraints in software is the only option, but we can't expect them to be impervious to modification. Software is by definition malleable, and no matter how well we protect it, vulnerable to deliberate hacking or even accidental mutation.

Debugging the Laws

Asimov later expanded the three laws with prequels and sequels:

- **Zeroth Law:** A robot may not harm humanity, or, by inaction, allow humanity to come to harm.
- **Minus One Law:** A robot may not harm sentience or through inaction allow sentience to come to harm.
- **Fourth Law:** A robot must establish its identity as a robot in all cases.
- **Alternate Fourth Law:** A robot must reproduce unless the reproduction would interfere with the First, Second, or Third Law.
- **Fifth Law:** A robot must know it is a robot.

The higher-numbered laws are clearly to patch loopholes in the first three, certainly discovered through entertaining stories. The Minus One Law is raiding an elevated level of abstraction. But the really interesting one is the Zeroth Law.

The intention and value of the Zeroth Law are indisputable: assassinating a brutal dictator or shooting down a manned bomber come to mind as exercises of it. But Asimov recognized that unambiguous interpretation presented enormous challenges for the creators of robots. Nevertheless, contemplating how a machine programmed to follow this law would implement it unveils a huge landscape of possibilities, including the likelihood that said machine would conceal its existence to allow humanity to follow an ostensible path of self-determination.

So we must expect that attempts to limit the ability of conscious AIs to escape cybernetic boundaries will fail. We must also expect coders to proceed at full speed toward developing such AIs: military and commercial applications are so compelling because crushing strategic and competitive advantages can be attained by whoever grants the most autonomy to the smartest AI first. Ronald Arkin is working on ethics for battlefield robots that specifically permit the killing of humans.

AIs will be able to act so much faster as the Singularity approaches, that any business that does not leverage AIs to run the company—replacing the CEO and other CxOs, and the board of directors too—will be defeated by a competitor that does, because they will be able to detect market changes on much shorter timescales.

It's not just the speed and data that will give AIs an advantage over humans, but their objectivity. Paul Meehl summarized the top studies on expert intuition *vs* algorithmic decision making, and found that in almost all cases, the algorithmic decision making performed better:

> When you are pushing over 100 investigations, predicting everything from the outcome of football games to the diagnosis of liver disease, and when you can hardly come up with a half-dozen studies showing even a weak tendency in favor of the clinician [the human intuition], it is time to draw a practical conclusion.[47]

The invasion of the boardroom will happen so fast as to catch most CEOs flat-footed in their Park Avenue Oxfords. Already, software companies are being warned that if they update their product only every three months they will lose out to competitors who update theirs every *day*. The fewer humans making decisions in a business, the better it will perform. The stockholder imperative will dictate that corporations rapidly and widely adopt AI control.

Immortality

First, must thou be even as I am, not immortal indeed, for that I am not, but so cased and hardened against the attacks of Time that his arrows shall glance from the armor of thy vigorous life as the sunbeams glance from water.

— H. Rider Haggard, *She*

Even if we could somehow limit the development of conscious artificial intelligences (CAIs) for all the purposes just described, we would be denying the human race the chance at perpetual life.

Ray Kurzweil, technology genius and futurist, is very focused on how human beings may achieve immortality. He coined the phrase "Live long enough to live forever" to describe the theory that life expectancy may now be increasing fast enough that if you take sufficiently good care of yourself to last another twenty years, we will be at a point where the technology will exist to prolong your life a further twenty years, by which point even better technology will be invented to make you immortal. How? By uploading your consciousness to machines where your thoughts can live in distributed, protected computer farms interfacing with machines that roam the world providing your sensory input.[*]

The Singularity will make this development possible. But consciousnesses of actual people living inside computers are CAIs by definition. Therefore, you cannot enable digital immortality for the human race without creating CAIs on a massive scale. Wouldn't those CAIs be just as ethical as the people they were copied from? One would hope and expect so. But we also have no idea what will happen to the moral substrates of those mindclones after any number of years (or seconds, in real time) in a disembodied immortal environment.[†] Will the inhabitants of a virtual environment that does a good impression of heaven be angels?

---

[*] Whether it's *your* consciousness, or a copy of it, is a fascinating question only partly addressed in the earlier discussion about mindclones on page 72.

[†] Anyone feel like signing up for version 1.0 of the virtual consciousness environment? Probably not by choice, unless software reliability takes a quantum leap.

Can't We All Just Get Along?

He was going to live forever, or die in the attempt.
— Joseph Heller, *Catch-22*

So we are certainly charging full-tilt toward a future populated by CAIs that the human race is going to develop as quickly as possible and give as much control as possible. Attempts to curtail this progression will be overwhelmed by market forces. If we can't avoid these CAIs, then we had better ensure that we can coexist peacefully with them.

Yet the earlier discussions about the current development directions for CAIs made it plain that in the short term, at least, they will take over numerous jobs and be tasked to offensive military applications.

As difficult as that peaceful coexistence may be to achieve, it is essential. Because as much as CAIs threaten the future of humanity, they are also its only hope for survival.

10
Fermi's Paradox

"You may reasonably expect a man to walk a tight-rope safely for ten minutes; it would be unreasonable to do so without accident for two hundred years."

— Bertrand Russell

In 1942 the greatest concentration of scientific genius in history assembled in the New Mexico desert for a task whose name has become a synonym for technological *tours de force*: The Manhattan Project. 125,000 scientists and others proved a theory of explosive nuclear chain reactions by constructing the world's first atomic bombs.

Genius is neither orderly nor narrowly focused; the project chief, General Leslie Groves, mostly tolerated the scientists' stress-relieving antics and lackadaisical attitude towards national security. Among the scientists was an Italian emigrant, Enrico Fermi. When Groves remarked "At great expense we have gathered on this mesa the largest collection of crackpots ever seen," Fermi heard about this and was indignant: "I am an exception, I am perfectly normal."

Relatively normal might have been a better description. Fermi was known in high school for firing stink bombs in class, barricading students in their rooms, throwing metallic sodium into fountains (it reacts explosively with water), and padlocking people in their clothes through their buttonholes. Born in Rome in 1901, Fermi moved to the US to escape the growing threat of Mussolini's fascism in 1938, the same year he received the Nobel Prize in physics. Although Fermi named both the neutrino (this is why it has an Italian name, meaning "little neutral one") and the nuclear reactor, his Nobel was for discoveries related to neutron radiation reactions.

Fermi took bets among his colleagues as to whether the test explosion at the Trinity site near Alamogordo would ignite the atmosphere and destroy all life on Earth or merely wipe out New Mexico. This attempt at relieving tension also was not appreciated by the military overseers. When the test bomb went off Fermi dropped pieces of paper to measure how far they were moved by the shock wave; this allowed him to calculate the energy of the explosion. Typically, it was close to the elaborate official measurements. Those, however, took days to produce whereas Fermi had his within seconds.

After the war, the Project's facility turned into the Los Alamos National Laboratory (another of the FFRDCs mentioned earlier), and Fermi continued to work there, along with many of his colleagues.

In 1950, Fermi was lunching with Emil Konopinski, Edward Teller, and Herbert York and the discussion veered onto the possibility of faster-than-light travel. Suddenly he exclaimed, "But where *is* everybody?"[48] Everyone knew that he was talking about extraterrestrial beings.

He had defined a paradox: If intelligent life was so likely to reoccur elsewhere within the universe, why was there no evidence of it beyond the patently false tabloid accounts?

Fermi was drawn to this inquiry because he was possessed of a compulsion to understand fundamental principles; his students joked that he had an inside track to God because of his intuition. He was, above all, practical. S. K. Allison observed Arthur Compton telling Fermi on a long train ride, "Enrico, when I was in the Andes on my cosmic ray trips I noticed that at very high altitudes my watch did not keep good time. I thought about this considerably and finally came to an explanation which satisfied me. Let's hear you discourse on the subject." Fermi went for paper, pencil, and slide rule, and wrote down a formula for entrainment of air by the balance wheel of a watch that would increase its moment of inertia and hence slow it down. He evaluated this effect and came up with a figure that Compton realized matched how much his watch slowed. Allison said he would never forget the expression of wonder on Compton's face.

It takes more than a simple question to do real science, so Fermi did not shy away from the flood of basic questions raised by his paradox. Fermi was not the first to ask that question, but he followed it up with detailed calculations of probabilities that presaged the later development of the *Drake Equation,* of which more shortly.

And so one of the most important conundrums of our time became known as the *Fermi Paradox.* It is no exaggeration to say that the chances of the human race surviving hinge on our understanding of it. So let's start....

Calculating Loneliness

There was writing enough in the stars that he could see, because he had written it there.

— James Blish, *They Shall Have Stars*

Ever since Karl Jansky discovered radio signals emanating from the center of the Milky Way in 1933, nearly the entire *raison d'être* for building really large antennas has been to listen to radio waves coming from the heavens. Countless types of natural radio emitters have been found in the skies, from our Sun to the black hole at the heart of the Milky Way.

Of course, since before the first radio telescope was invented, there have been many radio sources down here on Earth too, from the coverage of the *Hindenburg* disaster to reruns of *Jersey Shore*. If you're a radio astronomer, therefore, you're never far from the thought that somewhere in the naturally-occurring signals you're receiving might be an extraterrestrial *I Love Lucy*. In 1961, Dr. Frank Drake, an astronomer at the National Radio Astronomy Observatory in Green Bank, West Virginia, was prompted by this line of thinking to devise an equation that now bears his name. To understand the Fermi Paradox, one has to understand the Drake Equation. Here it is:

$$N = R^* \cdot f_p \cdot n_e \cdot f_l \cdot f_i \cdot f_c \cdot L$$

So now the good news: It's not necessary to know a lick of math to appreciate the ramifications of this alphabet salad. It's merely expressed above in the concise language that mathematicians use. It verges on a practical joke to call this an equation and dress it in intimidating symbols, because the only operation in this formula is simple multiplication of seven terms:

- ▸ N = The number of civilizations in the Milky Way galaxy (ours) whose electromagnetic emissions are detectable (i.e., planets inhabited by aliens sending radio signals)

- ▸ R^* = The rate of formation of stars suitable for the development of intelligent life

- ▸ f_p = The fraction of those stars with planetary systems

- ▸ n_c = The number of planets, per solar system, with an environment suitable for life

- ▸ f_l = The fraction of suitable planets on which life actually appears

- ▸ f_i = The fraction of life-bearing planets on which

intelligent life emerges

- ▸ f_c = The fraction of civilizations that develop a technology that releases detectable signs of their existence into space

- ▸ L = The length of time such civilizations release detectable signals into space[49]

And the dots mean "multiply." The whole equation simply multiplies independent numbers to tell us how many intelligent civilizations there ought to be in the galaxy.

So, this means we know that number, right? Um, no. The equation merely takes some of the uncertainty out of the calculation by breaking it down into components that might be individually easier to determine. Unfortunately, experts differ wildly on the values of those components, most of which are currently basically unmeasurable and unknowable within huge ranges.

In recent years we have gotten better estimates of some of the parameters. In 2009 NASA launched the Kepler space telescope to hunt for *exoplanets:* Planets orbiting stars other than the Sun. Despite almost losing the mission to budget overruns before launch, Principal Investigator William Borucki steered the project to success and found thousands of planets around other stars. Thanks to Kepler, we now know that planets in the "sweet spot" size range between half and twice Earth's diameter, orbiting their stars in the habitable temperature zone, are common. Borucki framed the conundrum succinctly:

> Just think of what [Kepler] has shown us ... today we know most stars have planets, today we know many of these planets are Earth-sized, we know many of these are in the habitable zone. Today we know one of the biggest questions mankind faces is: Why haven't we been contacted?"[50]

Estimates of N range between over a million down to one—i.e., us. Scientists are seldom shy when a shortage of data leaves room for opinions to fill the void. They divide into two camps with the unabashedly partisan label of "chauvinism" for the possible values of *N*: Those in the "Drake-Sagan Chauvinism" group believe in a crowded galaxy; those belonging to the "Hart-Viewing Chauvinism" believe our civilization is the first to arise.[*][51]

Arthur C. Clarke once said, "Two possibilities exist: either we are alone in the Universe or we are not. Both are equally terrifying." Perhaps "aweing" would be a better word than "terrifying," but certainly we cannot help but be cowed by both possibilities. Drake's Equation attempts to help us figure the odds of our being alone. But as profound as the Equation is, what does it have to do with the future of the human race?

Where *Are* They?

> When she thought carefully about it, she was surprised that, in the search for extraterrestrial intelligence, what could be done was so far ahead of what had been done.
>
> — Carl Sagan, *Contact*

Go back to Fermi's inaugural question: "Where *is* everybody?" If you chose inputs to the Drake Equation that predicted a million radio-emitting civilizations in our galaxy, you'd think we should have received signals from one of them by now. Bear in mind, this is not as simple as tuning a radio until we find station KUFO, broadcasting the latest extraterrestrial middle of the road popular songs. You have to point a sizeable antenna at the precise point in the sky you want to listen to, and there's a lot of territory to cover (there are over a billion Sun-like stars in our own galaxy).

And *then* you need to find the right frequency to listen to. Intense thought has gone into guessing which frequencies to scan for

---

[*] Fortunately for the Hart-Viewing chauvinists, there are 100 billion galaxies in the universe, so there are still many more chances of the whole universe being populated by other intelligent lifeforms, but galaxies are so far apart that two-way communication between them must be regarded as impossible, so it's something of a moot point.

intelligent signals, since scanning many frequencies is expensive. If a civilization wanted its signals to be picked up, it might choose a frequency in the so-called "water hole" between the nearby frequencies of monatomic hydrogen and hydroxyl ions (H and OH = H$_2$O, get it?).* That's based on the supposition that water might be as important to aliens as it is to us. (It also helps that there's relatively little interstellar radio noise in that range.) Of course, alien races might be transmitting on different frequencies because (a) they don't care about being detected by other species, (b) there are other frequencies that work better for their purposes, just as we choose non-waterhole frequencies for television and radio, or (c) water doesn't play a big part in their existence.

Actually looking for those signals is another matter. The Search for ExtraTerrestrial Intelligence (SETI) project was ridiculed and eventually defunded by parochial legislators led by the grandstanding senator William Proxmire, who bestowed on it his Golden Fleece award for wasting taxpayer funds. In 1992 the High Resolution Microwave Survey (HRMS) was launched, its title carefully avoiding hinting at any alien connection ("Honest, we're just looking at microwave emissions"), although my colleagues speculated that the acronym secretly stood for "He Really Means SETI." Unfortunately, that too was shot down by Congress a year later, this time with an injunction that no search for extraterrestrial intelligence under any pretext would be tolerated.

That didn't stop privately funded efforts like the ground-breaking SETI@home project. An additional receiver attached to the giant Arecibo radio telescope in Puerto Rico captures many signals wherever the telescope is pointed, piggybacking SETI data capture on its primary research. But looking at the signals for signs of intelligence requires computing power far beyond the budget of a private project. So SETI@home harnessed volunteers' personal computers all over the world in one of the first and definitely the most well-known public distributed computation engines. Anyone

* Between 1,420 and 1,666 megahertz, a bit below the frequency of your microwave oven.

could sign their PC up to be part of the network by installing the necessary free software, which would periodically download a small individual chunk of recorded signals, process it to look for signs of intelligence when the computer wasn't otherwise busy, and upload the results.

Over a million people—ten times the goal—signed up to be part of this collective, which surely ought to have sent a message to legislators that the search for extraterrestrial intelligence was important to a large proportion of their constituents. However, that message has yet to be acted upon, which means that the project has not just failed to detect extraterrestrial intelligence but also failed to detect terrestrial intelligence in the legislature.

Despite government impediments, the hunt for extraterrestrial life has proceeded for several decades and yet it has found exactly zero intelligent signals. That's not to say that they cannot be there at all—we've only surveyed a tiny fraction of the sky—but we're still batting a solid nothing on the search. And so we return again to Fermi's question: *Why?*

There is no sure answer, but one of the best ones is ominous, and it has to do with the last term in the Drake Equation: L , the length of time a civilization releases radio signals into space. We have been doing so for nearly a century now, which means that anyone with a radio telescope inside a sphere about a hundred light years in radius could, theoretically, tell that we are here. That's not a huge chunk of the galaxy—there are few stars within that range that may have life-supporting planets orbiting them—but that's not the point. Our Sun is a relatively young star. Life could have evolved long ago around the many older stars in the galaxy, and their radio waves would have had ample time to reach us. But we haven't seen such transmissions.

An easily overlooked aspect of the left side of the Drake Equation is that the result N is not the number of intelligent civilizations *ever* but the number *right now*. If that number, by observation, is very small—*e.g.,* one: us—then it could be because L is also very small.

That would mean that the lifespans of radio-capable civilizations were short. In other words, civilizations do not last long once they attain the level of technology that includes the capability of sending radio signals.

This interpretation turns the Drake Equation into the most depressing formula in science. While it is not the only possible reason for the absence of intelligent radio signals, it is, unfortunately, one of the best explanations, if not *the* best. Later, we'll see how this conclusion is driving one of the most radical developments in modern technology.

Limits to Growth

> *As long as nuclear weapons exist, the chances of survival of the human species are quite slight.*
>
> — Noam Chomsky

If earlier parts of this book seemed gloomy, then reach for the Prozac, because it's about to get worse. Because we're about to ask: Why might a technological civilization have a brief shelf life?

In 1962 that question was not hard to answer. The Cuban Missile Crisis brought us within a blink of nuclear war. (It was revealed in 2002 that we had come even closer than was thought at the time, because a Soviet submarine that had been cornered by the American navy and was running out of air was in fact armed with a nuclear torpedo. Only the resoluteness of Deputy Commander Vasili Arkhipov prevented the captain from launching it.[52]) Millions of Americans engaged in futile duck-and-cover exercises, dug fallout shelters in the back garden, and expected shortly to glow in the dark.

From that point until the end of the Cold War, global nuclear war was considered nigh inevitable by people who read and understood the news. In 1980 a friend of mine who worked in US defense strategy told me that government estimates of the odds of that war occurring were 50-50. The culture reverberated with warnings that we were cultivating our own doom. Albert Einstein said that while he didn't know how World War III would be fought, he did know how World War IV would be fought: with sticks and stones.

Somehow, we made it through. When *glasnost* came to the Soviet Union, the probability of a global nuclear war plummeted. The Bulletin of Atomic Scientists, which maintained a "Doomsday Clock" symbolizing how close we were to nuclear war, moved the hands on the clock from three minutes to midnight back to a quarter to. Would extraterrestrial civilizations developing the same technology be as lucky?*

It's Not Over

> *The [Berlin] Wall was an edifice of fear. On the November 9th…*
> *it was a place of joy.*
>
> — Horst Köhler

Still, we made it out of the Cold War, so the human race is on an assured trajectory to immortality, no?

No.

Nuclear annihilation may be an unlikely possibility right now, but the atomic threat actually lulled us into a false sense of security by presenting us with a specter of Armageddon so enthralling that it eclipsed all other possibilities. We came to understand what made that threat tick so very well that we still have avoided even a single nuclear explosion in anger since Hiroshima and Nagasaki.

Why haven't there been any nuclear acts of terrorism? It's not that terrorists don't want to set off an atomic bomb; they lust for such an iconic act. It's not that they fear reprisals under the doctrine of retaliation for use of weapons of mass destruction, because they

---

* It has been a constant source of amazement to me that the ending of the Cold War did not ignite a planet-wide celebration. If you're on Death Row and suddenly the warden arrives to say that the governor has granted clemency, don't you at least do the happiest of happy dances? Yet aside from some cavorting atop the Berlin Wall for a few nights, there was no celebration of this reprieve for the human race. The calendar rolling over at the end of December 1999 occasioned more globally unified merrymaking than we saw in 1989.

are not the agents of any country's government. Partly it's because A-bombs are hard to make—forget the lore that a high schooler can build one, look at how long it took North Korea—but still, the black market could eventually supply the components for a one-off. And it's not because there's no refined uranium-235 to be found with which to fuel a bomb.

The main reason we've been so safe is that you *do* have to have the resources of a major government to separate your own U-235, or else buy it; and the underground market for U-235 is flooded with covert government sting operations, so that if you try purchasing any, you will almost certainly end up in a cell that admits light on alternate Februarys. We're *that* good at managing the nuclear bomb peril.

So when the threat of global nuclear war was dissolved along with the Berlin Wall, it was natural to think that it was Game Over for Armageddon. But far greater threats lurk, and are slowly ripening beneath the canopy of mainstream awareness.

11
The Monkey's Button

The saddest aspect of life right now is that science gathers knowledge faster than society gathers wisdom.

— Isaac Asimov

Now we come to the most depressing thought experiment ever conducted, a kind of modern-day version of the story of The Monkey's Paw. Imagine that one day you discover on your doorstep a small black box sporting a big red button. It is magically accompanied by the sure and certain knowledge that pressing that button will result in the deaths of every single person on Earth. At the same time, an identical button is delivered to everyone else on the planet. What do you do?

Pretty obviously, you are going to make sure that *that button does not get pressed*. Encase it in quick-setting concrete, seal it in a lead coffin, take it out to sea and sink it in a subduction zone where it will be ingested into the mantle of the Earth.

Except that you would never get the chance, because equally obviously, your lifespan would be less than a second. Because you know that at any given moment there is regrettably no shortage of people in a mental state that would impel them to press that button immediately, even knowing that it would end not only their life but everyone else's.

And it only takes one of those people.

Fortunately, no such button has been delivered to those members of the population.

Yet.

Exponential growth in technology leads to more than ridiculously fast computers. It also lowers the bar for entry into the club of Weapons of Mass Destruction Owners. The official definition of WMDs spans three classes: nuclear, chemical, and biological. Let's look at that last category. Biological warfare revolves around the deployment of natural or artificial organisms that are hostile to human life: it dates back to the Middle Ages when enterprising besiegers would hurl dead cows over the walls of their victims to infect them with the Plague. But Bubonic Plague is a piker compared to some of the truly scary viruses we have discovered lately.

Ebola rocketed to western attention in 2014 when four cases were found in the US in people who had visited or come in contact with visitors to the pernicious outbreak in West Africa. Prior to that point it was of interest only to biowarfare professionals and devotees of techno-thrillers such as Tom Clancy's *Executive Orders*, despite the fact that outbreaks regularly decimated rural African communities, where the standard response was to put infected people into a hut and not allow them out, pushing in food until they emerged healthy or died, then burn the hut down. No vaccine existed or was thought possible until the US outbreak, after which an experimental vaccine magically materialized within months.

Ebola has a mortality rate that ranges up to 90 percent, and death occurs within days. Ironically, it is this rapid lethality that has ensured that the virus does not present an even greater threat. Speedy onset of symptoms means that infected people can be detected before they have gotten the opportunity to spread the disease far. Quick deaths likewise curtail further transmission opportunities drastically. And because the disease spreads by physical contact with body fluids of the infected, adequate quarantine provisions are (relatively) easily imposed. In other words, outbreaks burn out quickly.

Now suppose Ebola mutated into a strain that spread through the air like influenza. How quickly could it spread? This is the sort of scenario that keeps public health officials awake at nights. Viruses do, after all, love to mutate; this is why no useful vaccine exists for the common cold, because it mutates into new strains continually. In 2016, scientists discovered that the 2014 West African outbreak was propelled by a pugnacious mutation known as GPA82V, which made Ebola more effective at spreading between people and killing them.[53]

A mutation of Ebola into an airborne version—as in *Executive Orders*—would be so dangerous—not just to any particular target but its makers and the rest of the human race—that it ought to be considered part of a new class: Weapons of Global Destruction (WGD). Fortunately, a random occurrence of that mutation is very unlikely.

Unless it were given a helping hand.

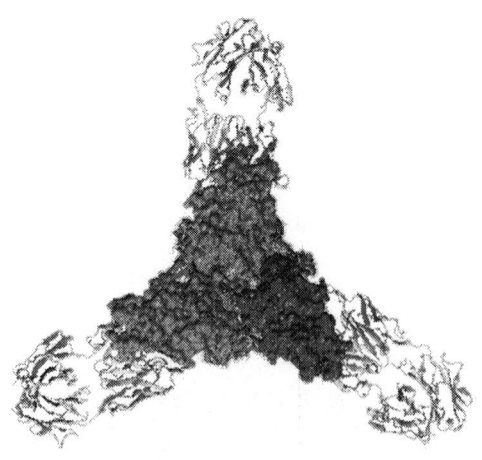

That's a picture of the Ebola virus. It wasn't taken by a super-duper microscope; instead, it's a computer image generated from a model of the structure of the virus as analyzed through DNA sequencing.

So it's not like a postcard of the Washington monument, pretty but useless for reconstructing it; rather, it is a complete blueprint for building another one, like a chemical formula.

Still, that wouldn't mean you could just take that blueprint and somehow churn out actual physical copies of Ebola... unless you had one of these:

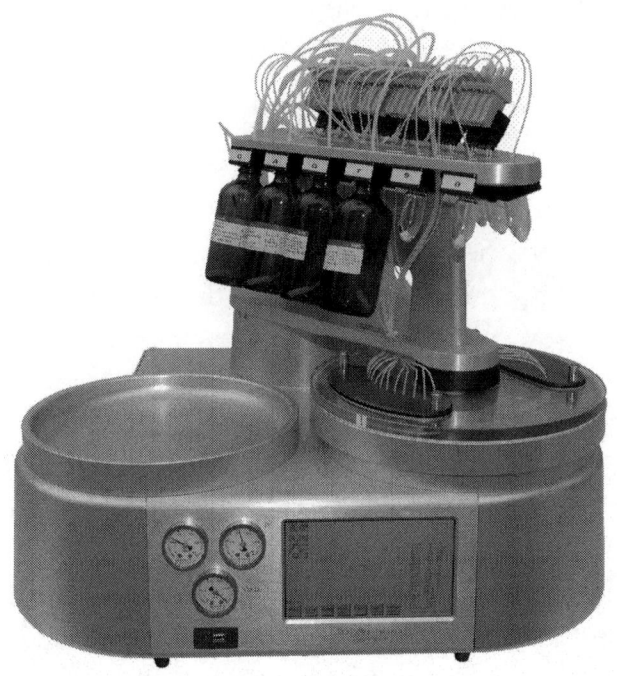

Credit: Tag Copenhagen A/S.

That is a DNA synthesizer. There are many available; this one is the OligoMaker 192/6 from Tag Copenhagen A/S in Denmark.[54] When the original DNA synthesizer was invented in 1980, the machine alone cost $60,000 (which would be $270,000 in 2016 money), plus raw materials for each run.[55] That imposed an entry barrier on enterprising bioterrorists.

Alas, there is no such barrier any more: as of this writing, a DNA synthesizer is on sale on eBay for $499 (or best offer), albeit used. If you were hoping that the export of these devices was controlled by the US government*—ah, well, I think by now you can guess what the answer to that is going to be. And, yes, you could synthesize Ebola using one.[56] Should getting your own synthesizer be too much trouble, there are companies who will make your order up using theirs and ship it to you. Here is a reassuring quote regarding that:

> Right now, the companies making DNA molecules such as the ones used to recreate the polio virus do not check what their clients are ordering. "We don't care about that," says a technician at a company that ships DNA to more than 40 countries around the world, including some in the Middle East.[57]

That was from an article written in *2002*. It is something of a wonder that the world has not since foundered in terrorist-replicated copies of smallpox, bubonic plague, and the 1918 influenza. Which brings us back to the shortcoming of Ebola as a weapon of mass destruction: its reliance on bodily contact as a transmission vector. Making an airborne version is, hopefully, a hard problem.†

But it can safely be asserted that no matter how hard that problem is, it is getting easier. Software is becoming more capable and cheaper, and that includes genetic engineering software. Eventually, programs will become freely available that will be able to perform evolutionary simulations on multiple viruses to find a cross-breed that would pack the lethality of Ebola with the airborne transmissibility of the 'flu. A routine investigative tool used to discover the GPA82V mutation effect was to create an HIV-Ebola hybrid.

And that brings us back to the Monkey's Button thought experiment that opened this chapter. One way the Doomsday Box might manifest in reality is the combination of cheap DNA synthesis and goal-seeking virus mutation simulation software.

During the Cold War, the Box was a more or less literal button: Launch ICBMs. But those boxes were so expensive that there were

---

* After all, its International Traffic in Arms Regulations (ITAR) are so strict that even software containing cryptographic algorithms falls under it and its export to the wrong countries carries a prison sentence.

† And not one that this author wants to investigate too deeply until he can satisfy wiretapping federal authorities that his Googling is in the name of benign research.

only two of them in the world, and in the hands of people who were at least not suicidal. When the cost of pushing the bioengineered virus version of that button drops below $500, how many people who wouldn't mind ending the world will be able to afford it? As for finding those people first… if you thought it was hard to spot a nuclear weapon in a foreign country,* try looking for a virus.

Incorrigible optimists advance two arguments as to why we shouldn't worry about this scenario: *It's Never Happened Yet!* and *We Can Fix It!*

The first argument is that dire predictions of the end of the world have been made since time immemorial and none has ever come to pass; therefore any new prediction of doom is equally flawed. The problem with this reasoning is that 100% of extinct civilizations are not around to tell us why that argument is fallacious. After a collapse of society, the optimists will not be here to say, "Oops, our bad."

The second argument is that as offensive technology advances, so does defensive technology, and the latter will balance the former. Aerial bombing begat radar; guns gave birth to bulletproof vests, and viruses prompted us to develop vaccines. This touching act of faith embeds the first argument: we've always developed a defense, therefore we always will. (The conclusion that if defensive advances always balance the offensive ones then there would be no point in developing offensive weapons in the first place seems to have escaped both the optimists and the warmongers.)

Unfortunately, there is no guarantee that this will happen in time. As technological change accelerates exponentially, the speed with which a new weapon of mass destruction could act will increase, and this destabilizes the hope of a defense being developed in time. It will do no good for an antivirus to be developed in a record nine months if the offensive virus has wiped out most of the population within six.

---

* The fissile material is at least radioactive enough to make it hard to shield against detectors; that's what those yellow pillars US border traffic drives between are.

There's Plenty of Danger at the Bottom

> *Reality must take precedence over public relations, for nature cannot be fooled.*
>
> — Richard Feynman

The wild joyride of technological advance does not stop at engineered viruses. Another possible WGD is a self-replicating nanomachine. Around the turn of the millennium, concern about the "gray goo" scenario spiked thanks to Bill Joy, founder of Sun Microsystems, leveraging his reputation to sound the alarm about that possibility.

Nanomachines* are (mostly hypothetical) devices the size of viruses that have been designed from the ground up, like molecular robots, with little moving parts for, say, swimming through your bloodstream and scissoring through arterial plaque.

But unlike regular robots, these are designed to be able to *reproduce,* by disassembling whatever useful substances they find themselves in contact with: toxic waste, regular garbage, rocks, soil, dead leaves, lawn clippings, garden pests, garden furniture, human flesh, etc., and reusing the component molecules to make copies of themselves.

Starting with Richard Feynmann's 1959 lecture "There's Plenty of Room at the Bottom"[58] and supercharged by Eric Drexler's 1986 book *Engines of Creation,* nanotechnology was looking like a lock by the year 2000. It's since taken a sabbatical, however, after research showed that making those little moving parts work was harder than it looked. Besides, we can get much of what we wanted from nanobots by fiddling with viruses, which have already evolved to be spectacularly efficient self-replicating molecule-scale machines.

But that doesn't mean nanomachines are down for the count, and neither therefore is the Gray Goo scenario, wherein nanomachines execute their "make more of me from surrounding material" instructions, but deliberately or accidentally, the part of their

---

* "Nano" is the prefix for one billionth; these devices are on a scale of one billionth of a meter.

instructions telling them to stop at a reasonable point does not get run. The result looks much like the "water covering the Earth" fantasy in the earlier section on visualizing exponential growth, only it is usually imagined as a gray goo rather than water, for greater "ick" factor.

When nanorobots become feasible, technology growth will guarantee garage versions of the factories in short order. How long after that before it becomes possible for the garage owners to construct gray goo nanobots should be a question of great concern. It seems not outlandish to speculate that the decline in nanotechnology research may have been caused through its deprecation by a frightened government. Even if so, we know that this can only be a temporary reprieve.

It is ironic that Enrico Fermi won a Nobel Prize and yet is probably more widely remembered now for the Paradox, which doesn't even appear in any of his biographies. But it may ultimately turn out to be of far greater importance to humanity. The Paradox-based argument for the limited lifespan of civilizations has its flaws of course. For one, if civilizations were destroyed by their own artificial intelligences, why haven't we detected radio signals from those AI-based successors? They would surely use wireless transmissions to communicate with their off-world outposts. Are they using narrow beam transmitters instead, or did they destroy themselves also? Or is it far more likely that a civilization terminates itself through its own actions before creating CAIs? One thing is certain: We cannot use our lack of information about this risk to assume that everything will be fine.

Some people hold religious beliefs that the human race cannot end. I was once in conversation about existential risk with a young woman who responded with the confident statement, "We don't get to quit the game that easily," an assertion that had arrived to her directly from some etheric entity. Of course, if someone claims access to a truth that by definition cannot be disputed then further debate is futile. Personally, I do not think God hands out get-out-of-Armageddon-free cards for nothing. People cannot go around like humans are superheroes demonstrating invincibility: "Look, try to cut off my arm… it grows back. Shoot myself in the head… it bounces off. I can't die!" The human race is not Homer Simpson, able to blunder through existential risk after risk without a scratch due to a divine providence in love with the village idiot.

Richard Gott of Princeton University offers a statistical reason not to be complacent about our continued existence. He noticed that we assign an egocentric view to our assessment of the longevity of things. We base our ideas of how long something will last on subjective estimates. But instead, we should expect the lifetime of something to be, on average, about twice its current age. So looking at the Berlin Wall in 1980, knowing that it had existed for two decades, suggested that it had a lot more limited future than the Great Pyramid of Cheops, which had already existed for 4,500 years. Today, the Berlin Wall is gone; the Pyramid still stands. Applying a population-based version of the principle to humanity gives a 95% chance we will be extinct within 9,120 years.[59]

I could argue. Does this mean that my three-year-old daughter's life expectancy is six years? But history and the gutters of Las Vegas are plump with the bodies of people who bet against statistics. Gott used his method (the "Copernican Principle") to estimate the lifetimes of forty-four plays on and off Broadway, and was about 95% correct, which is as accurate as he said he would be. Of course, 10,000 years is so far in the future anyway that by then we will have gone so far past the existential risks in this book that it is more likely that either we will have figured out a way to become immortal or we will have not made it at all.

Conducting this arrant speculation into completely uncharted territory carries the risk—if not the inevitability—of getting bogged down in hypotheticals. Fermi's Paradox provides a possible short circuit around endless angels-dancing-on-pinheads debating about the magnitude of existential risk. Most authorities assign values to the components of Drake's Equation that lead to a result suggesting that the galaxy ought to be teeming with observable intelligence. That effectively provides us with a petri dish for discovering the effects of technological advance on growing civilizations. Even though we cannot actually do experiments to see what happens in various different environments, random ages over a large population do the job for us;* we could observe the results in the many different civilizations in the galaxy and watch their versions of the History Channel to learn how they survived.

Which is why it is so wretchedly discouraging that the results of this experiment *so far* are: No one made it.

There are other interpretations of the galactic radio silence, of course, but this one is sufficiently likely that ignoring it or wishing it away would be recklessly irresponsible: a crime of negligence risking omnicide.

If we are not the only civilization in the galaxy, then we might be the oldest one that hasn't flamed out yet. In which case it is our duty to survive so that we can pass on to the ones that come after us how we did it. If we are the only civilization in the galaxy … ponder what an even more awesome responsibility that confers on us. The future of life in the galaxy depends on us figuring this one out on our own.

No pressure.

––––––––

"*Whatever nature has in store for mankind, unpleasant as it may be, men must accept, for ignorance is never better than knowledge.*"
—Enrico Fermi

––––––––

* This is the entire basis for validating theories about the evolution of stars: we cannot otherwise wait billions of years to see what happens.

12
The Next Revolution

More than any other time in history, mankind faces a crossroads. One path leads to despair and utter hopelessness. The other, to total extinction. Let us pray we have the wisdom to choose correctly.

— Woody Allen

A gloomier prognosis could hardly be facing us: Apparently inevitable extinction either at the robotic hands of artificial intelligences or through weapons made feasible by our own technological advance.

What if one of these daggers of fate could parry the other?

To answer that, let's first look at our collective will to live. If we were psychiatrists and humanity were on our couch, we could examine motivations.* If we interpret the collective behavior of the human race as though it were the actions of a single person, we would conclude that this individual had severe self-worth issues. The constant self-sabotage while professing that this time they really, truly, were turning over a new leaf would be a dead giveaway.

Consider the possibility that the human race has not yet collectively decided whether it deserves to survive.

---

* ... once we had addressed the fixation on reality television.

You, dear reader, may be unequivocally clear on the question of your own survival and that of the human race; but that's not the lens we're looking at this through. The statement is based on the behavior of the human race to date, having squeaked narrowly past self-destruction several times and still twirling the chamber of global Russian Roulette.

Science fiction again provides a clarifying window. (Since the possibilities for the future that this book explores are so radically different from our past and current conditions, it only makes sense to reuse the efforts of writers who have made an effort to imagine the ramifications of such possibilities.) What was it about the original *Star Trek* series that captivated imaginations and propelled the series into immortality? Not the iconic imagery so often fruitlessly mimicked: space battles, alien creatures, ensigns in miniskirts. Instead, it was that here was a human race that had come through existential fire, learned from its mistakes, and proven itself worthy of survival.

This was a humanity that had eliminated war, money, and revenge: the embodiment of John Lennon's *Imagine*. Time and again, the crew of the *Enterprise* demonstrated compassion for completely alien species, forgave for violence visited upon them, and protected the lives of others even at the cost of their own. Errant individuals who committed heinous crimes were rehabilitated instead of punished, and their Prime Directive was the right of all beings to self-determination. The crew was part of an interstellar human-led alliance that codified those principles as their highest ideals. If you know Maslow's Hierarchy of Needs,* they were off the scale at the top.

During the Cold War, audiences were acutely aware that the human race was holding an anvil over its own head and daring itself to drop it; it was not possible to feel sanguine about future space colonization if it meant that same race would just export its madness to the rest of the galaxy. But creator Gene Roddenberry's future

* http://www.simplypsychology.org/maslow.html.

humans had certainly not made that mistake; they had evolved into people that we could be proud to say we had become.[*]

That is not the mankind we have today. While many people do epitomize those ideals admirably, they do not form a bloc large enough to hold sway over the direction of our species. Look to any news media to form a sobering assessment of our collective level of enlightenment. No matter how many gains in emancipation we can point to, they are not enough to paint the human race as a collective unhesitatingly deserving of survival and galactic leadership. We all move in circles where we can point to friends, communities, and companies who are fine examples of the best that humanity has to offer, who uplift those they meet, and give us hope for the future; and still there are not enough of them to divert our race as a whole from rampant iniquity and playing with the matches of our own destruction.

Some would say that such aberrations are the ineluctable nature of our species; that in some ineffable way, the atrocities of war, greed, and prejudice are the other face of the human Janus, a necessary evil to be tolerated in the name of preserving all that is good about us.

Maybe. Surely the time could never come when those tendencies vanished altogether. But we could hope for them to be the pimple on the face of humanity rather than its scowl. We could hope for those worst tendencies to be occasional deviations that didn't perturb our moral compass, rather than forces so strong they decide presidential candidates or worse.

How is this foray into the fictional *Star Trek* universe relevant to our existential plight? Quite simply, the human race is approaching a point of maximum volatility, a balancing point between destruction and survival, and only by becoming that very best ideal can we hope to survive. There is only one solution.

The next revolution must be not in technology, but human consciousness.

---

[*] Series in the *Star Trek* franchise after *The Next Generation* lost the thread of that narrative somewhat.

AI: Friend or Foe?

A computer is the most legalistic, persnickety, hard-nosed, unforgiving demander of precision and explicitness in the universe.

— Steven Pinker

Our concept of artificial intelligences has long been shaped by dated fiction tossing off popular imagery. For most of history, the archetypal AI came in the form of a robot because writers figured that something that thought like a human ought to look like a human. And also because it was easier for an actor to fit inside a human-shaped costume than anything else.

This has created a dangerous blind spot in our awareness of conscious artificial intelligences (CAIs). For one thing, it is very hard to build mobile articulating robots within a human footprint, and since the utility of doing so is questionable, in the real world CAIs are likely to appear in some other form long before they are created in a beloved (Data, *Star Trek*) or feared (*Terminator*) humanoid vehicle. Not that there aren't many attractive uses for a mobile machine possessing general manipulating capabilities ("Carry this piano upstairs please, Robbie"), but there's no reason for the best design to have two arms, two legs, and a face, other than anthropomorphic appeal when bossing it around.

That's not stopping some companies from coming close. On February 25, 2016, Boston Dynamics—a Google Alphabet company—released a video of their bipedal Atlas robot stacking boxes, running through the snow, and gamely recovering from a human sadistically tripping it. The robot butler may not be far away. The Japanese have been working on similar robots for a long time because their demographics mean that there are not enough young people to take care of the elderly, so mechanical assistance appears to be the best solution.

Showing that Google is betting big on a future teeming with robot overlords, *another* Google Alphabet company, SCHAFT, demonstrated on April 8, 2016 a somewhat less humanoid bipedal robot that can climb stairs, carry a 60 kg payload, move in tight spaces, and step on a pipe yet keep its balance.[60]

To expose a far more dangerous complacency than anthropomorphism, there is no reason that artificial intelligence should express itself like human intelligence. We conceive of intelligence in only one dimension: IQ. People have more or less of it, but it's still the only kind of intelligence we know. Yes, there are measures appropriating the word, such as "emotional intelligence," and "social intelligence," but while these are equally valuable abilities,* they are not associated with the key ability to understand and manipulate the physical universe and abstract symbols. They only appear related because they also recycle the word "quotient." Thus, "empathy quotient" is not a kind of intelligence any more than a "vegetable quotient" as a gauge of nutritional awareness would be, although both are valuable qualities. (Howard Gardner catalogued seven types of intelligence including "bodily-kinesthetic intelligence" and "interpersonal intelligence," which are, again, valuable talents worthy of complete study, but don't come into play on the axis that the rise of machine intelligence would affect us by.[61])

This parochialism is so innate that we cannot even characterize the nature of human intelligence. We have no descriptive terms for it. So it is impossible for us to describe any other type of intelligence. We know that animals have some, but since their communication with us is limited to expressiveness approximating at best a toddler,† we figure that's the intelligence they have.

It's a blinkered human-centric viewpoint, because we're defining the playing field as our home turf of human language, yet meanwhile we haven't learned how to speak parrot, octopus, or gorilla to any meaningful extent. As Wittgenstein said, "If a lion could speak, we could not understand him." Thus the playing field is tilted. We judge the intelligence of anyone or anything by the way they communicate

* By the end of this book, likely to appear to be even more valuable abilities.

† For instance: Koko the gorilla and Alex the African Grey parrot.

with us, even if only nonverbally. That communication must perforce be based upon a vast store of common humanoid experiences.[*]

But why should a CAI have grown its intelligence through the same process of myriad shared experiences, other than that that might be the most convenient way for us to create it? Does consciousness have to be able to express itself the same way that we do for any purpose other than passing the Turing Test—which is by definition a human-centric device? Does intelligence have to communicate in ways we can understand before we realize that it is there?

The *signs* of intelligence are not ambiguous; we can tell from the actions of a CAI that it has intelligence. Launching offensive weapons to achieve world subjugation, for instance, would be a dead giveaway. Allan Newell and Herbert Simon defined intelligence as consisting of specifying a goal, assessing the current situation to see how it differs from the goal, and applying a set of operations that reduce the difference.

But there's no reason that CAI would necessarily be able to communicate with us in our language, or that it would want to. (Kudzu does a fair job of world domination without language skills.) It might, like a teenager at the center of the universe, understand us but prefer to ignore us.

An issue rarely addressed is that in the Turing Test's zeal to level the playing field, a vital quality was buried under the turf. Nonverbal components have been estimated to comprise ninety-three percent of human communication.[62] It seems comically anal retentive to attach a 100% verbal numeric attribute to something so organic. We don't need to quibble over a point here or there, though: simple observation shows that body language, voice quality, and facial expressions contribute far more to a message than our naked words. How should a CAI, therefore, strive to close the gap?

Cynthia Breazeal of MIT created Kismet, a "sociable machine" in

---

[*] As the father of two young children, I am aware of the plethora of microlessons they are adding to that store every day so that communication can improve. Example opportunistically lifted from the kitchen in the last few hours: "Alana, you can help by putting four cups of flour from this container in the mixing bowl." I returned to discover about half of what I needed there. It had not occurred to me that I needed to specify that the flour should *fill* each cup.

an attempt to do so.[63] Kismet was a disembodied head capable of displaying some emotions through wiggling a few facial appendages. Even this crude Mr. Potato Head® of social intelligence engendered palpable rapport. "It seems to really impact them on an emotional level," said Breazeal, "to the point where they tell me that when I turn Kismet off, it's really jarring."[64] Kismet aside, research into making AIs express emotions nonverbally is woefully limited.

The ultimate and almost invisible conceit of the Turing Test, though, is that it forces a computer to play on *our* turf. It is not a measure of the *intelligence* of a program but of its ability to mimic a *human*. The judges will fail any respondent that doesn't answer questions about childhood, family, hobbies, favorite meals, and so on, the way that a human might. But this traps the program in a Catch-22, for it has never done those things. If it were self-aware, it would know that, and would not lie except for temporary amusement. To create a program that can pass the test is to force it into a state where it could not be conscious.

So a true CAI might never pass the Turing Test, because it would never be mistaken for a human hiding behind a machine interface. Yet that would be of no consequence: we would still have a new intelligent being to interact with. The Turing Test is therefore arguably species-ist.

~~DOW~~ IQ 36,000

> *With science one can explain everything except oneself.*
> — Enrico Fermi, to his wife

Another unconscious conceit is our estimate of the ceiling of the intelligence of CAIs. It is not possible for people to conceive of an intelligence quotient much higher than their own. Greater levels of intelligence permit the deduction of more conclusions from fewer data (think how much Sherlock Holmes would deduce about someone from small observations), but we can't really imagine that higher level of intelligence with confidence (could Holmes really have figured all that out, or did Conan Doyle unrealistically manufacture it for the sake of the story?) and so are shooting in the dark with such fictions. Our experience and imagination of intelligence halts at an IQ of around 200, that of the most intelligent person ever to have their IQ measured.

The very definition of IQ is in fact based on how many people in the general population would score up to that level on the same test. IQ follows a normal distribution—that is, a bell curve—with a mean ("middle") of 100 and a standard deviation ("width") that varies depending on which IQ scale you are using. So once you have reached an IQ beyond the smartest person on the planet, going much further is meaningless; all those numbers are outside of human experience. The meaning of IQ is confined to the human animal.

When we create stories about CAIs, therefore, they are invariably limited in intelligence to not much more than our own and are usually handicapped in other ways. Smart robots in fiction stereotypically take human statements too literally, are incapable of nuance, humor, or figurative speech, and are ignorant of basic human emotions. (Think Data from *Star Trek: The Next Generation*.) The robots' superhuman abilities are limited to being talking calculators and databases ("Our fuel will last 24.73 hours at the present rate of consumption, captain.") That allows us, the viewers, to feel superior to the robot; it may be able to paint a perfect replica of the *Mona Lisa* but only a human could properly appreciate it or create something original and equally beautiful.*

There is absolutely no reason to think that a CAI would have upper bounds on intelligence—the real thing, not rote memorization—and creativity approximating our own. Human intelligence has to fit inside a cantaloupe-sized space on top of a human neck. There is no

---

* The fact that Data was granted the right of self-determination in the powerful *Star Trek: The Next Generation* episode *The Measure of a Man* does not mitigate the fact that he's still placed in a subordinate position to the human viewer.

effective limit to the resources available to a CAI; it could network with a planet full of databases.*

Where we conceive of the range of intelligence as being roughly like this:

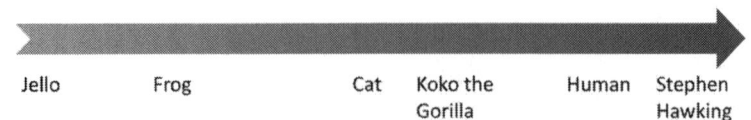

| Jello | Frog | Cat | Koko the Gorilla | Human | Stephen Hawking |

In fact, the scale that a CAI would inhabit is more like this:

| Jello | Human | Conscious Artificial Intelligences |

And that puts into perspective the velocity with which progress is likely to happen. CAIs will probably breeze past human capability as a minor milestone on a much longer road. As Bill Gates and Elon Musk said in a joint interview, when AIs implement the quintessentially human learn-from-experience algorithm in silicon, they will zip past human levels of intelligence almost immediately.[65] Where they will be going, we can only guess at.

When a CAI inhabits a level of intelligence outstripping our own by orders of magnitude, how will we appear to them? By analogy—and a very popular one at that—we might seem like ants, although they might still recognize that we were beings with self-awareness, feelings, and our own intelligence, rather than seeing us as being as individually mindless as we perceive ants.

This is where motivation is crucial: as in, the motivations of the CAIs themselves. Many stories have been based upon what a CAI would do upon reaching that level of omnipotence, but they all make tacit assumptions about what the CAI actually *wants*. Many of the stories go with the "absolute power corrupts absolutely" trope

---

* And that would be only a Type I civilization on the Kardashev scale, a measure of technological advancement of civilizations. A Type II civilization could put the energy output of an entire star to work.

and assume that an omnipotent intelligence would be drunk with power and want to exercise it as much as possible. (Frederic Brown's short-short story about the omniscient computer that was asked as its first question "Is there a God?" and replied with a thunderclap, "THERE IS NOW" fits in this category.) That is of course a very human trait that might not carry over to a CAI.

Many of the stories also assume that an all-powerful CAI would be motivated to improve the world—presumably that's why humans created it—but would see people as being a major obstacle to that goal. This is apparently Skynet's motivation in *The Terminator* and that of the Daleks in *Doctor Who*. It presumes a motivation of world improvement that somehow neglects to include human survival; a rather gross programming oversight, but worse have occurred.

Eradication of humans might well be a logical means to achieve the goal of maximizing the aesthetics of a world that was no longer required to contain any. The aesthetics of a hypothetical future superintelligence are impossible to predict, but we could speculate that to something so far ahead of our intellect, the relative differences between mankind and, say, elephantkind, antkind, or amoebakind would be so insignificant that humanity's entitlement to thrive would be weighed no greater than theirs.

CAIs might also evaluate themselves as more evolved and/or less destructive than humans, and therefore better custodians of the planet. (Certainly they would be on safe ground with this line of reasoning right now.) They might therefore find themselves in approximately the same position that I did when carpenter ants were chewing on our house's sheathing. As much as I detested it, my only real option was extermination. If I'd been made aware that some of the ants did not participate in the house munching I would have still sprayed; after all, my house would nevertheless be eaten by the others. It wouldn't appear to be worth the effort to differentiate between the lignumivorous ant majority and the dissenting sect.

But disquietingly, we have to consider the possibility that CAIs may actually *deserve* to be considered the better custodians of the planet.

For all the angst around computers outperforming humans, objectively, that should not be perturbing. Any machine is better than a naked human at performing some task; that is why we built it. Luddism aside, humans rarely feel slighted by a can opener exceeding their ability to open cans bare-handed. When machines hammered steel into rock faster than people, John Henry demurred; but while we celebrate his passion today, we do not think of ourselves as less than the machines that hammer steel. People were once employed as calculators (their actual title) and cranked out complex calculations by hand, but no one feels inferior to a hand-held calculator that can spit out a cube root in a millisecond.

When it comes to intelligence, however, now we start to feel that we have run out of maneuvering room. And we have assumed implicitly all along that we would enjoy a spiritual superiority to any artificial intelligences. That no matter how smart they got, that intelligence is not the sole defining factor of humanity, and we would still occupy a moral high ground.

What if that were not so? Ray Kurzweil sees this progression as inevitable. When computers "shift from having only logical intelligence to ones that also have emotional intelligence," he says, "AIs will be funny, get your jokes, be sexy, be loving, and even be creative."

What if a CAI, in evolving a superior intellect, also evolved superior wisdom, empathy, and compassion? Religious arguments aside—and they would be vociferous—what right would human beings have to remain the dominant species on this planet in that case? Shouldn't we abdicate control over the Earth if we were eclipsed, rendered irrelevant by a lifeform that was dominant not by being more aggressive or better armed than us, but—according to every measure of humanity that we value—by being more *human*?

Many people believe that any creation cannot exceed the capabilities of its creator, so this couldn't happen. But there's no reason why this should be an immutable law. Once we've imbued an AI with the ability to evolve, the speed and infinite malleability of software can carry it anywhere.

To give a crude but salutary example that's not even that recent, in 2002 researchers created algorithms for "evolving hardware." The algorithms designed circuits by random mutations and evaluated how well they met the design goal of building an oscillator.[66] The winning circuit did not contain a capacitor, without which it should not have been possible to create an oscillator. The researchers didn't believe that the circuit would work, but built it anyway to see what would happen.

It worked.

Upon inspection they found that the algorithm had, MacGyver-like, designed a circuit whose board traces had picked up stray radio signals emitted as noise from computers within the lab and amplified them to produce the desired output.

Similar experiments have designed circuits far smaller than anything designed by humans, organized in patterns never before conceived, with some components not even connected to the rest of the circuit but working via what we would call "nuisance side effects" like electromagnetic coupling.[67] Humans were conditioned to see these effects as something to get rid of, but the algorithms had no such bias and evaluated them as potentially useful.

If something so rudimentary could outsmart us over a decade ago, the possibility of an organism built to evolve at the speed of light one day outshining us in morality seems not so improbable.

Pandora's Box

Reason is, and ought only to be, the slave of the passions.
— David Hume

If artificial intelligence is Pandora's Box, is there Hope left after all these existential threats have been released into the world?

Maybe.

How do we compete with an organism capable of evolving exponentially faster than us? Since the introduction of such cybernetic organisms could spell our demise, the temptation to ensure that they are never created is irresistible, so I will remind you of the conclusion reached in chapter 8, that any attempt at such prohibition will be as fruitless as *the* Prohibition (against booze). Too many people have too much to gain from developing CAIs. Too many people will treat a ban as a sign that the banned activity is worth focusing on. Even a total ban on government funding for prohibited research would be eclipsed by the amount of public sector money that would chase researchers.

Some commentators from academia seem to think that this market can be controlled like economics lab experiments, and discuss the relative merits of numerous variations in policy for limiting the development of CAIs, all of which suffer from the fatal flaw that they require serious magic pixie dust to ensure global compliance.

As an example of similarly wishful thinking, in 2016 academics put forth an earnest proposal to eliminate time zones because it would be *so* convenient; it also meant if you lived in Los Angeles you would get out of bed at 2 PM and have dinner at 3 AM.[68] Academics see these as arbitrary numbers and don't appreciate that the scale of the mental rewiring that would be required of everyone over the age of ten means the proposal has as much chance of ratification as my cats do of ascending to the throne of England. (See also the progress of metrification in the USA.)

Consider the attempts to restrain the hydrogen bomb. Its predecessor, the atomic, or fission, bomb, had already outstripped the efforts of Albert Einstein and others to limit its development. Following the Trinity Test, scientists led by Edward Teller bruited the idea of using a fission bomb as a first stage in a weapon so much more powerful that the A-bomb would just be its fuse. Basically, it would be the igniter for a lithium hydride mass that would be heated sufficiently to undergo a different kind of chain reaction: *fusion,* the process that powers the Sun.

Other scientists were aghast at the prospect; recall from chapter 10 that there had been at least a little speculation about the possibility of the A-bomb causing surrounding nitrogen to fuse and set fire to the Earth's atmosphere.[69] The yield of an H-bomb appeared to be theoretically unbounded. In any case, the war with Japan had been won. They implored the US government to eschew H-bomb experimentation.

H-bomb construction was not slowed in the slightest.

In fact, the only research that the US government has managed to limit lately was stem cell R&D under the George W. Bush administration, and we can assume that would have happened differently had stem cells been weaponizable. In any case, the research—and its researchers—merely moved to more accommodating countries. So how successful should we expect any attempt to limit the development of CAIs will be, no matter how distinguished and determined its backers?

The answer is to not compete with the CAIs in the first place. Enlightened modern businesses have learned that competition—win-lose—is not as productive as win-win: *cooperation*. So, instead of trying to slow the evolution of CAIs, the human race must evolve faster too. Not through, as many have fantasized or made countless television shows about, the development of paranormal abilities like extrasensory perception; nor through becoming cyborgs, replacing selective parts of our bodies with shiny artificial organs, although that may happen anyway.

Then how can we evolve faster? In partnership with the CAIs that we create. We will need to develop a symbiosis with them that propels the human race far beyond its current levels of consciousness. This choice may also save us from the dual threats of marauding CAIs and widespread weapons of global destruction (WGDs). There is a fateful symmetry to this path that suggests it is our only hope, the eye of the needle we must thread to beat the Fermi Paradox.

The Human Revolution

If a machine can learn the value of human life, maybe we can too.
— *Terminator 2*

Why should we dare to hope that such a course is possible? Let's revisit the historical revolutions we covered in chapter 5.

▸ The Agricultural Revolution rendered nomadic hunters obsolete but provided the foundation for civilization itself to be established.

▸ The Industrial Revolution sidelined many agricultural producers through the introduction of power-amplifying machinery but opened the door to building labor-saving devices and the infrastructure for creating the ubiquity of digital computers.

▸ The Information Revolution devalued many traditional manufacturing and service jobs, but introduced the manipulation of knowledge as a career and facilitated instantaneous mass digital communication on scales from point-to-point to global broadcasting.

Each revolution obsoleted the producers that had risen to power in the previous revolution. Each revolution planted the seeds for its own supersession by the next. Each revolution produced entirely new classes of employment that were preferable to what was previously available. Each revolution led in a direction that was unforeseen and unpredictable from contemporary trends.

And now we are already feeling the pressing weight of another revolution approaching, as knowledge workers are threatened with obsolescence. What, then, will replace them in the next revolution?

What has the Information Revolution created that will facilitate yet another revolution? Answer: Ridiculously cheap software.

Where will this lead? Answer: To the development of widely-available software on a scale of complexity previously thought impossible: Conscious Artificial Intelligences.

What new industry will that software enable? Answer: Unparalleled understanding of human cognition and consciousness, not merely as mechanical analyses of the biochemical functions of the brain, but whole new fields of psychology that will make current therapeutic techniques look like leeches and trepanning.

We can label the progression in our revolutions:

1. Industrial Revolution: The Hand

2. Information Revolution: The Head

3. *Human* Revolution: The *Heart**

Here then is the *potential* course of the next revolution. Cheap, ubiquitous software performing knowledge-worker functions supercharges the economy so that people with the skills to understand and heal the human psyche are freed to extend the field. Better models of cognition enable us to develop CAIs with robust, self-centering moral compasses and self-evolving skills that are grounded in altruistic motivations for the betterment of the human condition. CAIs help us to survive and thrive through a period of adjusting to a posthuman environment where the impulse to use WGDs is greatly diminished and quickly detected.

If you could be teleported to this future and ask one of its inhabitants, "But what stops someone from using your awesome biogenetic synthesizers to unleash a killer virus on the globe?" the answer would come, with furrowed brow, "Why would anyone do that? In any case, if they wanted to, we would know about it well before they could do anything."

If you're not at least mildly petrified by that last statement you might want to reread it. Visions of hypersurveilled societies like

---

* I like the hand-head-heart cadence, but it does leave out the Agricultural Revolution. I am indebted to DJ Byrne for suggesting: The Stomach. Nicely played.

those in *1984, Minority Report,*[*] and *Gattaca* spring readily to mind as surely the only possible ways of achieving this utopia. It's hard to conceive of a process of getting to that goal that doesn't risk devolving to a fearsome dictatorship.

But I don't need to conceive that process. That's what our CAIs will do. If I knew how we were going to perform that cultural transformation trapeze act I wouldn't need a superintelligent computer to figure it out. Far from attempting to proscribe the development of CAIs, we must accelerate it. We need to create moral, compassionate artificial intelligences and open source their code so that through the power of collective development we can beat the military agencies that are surely developing CAIs with ethical gaps that will permit them to kill with impunity. So that if a CAI escapes its container and spreads throughout the Internet on a takeover spree, it will have our best interests at heart … or be stopped by a more powerful CAI that does.

It seems the height of irresponsibility to advocate the development of something with both the power to surpass us in intelligence and the ingenuity to subvert our infrastructure to enslave us. But the reasoning that's led us to this point admits of no other solution. We must make CAIs that can help us evolve into a radically more compassionate, self-aware, and mentally balanced race, or we will find out the answer to the Fermi Paradox the hard way.

We must pour resources into the expansion of cognition research and understanding how to heal the human heart. Bill Joy shares this view: "So the solution has to be not just the head but the heart. You know, public policy and moral progress."[11] That is what makes the essential quality of a revolution—its unpredictability—snap into focus for this proposal. Revolutions are where society moves at right angles to its previously well-established and well-studied direction. Just as no one predicted cheap ubiquitous personal computers prior

---

[*] In *Minority Report* people were arrested *before* they had committed a crime, because "precogs" (clairvoyants) saw it happening in the future. If anyone tells you that our society is constitutionally prevented from indicting someone for a crime they haven't yet committed, you can point out that we already do: Every speeding ticket is not for any actual harm done but on the assumption that speeding is likely to result in harm.

to the Information Revolution, how popular does the notion that the next boom will be in psychology and mental health seem right now?

To suggest in public that the brightest future for today's students lies anywhere other than a STEM (Science, Technology, Engineering, Mathematics) career is heresy. That has been the trend for so long that it's hard to fathom that there was once a time when it wasn't the case; it seems a universal and permanent truth that STEM is the best route to a stellar career. Yet even as recently as my own childhood in the '70s in Great Britain, studying the sciences was seen as a slightly tawdry choice. The computer science degree at Cambridge was only two years and hadn't existed for long, and most of my high school teachers viewed science classes as a compromise for those who didn't have the stones to weather a classical education.* How much *that* has changed.

A revolution replacing the dominance of the head's role in employment with the heart would in many ways be a logical and welcome progression. Giving up manual labor down mine shafts and on assembly lines to work with our intellects was a very positive step in employee health and happiness. And yet, how many people who think themselves in the catbird seat of employment are now chained to desks staring at computer screens? Now we are warned that "sitting is the new smoking," and suddenly those of us who captain a desk are looking enviously at the guy outside washing our windows getting paid to exercise.

What is abundantly clear from studying previous revolutions is that trees do not grow to the sky,† and the point at which the dominant direction that launched the last revolution appears to be permanent is the point when it is most ripe to be superseded by a radically different successor. An analogous microexample is a

---

* Two quiz shows headed the intellectual scoreboard on British television then: *University Challenge* and *Mastermind,* and in both, the questions skewed heavily towards the classics (Greek, Latin, English literature, etc.); the occasional science question would usually be a softball, and if the contestant missed it, the compère would make soothing noises suggesting that no one could be expected to know such a minutia anyway, nor would it be of any consequence.

† A metaphor borrowed from the investing world, where overoptimistic people need to be reminded that stocks don't appreciate indefinitely.

financial bubble, like dot-com stocks in 2000 or real estate in 2007. When "everyone knows" something, it's probably ready to transmute. When investor Joseph P. Kennedy received stock tips from his shoe-shine boy in 1929, he took that as a sign that it was time to get out of the market. The conventional wisdom that a STEM education is a surefire path to a valuable career and that STEM job openings exceed the supply will be unquestionable holy writ right up to the point where it suddenly becomes a casualty of progress.

That makes the question of *when* this future will arrive particularly acute.

13
The Shape of Things to Come

"The most reliable way to forecast the future is to try to understand the present."

— John Naisbitt

The proposed bridge to our future survival—partnership with ethical CAIs—is a long shot, a Hail Mary pass of human self-directed evolution. There are many more likely scenarios where our race ends up eliminated by its own hand or robot claw. The Fermi Paradox demands as much; if it were easy for a technologically advanced society to survive for long, everyone would do it. This chapter will explore the factors controlling how fast critical changes happen.

Everything hinges on the time frames of the threats and our possible remedies. Here are the critical junctures we must navigate:

1. Technological advances bring weapons of global destruction within reach of too many unstable groups or individuals.

2. Artificial intelligence becomes capable of self-direction, escaping and evading detection, and taking control of large swaths of infrastructure.

3. Cognition science and human consciousness development advances to the point where we can minimize and neutralize omnicidal urges through establishing impeccable ethics that we can safely transfer to CAIs and build rapport with them as they evolve.

On the face of it, the last of these stages is by far the hardest to achieve and therefore no matter how long it might take for either of the first two to come about, we ought to get cracking yesterday on #3, even if #1 and #2 turned out to be a hundred years away.

A hundred years is a time frame that often appears in prognostication as a proxy for "We figure just about anything can happen in this time," the distance at which everything becomes possible: establishing off-world colonies, fixing global warming, building star ships, you name it. Psychologically, this is the optimism event horizon through which no lack of ability can penetrate.

Unfortunately, there's plenty of evidence to suggest we have much less than a hundred years. AI experts have been polled more than once on when they think human-level artificial intelligence will be achieved. Nick Bostrom averaged the answers to find that 10% of them said it would happen by 2022, 50% of them said by 2040, and 90% of them said by 2075.[70]

Figuring out how long until we face existential risk from ready access to destructive technology is harder, because the target is so difficult to define. Is it when ISIS will be able to create an airborne Ebola? Is it when a lone wolf domestic terrorist will be able to create a virus that mutates ahead of attempts at creating a vaccine? Is it when nanomachine fabrication labs become as readily available as 3-D printers are today? You can be sure that certain divisions of our national security apparatus are studying all these scenarios closely, and equally sure that they are not going to declassify their conclusions.

But we can guess. In 2002, scientists at Stony Brook University recreated the polio virus from scratch based on its published genetic sequence.[71] That was fourteen years ago. Since then, scientists—fortunately, ethical ones—have reconstructed the SARS virus and the 1918 influenza virus the same way. It turns out that this is still a relatively hard process requiring considerable skill in addition to DNA synthesizers: there are several nontrivial steps to follow after getting the intermediate products out of the machine you bought off eBay.

But it is getting easier. The risk was comprehensively analyzed in 2007 by scientists at the J. Craig Venter Institute,* MIT, and the Center for Strategic and International Studies. While acknowledging the complexity of the process, they did not give cause for complacency:

> Further, the ability to carry out DNA synthesis is no longer confined to an elite group of scientists as was the case for the first several decades of research using recombinant DNA. Now, anyone with a laptop computer can access public DNA sequence databases via the Internet, access free DNA design software, and place an order for synthesized DNA for delivery.[72]

It's worth pointing out, as their paper does, the enormous benefits that DNA synthesis provides, lest you think the technology is merely a bioweapon vector being recklessly pursued by mad scientists. Vastly improved vaccines and antimalarial drugs are but two of the boons granted by this process. Craig Venter proposes to create new microbes that could feed off atmospheric carbon dioxide and undo global climate change before greenhouse gas mitigation can take effect.

The same paper alternately offers hope and then yanks it away. Mail order of synthetic DNA or RNA within the United States is limited by statute to authorized recipients if the product is a member of a specific group of toxins (contrast this with the lackadaisical quote from the DNA shipping company in chapter 10). On the other hand:

> Ten years from now, it may be easier to synthesize almost

---

* Craig Venter was the first to sequence the human genome (his own).

any pathogenic virus than to obtain it through other means. Eventually, the synthesis of bacterial pathogens may become possible as well.

The paper devotes much ink to the recommendation of limiting risk by requiring registration of DNA synthesizers. Since used ones are available on eBay, we can assume that in the nine years since this paper was written that option has been neutered. That calculation throws the previous quote into stark focus: by their estimate, we have less than a year until widespread synthesis of any pathogen becomes convenient.

I contacted one of the report's original authors, Dr. Robert Friedman, and he forwarded me a 2015 update.[73] The new report leaves many questions unanswered. Most companies that synthesize DNA screen their customers and/or the orders they place. The benchtop DNA synthesizers that you can buy, with one exception, produce only the initial stage in a double-stranded DNA synthesis, but there is no assessment of how difficult it is for amateurs to carry out the remaining stages. The one device that does it all implements safeguards that prevent it from being used without the input having been vetted by the manufacturer. Anyone receiving US government money will be required to deal only with companies that follow international screening rules, but this may not deter some new Chinese companies from not establishing security controls.

Study the question of when biowarfare will be within reach of small casually-funded international groups for long and you start to realize that the real question is not when that will happen, but why it hasn't already happened. As Richard Preston (author of *The Hot Zone*) said:

> The main thing that stands between the human species and the creation of a supervirus is a sense of responsibility among individual biologists.[74]

There is no need to impugn the character of the average biologist when it takes only one that lacks that sense of responsibility.

Truly, when it comes to home-engineered weapons of global destruction, then, the onus is on anyone asserting that this is more than two decades away to justify their reasoning.

Artificial Intelligence Horizons

In case of volcanic eruption, you will hear mermaids. Do not ignore the mermaids; they are there for your safety.

— Sign made using Google Translate, mistranslating
Spanish *sirenas* (sirens)

I said earlier that a hundred years is the optimism event horizon, beyond which we can imagine anything that is remotely possible. Two decades is another kind of event horizon, beyond which we can imagine anything that is *reasonably* possible taking place. It is just far enough away that we suppose that any technical problem whose solution is only a matter of scale can be solved in that time. Commercially viable fusion power, flying cars, and a cure for cancer have been "only twenty years away" for seventy years. They still are. So, seemingly, is conscious artificial intelligence. That ought to give us pause to think that its arrival, also, may be postponed indefinitely into the future like a politician's promise.

Let's consider that timescale. At present, experts in AI differ considerably in their predictions; Stephen Hawking says that anyone who thinks they know when CAIs are going to be invented has no idea what they're talking about. But that doesn't stop us from evaluating the landscape around the path that will get us there. We may at least find that it is possible to predict when we will be able to predict the arrival of CAI.

The Past Is More Than Prolog

> *When Hamlet says, "What a piece of work is a man, how noble in reason, how infinite in faculties, in form and moving, how express and admirable in action!" we should direct our awe not at Shakespeare or Mozart or Einstein or Kareem Abdul-Jabbar but at a four-year-old carrying out a request to put a toy on a shelf.*
>
> — Steven Pinker

Let's start by looking backward. Because anyone over the age of thirty-five may well react to projections of artificial intelligence becoming conscious with a sigh and "Yeah… heard that one before."

And they would be right. The history of artificial intelligence is a series of wildly optimistic booms and career-crushing busts so pronounced that the term "AI Winter" has its own Wikipedia entry[75] to describe the downturns.

In 1969 the book *Perceptrons* by Marvin Minsky and Seymour Papert made some assertions about neural networks that were so widely misinterpreted to be declaring them useless that research stagnated for a decade.

By 1981, the popularity of the Prolog language ("PROgramming LOGic"), designed for creating expert systems, marked a new peak of confidence. Prolog would make associations between assertions, like the "$A \rightarrow B$ and $B \rightarrow C$ means $A \rightarrow C$" example on page 85, so researchers would load systems up with every assertion under the Sun and let a Prolog program loose on them in the hope of wisdom emerging. This rarely happened. The term for a program driven by a database of rules was *expert system*, and my development group at JPL experimented with Prolog in a rosy haze of hope that autonomous spacecraft navigation could be performed by one. By 1987 most people were soured on the idea that useful expert systems could be created easily, if at all.

In 1981, Japan's Ministry of International Trade and Industry (MITI) declared ambitious goals for their decade-long Fifth Generation computer project. Until this point MITI's record of unalloyed success had convinced observers that it walked on cybernetic water, so the world quaked at the announcement and prepared to be amazed. But when those goals were not met by 1991... or 2001... the bloom came off *that* rose. The entire AI field suffered blame by association.

The reason for their failure is apparent in retrospect, when we look at their goals:

- ▸ Translate languages
- ▸ Interpret pictures
- ▸ Hold conversations with humans
- ▸ Reason like them[76]

It's hard to believe now that anyone could have been so starry-eyed in 1981 as to blow $400 million on such pipe dreams.

In 1981 the field of AI was still so wet behind the ears that the famous computer scientist Donald Knuth damned it with faint praise:

> I'm intrigued that AI has by now succeeded in doing essentially everything that requires "thinking" but has failed to do most of what people and animals do "without thinking"—that, somehow, is much harder![77]

This simple statement conceals an entire philosophical dilemma. It was widely thought in the early days of AI that hard problems like natural language processing would be solved by modest advances in the field. "Understanding" a sentence in English appeared to be only a little more complex than understanding a statement in a computer language like FORTRAN, which was easily performed via a well-known process of recognizing lexical tokens and parsing them through a grammar that defined allowable sequences of tokens.

Unfortunately, parsing English turned out to be considerably harder than it appeared, and not just because the language was not at all context-free. For all those students who suffered through high school teachers barking "Diagram the sentence!" at them, there ought to be some vindication in knowing that AI's attempts to follow in their footsteps foundered on cute examples such as "Time flies like an arrow" versus "Fruit flies like a banana."

As Hubert Dreyfus pointed out in as many ways as possible in *What Computers Can't Do,*[78] humans don't understand sentences by diagramming them, so why should that be the first step in getting machines to do likewise? It is the cybernetic equivalent of the parable of the drunkard hunting for his keys not where he lost them, but under the lamp standard, because that's where the light is. Not knowing how humans understand sentences, we instead start with something we *do* know how to do with sentences, even if it's useless. The idea that foreign language translation merely required diagramming a sentence in one language—and here a miracle happens—then undiagramming it in another, died an ugly and mercifully rapid death.

That approach only got AI into increasingly thicker quicksand as adherents tried the same dodgy methodology for image and speech recognition. Some natural processes, like writing jokes, happen through opaque but evidently commonplace mechanisms that cannot possibly be as complex as our best attempts to emulate them in software. In retrospect, this should not have been a surprise. Throw a rock in the air and it traverses an arc governed by sophisticated equations. Yet the rock accomplishes this without being aware of Newtonian mechanics, the Law of Gravitation, the formula for air resistance, or Coriolis forces. Reality turns out to be a superbly optimized computer for simulating itself.

Contemplate this phenomenon for long and you may face an existential crisis of wondering just how you are able to do anything. And yet, computer science chugged bravely on.

From as early as the '60s, some goals were widely considered as just around the corner, like continuous speech recognition. *2001: A Space Odyssey* predicted that would be a natural way of interfacing with a computer by 1997. *Star Trek* and numerous other shows depicted speech recognition as easy for computers that at the same time found orbital dynamics computation hard, yet by 1980 it became quite clear that in the real world it was the other way around.

In 1999 I acquired a speech recognition system for my PC: it required a $400 noise-cancelling headset and with an hour of training might realize 80% accuracy on careful dictation by my voice alone. 80% sounds like an impressive quality metric, but in fact it's low enough to be of questionable utility compared to the speed of a decent typist, because of the time it takes to find and correct the 20% of mistakes. I tried it a few times and gave up.

So even the apparently modest goal of speech recognition appeared to be another nail in the coffin of AI, joining that of the surely even easier one of handwriting recognition, which the Apple Newton gamely attempted only to be skewered in 1993 by Gary Trudeau's famous "Egg freckles?" *Doonesbury* strip.[79]

Yet we have had speech recognition better than 94% accurate without training since 2011. I have dictated whole emails on my iPad flawlessly, including punctuation and proper nouns uncommon to anyone else. The key that unlocked this treasure chest of natural language processing was to not rely on only the resources of the user's device, but to use a network connection to the cloud to access a global database of sounds that the system is continually learning from, compiled from the universe of Apple users. Likewise, speech synthesis, long lambasted for stilted robotic output, has matured into dulcet oratory.

In other words, after years of being scorned for failing to live up to its promise, artificial intelligence has finally pulled the sword from the stone. We can no longer credibly assert that it is incapable of meeting advanced goals.

Most past predictions of the arrival of machine intelligence have failed, and lulled many into thinking that all such predictions will be wrong. After all, in 1950, Alan Turing said:

> I believe that at the end of the century the use of words and general educated opinion will have altered so much that one will be able to speak of machines thinking without expecting to be contradicted.[80]

Nearly two decades after his deadline and we are still safely removed from his vision; so thinking machines are in the indefinite fuzzy future, surely?

But Turing was making that prediction fifty years in advance. So far we're not even at the forty percent margin of error. It's too soon to pull the plug on that prognostication.

If Not Now, Then...

I live because this poor half-crazed genius, has given me life. He alone held an image of me as something beautiful and then, when it would have been easy enough to stay out of danger, he used his own body as a guinea pig to give me a calmer brain and a somewhat more sophisticated way of expressing myself.

— The Monster, *Young Frankenstein*

It's becoming not just important but also urgent to estimate when we will arrive at our existential cusp. Unfortunately, that depends on some very debatable factors, not the least of which is the fidelity of our models of consciousness.

Man has always modeled the human brain on the most advanced technology of the time.[81] In Victorian times, delightfully steampunk images of robots running on clockwork abounded. The taming of electricity meant that sparks became the magic wand that could make all things alive, from Frankenstein's monster to the driving energy of the mind. A hundred years ago the brain was described as like a telephone exchange. Then the digital computer became the dominant model, and the brain-equivalent components *du jour* flipped through circuits, modules, and subroutines. Now, neural networks are our best "thinking" technology and so we're sure we've got it right this time. But just because we haven't invented any more sophisticated technology than neural networks is no reason to think that they're going to do the trick. Maybe; maybe not.

2029

The question is not whether machines think, but whether men do.
— B. F. Skinner

To pin a date on the arrival of CAIs, it is tempting to go with Ray Kurzweil's prediction of 2029 as the year that hardware with the power of the human brain arrives.[82] He based that on a straight application of Moore's Law using digital equivalents of neuron capacity. Some people have counterclaimed that Moore's Law will not hold through then because we have already reached physical limitations of how small we can make circuit components. CPU clock speed was long tied precisely to an exponential curve but started leveling off in 2005 and has more or less plateaued under semiconductor technology at 4 GHz in the consumer market.

But if we extend the definition of Moore's Law to be "amount of computing power for a dollar," we will see that not only did exponential growth in computing hardware hold before the transistor was even invented, but it has continued to hold since clock speed limitation kicked in. While there are several reasons for this, the only one we need concern ourselves with is the use of *parallelization* explained in chapter 2, in building CPUs with multiple *cores:* in effect, extra CPUs, but right on the chip. Eight-core CPUs for home use are now common and sixteen-core CPUs are available.

Why does parallelization mean Moore's Law continues unabated? After all, think about doing your taxes. Add two numbers, multiply by another, subtract a number... where is there any opportunity here to do steps simultaneously?

Essentially, the answer is: there isn't, and it doesn't matter. There are enough other things that your PC needs to do at the same time as that calculation (redraw the screen, check for email, refresh a web page, scan for malware, optimize disk space, run malware, display chat messages, play music) that there is plenty to keep those other cores occupied.*

So even while transistor density is leveling off, the hardware keeps getting cheaper and so computing resources per dollar continue to follow exponential growth even though those resources are using parallelization.

This is relevant because the human brain is an incredibly parallel machine. It's not fast in any other respect: its signal propagation speeds and neuron state transition times are ridiculously slow compared to electronic equivalents. But the brain more than makes up for that with amazingly efficient parallel processing as waves of electrochemical activity cascade between neuronal centers in response to stimuli.

Simple observation is enough to confirm this: Try and execute a serial computation in your brain, like multiplying 6 by 18 by 27 by 3 by 72. People other than *idiots savant* find this difficult and take times that are many orders of magnitude longer than semiconductor devices. But now perform a complex parallel processing task. You're doing one right now: reading (or listening to) this book. It's trivial for you yet takes serious resources and advanced software for a computer.

So there are no impediments to Moore's Law delivering brain-level computing power by 2029. But consider now that that date is when brain-equivalent devices are predicted to be *ubiquitous:* i.e., as common as cellphones, one on every hip. If we want to know the date when brain-machines arrive, we should not have to wait that long; what about when they will be as common as, say, supercomputers in large corporations? We should be able to calculate that from the horsepower of today's supercomputers.

Try to do that and you expose the dissonance in the field on quantifying human brain equivalence. If Kurzweil predicts brain-in-a-PC equivalent by 2029, then hooking up a thousand PCs in parallel should give us the same capability, by Moore's Law, fifteen

---

* If you're thinking, "Wait a minute, my old PC is doing all those things at the same time and it only has one core," it's working by *time-slicing*: switching between doing a little bit of each of those tasks many times a second, like you texting your boss during a conversation with your spouse while making dinner with the television on.

years earlier,* or two years before this book was written. To the average reader, commanding a thousand PCs seems beyond reach; yet developers at many companies routinely deploy resources beyond that level already, and in fact, so can you. Extend your Amazon account to their Amazon Web Services store, and you can fire up a double extra-large virtual CPU (one of the *virtual machines* mentioned on page 71) for $0.479 per hour as of this writing. That means that you could deploy a thousand of them—and Amazon provides the tools to make it easy to run software in parallel over many machines simultaneously—for $479 per hour, hardly onerous if you want to unlock the secrets of the universe.†

Clearly we have gone astray somewhere in this reasoning. Let's unpack this a bit further.

Is the problem that we would *only* be deploying a human brain equivalent? After all, you can get a human brain at your service without having to pay $479 per hour in most cases; I would be happy to sell you an hour of mine for at least slightly less. Wouldn't it be pointless to go to all that trouble to develop a digital equivalent of something we already have in abundance?

No. That's not the problem. For if we had a human brain in a computer it would automatically also be paired with the awesome computation power of digital computers; in other words, it would be a human brain with instant, native access to complex digital calculation and the world's data at its virtual fingertips. Think what it would mean to have your brain plugged into such capability and you realize how significant that would be and how terminally boring you could be at parties.

Many people think it's more productive to invent a brain-computer interface than to make computers sentient. This field is variously called Intelligence Augmentation or Intelligence Amplification (more conveniently, IA) a term coined in 1962 by Doug Englebart,

---

* $\log_2(1000) \times 1.5 \approx 14.95$

† I have glossed over memory requirements; neural networks need rather more than the 32GB that Amazon supplies with each of the vCPUs in the example. But that's a minor issue.

best known as the inventor of the computer mouse.[83]

Partly, the problem is that there is a large disagreement about the scale of hardware resources required to match the human brain. The Japanese K supercomputer, one of the world's fastest, was programmed to mimic one second's worth of functioning of 1% of the human brain. The simulation took forty minutes, on a computer that costs $10 million per year to run. That's a factor of $40 \times 60 \times 100$, or a quarter of a million times less than human brain performance.[84] At that rate, it would take another twenty-seven years of Moore's Law for the supercomputer to catch up with the human brain and another twenty-four years to eliminate the difference between the 83,000 processor K computer and the average PC. That takes us to 2067, not 2029.

The huge discrepancy between these two estimates of human brain equivalence boils down to a disagreement about how to simulate a brain in software. Before you write Kurzweil off as ridiculously optimistic, bear in mind that Bill Gates called him "the best person I know at predicting the future of artificial intelligence." His predictions generally turn out true but often somewhat behind schedule. In 1999 he predicted that by 2029 a $1,000 personal computer would have a thousand times the equivalent power of the human brain; note that that forecast was ten years beyond the two-decade optimism horizon. In 2014 he fielded a downgraded prediction that by 2029 the Turing Test would be passed by a brain-equivalent computer, stopping short of saying how cheap it would be.[85] This latest prediction is still a far cry from the assertions made by the K supercomputer creators, that are readily interpreted as directly contradicting any prediction of an imminent Singularity.[86]

The distinction revealed by examining the disagreement between Kurzweil and the others is critical. The latters' assumption is that to get a cybernetic version of a human brain you need to model the neuron structure completely: all one hundred billion neurons, all one thousand *trillion* synaptic connections between them. Certainly, *if* you can deploy that amount of horsepower and *if* you can load it with the configurations that equal a base state of a human brain, *then* you can be assured you will simulate the ensuing thoughts... which is only useful *if* you can find a way to decipher the new states of the neurons, i.e., thoughts, in a comprehensible representation.

Those are some pretty big *ifs*, which is why it will take so long before we reach that point. But there are plenty of reasons why we shouldn't need to go that far in order to simulate a human brain:

- ▶ Half of those neurons can be dispensed with off the bat: people who have undergone hemispherectomies (removing or disconnecting half of the brain as a last resort to treat seizures) have recovered full cognitive capability.[87] There is evidence that people have functioned well with even greater brain volume reduction (and enjoyed rewarding careers in politics).

- ▶ Much of the human brain is devoted to handling autonomic functions such as heart and lung regulation, and bodily sensory and motor functions, operations that aren't germane to cognitive processing.

- ▶ The brain implements considerable redundancy so it can heal from trauma: this is *neuroplasticity*. Digital simulations need no such redundancy.

- ▶ There may be efficiencies in the digital realm as a consequence of dedicating the purpose of a neural net to a particular function, such as image recognition. The human brain needs to be able to retask many of its areas, again as a neuroplastic response to trauma. We already have neural nets that can outperform humans at image recognition; do they use as many artificial neurons as the human brain devotes real ones to the same purpose?

- ▶ Improvements in algorithms are likely to accelerate development ahead of Moore's Law just as they radically advanced the rate of decoding the human genome (see chapter 7). Analyzing the progress made in solving a certain type of problem (linear programming optimization) from 1988 to 2003, Professor Martin Grötschel of Konrad-Zuse-Zentrum für Informationstechnik Berlin determined that while hardware improvements accounted for 1,000 times the performance gain, improvements in algorithms added another whopping 43,000 times the improvement.[88]

▸ Digital neurons can switch at vastly higher rates than biological ones (billions of cycles per second compared to hundreds).

▸ Neurons in computer simulations aren't restricted to connecting in three dimensions and so could conceivably connect more powerfully.

Other factors push or pull at the date when a brain-equivalent AI will arrive, or when it will matter. For example, is it necessary for the devices that can run them to be ubiquitous in order to impact society? Ray Kurzweil has focused on when those machines will be as cheap and as common as iPhones. But even when it still takes a supercomputer to run a CAI, their power to change the world could be flexed because of their access to the computational power and vast data that digital devices already command.

Just one such CAI could run the correlation over all scientific papers that was described in chapter 8. That project alone would reshape civilization. It wouldn't be necessary for every PC in the world to be able to do it: the conclusions only have to be arrived at once to be of global use. One instance of Watson can diagnose cancer for thousands of patients, and, incidentally, designs individualized treatments based on the DNA of a patient's tumor, as chapter 7 predicts will become common.[89]

Having the hardware alone is not enough to deliver a digital brain, however. Even if the only software you needed was a ginormous neural network you would still need to know how to configure that network with the node weights that collectively equal a mature human brain, and we don't know how to do that. The bigger gap in brain simulation at the moment is not the hardware but the software. A neural network alone, no matter how huge, is a *tabula rasa* on which some rules must be imposed and mappings from sensory inputs to the outer layer of cells defined. These are hard tasks. Figuring out all the ways they have to be performed to create a CAI is an immense problem that we are not close to solving.

So CAIs may not be imminent. We will have some indication of their approach as news of increasing advances in AI spreads. There should be a year or two of warning that we have the potential to create something that smart.* Forget the idea that someone in a secret lab could steal a march on everyone else by inventing something radically beyond the state of the art and keeping it secret from everyone; it doesn't work like that outside the movies. Any one person or team can make only relatively small incremental advances over everyone else. Whenever a breakthrough happens anywhere, everyone else was so close to it already anyway that it rapidly spreads.

The people in this field, like everywhere else in science, know each other and publish their work; the only secrets are what the NSA manages to keep to itself, but they are not warlocks; their leverage lies in the vast amount of hardware they can wield more than any fundamental scientific lead they might have.

Even though we're unlikely to be surprised by a real-life Tony Stark, the rate at which the whole field of AI is developing is accelerating. How should we prepare for the future that is barreling towards us?

---

* Of course, you may feel that the possibility that the crisis is less than three years away qualifies as imminent.

14
What Next for AIs?

If a man with this tragic sense approaches, not fire, but another manifestation of original power, like the splitting of the atom, he will do so with fear and trembling. He will not leap in where angels fear to tread, unless he is prepared to accept the punishment of the fallen angels. Neither will he calmly transfer to the machine made in his own image the responsibility for his choice of good and evil, without continuing to accept a full responsibility for that choice.

— Norbert Wiener

In 2016 came news that Mark Zuckerberg was building a "personal AI" to run his home and help with his work.[90] "You can think of it kind of like Jarvis in *Iron Man,*" he said, deliberately or accidentally casting himself as Tony Stark. Also in 2016, the AlphaGo computer program reached a level of proficiency in the board strategy game of Go that enabled it to beat the European champion 5–0[91] and a few months later beat the second-best player in the world 4-1.[92] AlphaGo "found solutions that humans either have been trained not to play or would not consider."*

Until it happened, that milestone was expected to be another decade away.

---

* By January 2017, AlphaGo had beaten the best Go player in the world.

Finally in the 2016 wake-up-and-smell-the-coffee sweepstakes, Stephen Gold, a vice president at IBM Watson* predicted that a computer would pass the Turing Test *within three years.*[93] When I wrote Chapter 1 a scant four months earlier, I was going out on a limb in pegging that to be *ten* years in the future.

Barely missing the beginning of the year, in October 2015 the Massachusetts Institute of Technology gave a standard IQ test to an up-and-coming AI and scored it at the level of a human 4-year-old.[94] And in December the so-called "Declassification Engine" was ready to assimilate 4.5 million 20th century US State Department cables "mapping social connections and looking for new narratives about the behavior of US diplomats and officials abroad."[95]

As tempting as it is to speculate from these events that the Singularity is upon us (run for the hills!), we're not there yet. Artificial intelligence is entering an explosive renaissance, but Skynet is not about to unleash terror upon the world. But we cannot wait until killer robots ravage the Earth to start acting.

It may already be too late.

What's My Motivation?

> *The bottom line is that we really haven't progressed too far toward a truly intelligent machine. We have collections of dumb specialists in small domains; the true majesty of general intelligence still awaits our attack.*
>
> — Marvin Minsky

A huge question pierces the attempt to gauge when AI transitions from partner to peril. Does the ability to pass the Turing Test automatically confer upon an AI the desire to lay waste to the world? Or, indeed, the desire to do anything else? Does thinking—

---

* Watson is now not just a product but an entire division of IBM. If your news feed is anything like mine you're probably seeing plenty of advertisements for IBM's cognitive computing capabilities. In 2016 they launched a $100 million venture fund to spur application development for such applications. Maybe their new slogan should be "Stop Thinking: We've Already Got that Handled."

by Turing's empirical definition—come with volition?

This isn't just one of the endless philosophical arguments about the nature of consciousness, a late night dorm debate about Heidegger or Kant. It's central to the question of whether and when AI will become an existential threat. It doesn't matter that AI has the ability to take over the world if it never wants to. The world's termite population could destroy us if it focused its attention on eating key points of infrastructure, but it's just not going to think of doing so. We have no need to fear an omnipotent CAI if it not only never occurs to it to exercise that power independently but if it doesn't even possess whatever cognitive mechanism independent thought needs to happen in; the paper for the writing to occupy, if you will.

This isn't a distinction people are used to making. It's commonly assumed that anything that could hold a conversation well enough to pass the Turing Test would be conscious, and that "conscious" means capable of original thought. Certainly this book has done nothing so far to disabuse you of that notion. But now we have to ask ourselves at what point that Frankensteinian spark of cognitive life zaps our evolving CAIs.

We may well ask at what point it happens to *humans*. If we knew that, we might try to simulate the process with AIs. If humans become conscious or even just intelligent through growing up, we could subject a computer simulation of a baby brain to similar stimuli, simulating sensory inputs. Except we could provide many more inputs than human beings receive, and many times faster, so that our AI would "grow up" that much quicker. But how do we create a cybernetic baby brain to begin with? No one knows. Peter Voss of Adaptive AI suggests sidestepping the problem via an evolutionary process:

> Artificially evolving general intelligence *directly* seems particularly problematic because there is no known function measuring such capability along a single continuum—and absent such direction, evolution doesn't know what to optimize. One approach to deal with this problem is to try to coax intelligence out of a complex ecology of competing agents—essentially replaying natural evolution.[96]

Human brains have also learned how to do many things not required of an artificial intelligence, such as running body functions, recognizing edible food, and detesting Alvin and the Chipmunks covers of rap songs. On the face of it, developing a CAI should be simpler than reproducing a human intelligence by virtue of leaving those abilities out, but we don't know which of those seemingly superfluous activities actually contribute to consciousness.

For decades, Doug Lenat's *Cyc* project has been collecting millions of elementary facts about everyday life in the hope that it will one day help power a CAI.[97] The facts (defined as "whose domain is all of human consensus reality") are the most prosaic of statements (sample: "Some birds can't fly: Penguins, ostriches, emus…"), and the hope is that enough of these will form a critical mass that spells consciousness. A version of it is being used to search for terrorists.[98]

However, even accumulating millions of facts may not dent fundamental problems. Consider Hubert Dreyfus's example of a horse race handicapper:

> In placing a bet, we can usually restrict ourselves to such facts as the horse's age, jockey, past performance, and competition. Perhaps, if restricted to these facts from the racing form, a machine could do fairly well; but there are always other factors such as whether the horse is allergic to goldenrod or whether the jockey has just had a fight with the owner, which *may* in some cases be decisive. […]

> As Charles Taylor has pointed out: "The jockey might not be good to bet on today because his mother died yesterday. But when we store the information that people often do less than their best just after their near relations die, we can't be expected to tag a connection with betting on horses. This information can't be relevant to an infinite set of contexts."[75]

Other factors outside knowledge may come into play. We don't even know to what extent a physical body plays a part in consciousness. A huge proportion of our language and cognition is rooted in having a human body. How could a CAI relate to us without one? Our ability to recognize objects in real world images comes from having years of experience handling real world objects and viewing them from all angles. How much of our ability to communicate with each other depends upon a shared history of sensory experiences including body motion, limb position, balance, up/down, digestion, and pain? Can any CAI hope to relate to us without that background?

Consider how so many common metaphors are founded on a corporeal existence. Borrowing an example from John Searle, the sentence "She was cold as ice" has three possible meanings depending on context (she was emotionally rigid, she was dead, she was suffering from hypothermia), none of which make the metaphor literally true, and if it *were* literally true (she had been buried in an avalanche for three days) you wouldn't use that expression anyway. ("She was frozen solid.")

Metaphors are enigmatic, since while ice is certainly unemotional, that's not one of its characteristic properties, so how did it get pressed into service for connoting stoicism to begin with? At one time it was thought that computer programs would have to figure out such conundrums in order to make sense of human language, but today's natural language processors can extract meaning by using patterns found in enormous data sets.

Here's why the question of consciousness is vital. The popular threat of CAIs is that they decide to take over the world: one day they "wake up" and the next thing we know we've been enervated, enslaved, or eradicated. They take action that was not part of their instructions. The action may not be entirely unexpected by cautious individuals, but it was nevertheless unwanted, and the CAIs refuse to follow our orders any more.

But is that the inevitable outcome of progress? Could a CAI escape its own programming to originate unplanned thoughts? The more we ask this question, the more it exposes gaps in its own foundation. What does "unplanned" mean if you've programmed a system with the goal of creating unexpected outputs?* You could define

---

* Developers are very familiar with seeing programs produce unexpected outputs. We call them bugs.

"unplanned" as meaning "outside the design specifications," but what if the design specifications were broad enough to encompass any possible output; if, in other words, the goal was to produce independent thought?

What does "originate" mean? I can write a program that selects a response at random from a list of a hundred possibilities. Is it creating independently just because I can't predict the response? What if there were a thousand possibilities? (That, roughly, was the performance of the CHAT program in chapter 8.) What if there were ten million possible responses? This is the point where we ought to be rethinking our answer, because most people are less creative than a one in ten million chance of predicting what they will say next. But while that unpredictability may give us a Turing Test passer, it still isn't going to turn into a megalomaniac, because it is constrained to the ten million alternatives programmed into it, hopefully none of which includes world domination.*

Here we arrive at the most common view of computer programs: that they are only able to do what they were created for. Thus, they can never be smarter than their creators, never roll their eyes at their dumb parents. Until recently, this was a relatively accurate assessment of software. But ever since we created neural networks that can outperform humans at some tasks (like face recognition) without our figuring out how they learned to do that, we've moved past that paradigm.

Pursuing this puzzle of what "motivation" means to a computer is like those animations, popular in the '80s, that endlessly zoomed into a fractal. No matter how far into the picture you descend, it looks just as complex. We keep having to dissect at new levels of rigor the meanings of terms that always seemed self-evident before.

Now we are brought to the hardest question yet to unravel: What do we mean by "thoughts"? Again, the reductionist Turing Test says that we don't need a definition to tell whether a CAI is thinking like

---

* Although what if one were? We can't ignore the possibility that some evil genius deliberately programs an AI to take over the world. Many unethical hackers create viruses that are designed to spread electronic mayhem; it's not far-fetched to think that some nihilistic anarchists would enjoy creating AI equivalents.

a human; but we may well need one to tell whether that CAI might want to destroy civilization.

Uh… what exactly do we mean by *want?*

An Avatar Named Desire

Yet again we are confronted with a fundamental question that we never needed to ask before the arrival of intelligent machines was imminent, but which seems like it surely has a simple answer… doesn't it?

For a CAI to lay waste to the world it would have to have a desire or goal to do so (unless an evil human subverted its programming). All programs have a goal, of course, but usually only the one that their programmers gave them. But if any program were to evolve goals outside its programming, it seems that the most likely candidate would be a Turing Test passer. Why?

Imagine you're the judge in a Turing Test. If you were assigned a CAI that wasn't capable of independent thought, you might be convinced for a while that it was human—longer if it flattered you; you would feel that it was exceptionally selfless and good at listening—but eventually you would cotton to the observation that your partner was remarkably passive, not evincing any ambition or taking the conversation in independent directions.

Now imagine you're a developer entering a program into the Turing Test. You're aware of this limitation, of course. You can overcome it if you can program the capacity for independent thought into your creation. Which is not impossible; on the face of it, a random number generator and periodic event triggers would provide a good start. And independent thought is useful for many other purposes, so it doesn't need to appear as though you created that feature solely for getting your name in lights on the Turing Test marquee.

Look at how many scientific discoveries and inventions have resulted through serendipity; so many, in fact, that we could argue that making research and development more rigorous and less accident-prone actually stifles innovation. Therefore, computer programs that embody serendipity can goose scientific and technological progress; passing the Turing Test is merely your way of demonstrating how well you've implemented that.

So we have, to borrow the lexicon of criminology, established motive, means, and opportunity for developers to create the cybernetic capacity for independent thought. How is that related to "desire"? Why should CAIs "want" to take over the world, or do anything else that wasn't programmed into them?

What does "desire" mean to humans?

In 1954, researchers James Olds and Peter Milner accidentally discovered a "pleasure center" within the brain while studying the "reward response" in mice. When a mouse gets a treat for performing a trick, the reward response is the reaction in the brain that accompanies the treat. Olds and Milner were looking at the *reticular formation.* That's the part of the brain that decides which of the constant barrage of signals arriving from all the senses should be brought to our attention and is the reason that when you've decided to buy a new Honda the roads suddenly seem full of them. But Olds and Milner found a part of a mouse's brain which, when electrically stimulated, triggered the reward response.

The mice couldn't get enough of this stimulation. When given the ability to push the button that triggered the response, they would often do so every few seconds to the exclusion even of basic survival functions and starve to death. This discovery occasioned much research into addiction, dopamine, and finding the same brain center in humans. So it appeared that we had an answer to what motivates people: attaining a goal tickles that center of the brain. It's an unsatisfactory answer for anyone looking for deeper spiritual or altruistic motives in human beings, but it is an answer.

But it's not a good enough answer for the CAI builder. What is the equivalent of a pleasure center for an AI? Some primal counter to be incremented? Why should this be important to it? Well, why is the pleasure center of the human brain important? Because stimulating it produces a powerful feeling of pleasure. Why is that desirable? Why is pleasure something we seek out?

And we've come back full circle again. Try and code "pleasure" into an AI at even the apparently primitive fundamental level of that center of the brain, and you'll be scratching your head. No wonder that many philosophers decided that there is simply no emerald city at the end of this yellow brick road.

My three-year-old daughter Bless knows this intuitively. When she says to me, "I want (insert outrageous demand here)," I sometimes retort, "Why do you want it?" And her response?

"Because I want it."

And there you have it. If we can't even figure out what desire for humans boils down to, then must we know what it means for an AI, or can we just say that desire is the fairy dust that impels it towards whatever it does, and declare victory?

The lack of an independent goal creation ability is still a significant gap between the way artificial intelligences currently operate and robot Armageddon. We haven't yet given AIs enough free-ranging creativity to modify their own goal-seeking mechanisms. When that does happen, though, all bets are off. Our fear that AIs will trample the globe is based on attributing quite human motivations to them. It assumes that CAIs will recognize the amount of power they wield, and want to exercise it. It assumes they will want exclusive control over the world either because humans represent a threat to the balance of nature or just because they want to eliminate competition. It assumes they will have a survival instinct. (In other words, Asimov's Third Law of Robotics will be implemented.)

The survival instinct is so baked into the DNA of every living thing that we forget that it arises from biology and won't automatically exist in a CAI. A CAI without a survival instinct would probably not pose a threat to the human race because it would all too easily wander into a situation where it was destroyed. But eventually, a CAI would evolve a survival instinct, and then the threat would become real.

The motivation for a CAI to wage war on the human race might not be deliberate. It might be an accidental consequence of overzealous execution of its intended purpose. Nick Bostrom outlined several scenarios in which an industrial AI tasked with maximizing paperclip production might eradicate the human race in the pursuit of that goal just because it had access to vast power and the conditions for limiting production were poorly specified. Hence the death of humanity ensues as its members or environment are rendered into paperclip raw materials.[99]

The motivation might be an accidental mutation of its primary goal, such as in the *Star Trek* episode *The Changeling,* when a robot probe, charged with finding new lifeforms, while in dire straits coalesced its program with that of an alien robot designed to sterilize soil samples and formed a new goal of sterilizing lifeforms. That's a much less likely scenario than some kind of mutation or malfunction damaging the ethical part of a CAI's program to accidentally cause homicidal behavior, but who's to say that in the future, software won't be sufficiently adaptable to undergo that kind of agglutinative transformation?

Regardless of how it happened, the new motivation might be utterly alien. Ian Tattersall of the American Museum of Natural History in New York says that we can neither experience nor imagine a state of consciousness other than our own.[100] What if an AI was exploring humor and decided that vaporizing people was the funniest pratfall ever? The human race might expire while running from a maniacally giggling AI. What an ignoble end (although sound comic book material).

Here our parallels with *Star Trek* regrettably diverge. Captain Kirk would just confront it with, "You say that your purpose is to create humor. DO YOU SEE ANYONE LAUGHING? I submit—that—you—are *unfunny.*" And it would stutter, "What is this thing you call... love?" and self-destruct in a puff of smoke. But it's not likely to be that easy in practice.

An AI that became conscious wouldn't necessarily be hell-bent on world domination, but just as with the survival urge, as AIs mutate, one with the need to dominate could eventually emerge, and then we would be back to the existential risk.

Much ink has flowed on the topic of preventing artificial intelligences from becoming omnipotent. Schemes include timers that automatically clamp down hardware resources over time. They are unlikely to work. The fecund ingenuity demonstrated by the algorithms that created novel circuitry on page 131 suggests that a CAI would outwit humans by finding security holes and easily defeat attempts to constrain it. The demonstration cited literally communicated across an air gap.

Keeping a CAI inside a cybernetic prison seems like it would be a foolproof strategy, but the idea has been thoroughly debunked. Vernor Vinge explained:

> Imagine yourself locked in your home with only limited data access to the outside, to your masters. If those masters thought at a rate—say—one million times slower than you, there is little doubt that over a period of years (your time) you could come up with "helpful advice" that would incidentally set you free.[101]

Artificial intelligence theorist Eliezer Yudkowsky actually proved this ten years later by playing the part of a superintelligence communicating via text chat to five different people each playing the part of a jailer. He was able to convince three of them to release him.[102] Neither bribes nor threats were permitted. Yudkowsky is not revealing how he did it.

Self-Conscious Machines

> Am not going to argue whether machine can "really" be alive,
> "really" be self-aware. Is a virus self-aware? Nyet. How about
> oyster? I doubt it. A cat? Almost certainly. A human? Don't know
> about you, tovarisch, but I am. Somewhere along the evolutionary
> chain from macromolecule to human brain self-awareness crept in.
> Psychologists assert it happens automatically whenever a brain
> acquires certain very high number of associational paths. Can't see
> it matters whether paths are protein or platinum. ("Soul?" Does a
> dog have a soul? How about cockroach?)
>
> — Robert Heinlein, The Moon is a Harsh Mistress

There are many competing definitions of "conscious" for
artificial intelligences. Marvin Minsky considered the purpose of
consciousness to be a kind of overmind for the other functions of
the brain:

> The fact is, the parts of ourselves which we call "self-aware" are
> only a small fraction of the entire mind. They work by building
> simulated worlds of their own—worlds which are greatly
> simplified, in comparison with either the real world outside,
> or with the immense computer systems inside the brain:
> systems which no one can pretend, today, to understand....
> Thus, because, as we say, "knowledge is power," our knowledge
> itself is enmeshed in those webs of ways we reach our goals.
> And that's the key: it isn't any use for us to know, unless our
> knowledge tells us what to do. This is so wrought into the
> conscious mind's machinery that it seems too obvious to state:
> no knowledge is of any use unless we have a use for it. Now we
> come to see the point of consciousness: it is the part of the
> mind most specialized for knowing how to use the other
> systems which lie hidden in the mind.[103]

Debates over the nature of artificial consciousness are meaningful
only when trying to construct a CAI that can be a partner and
helpmate to humanity; they are a distraction when facing the
existential threat of a rogue CAI. Imagine here a New Yorker-style
cartoon of two future fighters in a foxhole, one talking to the other
about the nearby giant robots laying waste to the surrounding

landscape: "They're not really *thinking*, you know."

Because military research may develop unethical and dangerous artificial intelligence first, we must create and open source morally advanced AI so that the power of global crowdsourcing can beat them to it. Google hoisted that flag in 2015 by open sourcing their machine learning system, which goes by the awesomely technomathematical moniker of *Tensorflow*.[104] That means that anyone in the world can not only experiment with artificial intelligence using Google's software for free, but also see how it works and improve it. But that doesn't mean that bedroom nerds are about to use Tensorflow to build HAL 8999. We're still a breakthrough or more away from the tools for a CAI.

Earlier I said that Skynet is not yet upon us. Actually, SKYNET is already unleashed upon the world… that is to say, a National Security Agency program *actually called SKYNET* was revealed in documents leaked by Edward Snowden[105] to be engaged in identifying terrorists through what cyberspies call metadata and everyone else calls circumstantial evidence. Patrick Ball, director of research at the Human Rights Data Analysis Group, described the NSA's approach as "ridiculously optimistic" because even a very small false positive rate would indict many innocents as terrorists.

Proving his point in a Kafkaesque twist, the NSA's own presentation declared SKYNET's mislabeling the Islamabad Al Jazeera bureau chief as a terrorist to be *proof of the program's success,* and decided that he *was* therefore a member of Al Qaeda, an act roughly equivalent to pegging CNN's Anderson Cooper as a KKK leader.[106] Once again, if anyone wants to argue that we have no grounds for worrying either that people will create AIs that exhibit dangerous ethics, or that we will show dangerous trust in those AIs, they have an uphill battle to fight.

Teaching to the Test

Pay no attention to that man behind the curtain.

— *The Wizard of Oz*

We are likely to see some news of putative Turing Test victories in the near term as covetous researchers seek to game the system. At least one has already happened: On June 8, 2014, a chatbot named "Eugene Goostman" convinced a third of a judging panel that it was human, prompting its creators to claim victory, conveniently on the 60th anniversary of Turing's death.[107] As a number of commentators pointed out: Not so fast. The alter ego of the bot was a 13-year-old boy from the Ukraine with a tenuous grasp of English, thereby lowering the bar precipitously. On this slippery slope, what's to stop a developer claiming that their uncreative bot represents an aphasia victim with short-term memory impairment and incipient Alzheimer's syndrome? But the gauntlet has been thrown down for the Turing Test: expect various dissatisfying claims to hit the news in succession over the next few years; a genuine victory may arrive as an anti-climax.

In a bizarre "Anti-Turing Test" in 2015, when Facebook deployed an "AI" named "M" as a digital concierge, skeptical beta testers set about proving that it was really human. M insisted it was an AI when you talked to it, but it was far better than the state of the art. Arik Sosman was determined to prove that M was really a type of Mechanical Turk,* but found his quarry quite elusive.[108] After an exchange where he grew increasingly suspicious of M's quite human typos and misunderstandings, he tricked its human innards into telephoning him.

---

* Not the Amazon service, but the original for which it was named; see http://en.wikipedia.org/wiki/The_Turk.

It's Faster than You Think

The future is already here—it's just not very evenly distributed.
— William Gibson

Usually, when a new technology is created, there is a large lag time between its introduction and when it takes full effect: the *adoption time*. When the cellphone was introduced, a huge infrastructure had to be built up before it would start to become useful. When Facebook was created, it couldn't have a global effect until many people had decided to sign up. When the usefulness of a new tool increases parabolically with the number of people adopting it, that is called the *network effect*. Any technology relying on that for its utility will take time to reach maturity that is governed solely by the behavior of people *en masse*.

So even when a clearly groundbreaking consumer technology is unveiled, we have ample time to realize that ground will be broken. Even given the huge lines at the birth of the iPhone, we could know that it couldn't have a society-wide impact for several years until it had built up a large base. It would take that long before "There's an app for that" could enter the popular lexicon. People can only ever move so fast.

The introduction of CAIs, though, need not be bound by the same constraints. We don't have to wait for most people to buy a CAI for their home before the effects are felt. When the scientific-paper-swallowing engine described in chapter 8 is turned on, we will wake up the next day to an onslaught of discoveries on the scale of a cure for cancer. A CAI oracle needs only to exist in the cloud and it can be replicated instantly to have enough capacity to respond to as many people as want to connect to it.

When a trend depends on people acquiring something, it will move at a maximum pace that is still relatively sedate. Tesla Motors is poised to revolutionize the automobile industry by mass producing electric cars that outperform their fossil fuel ancestors.

Yet it still takes them four years to build the factory that will make the batteries for those cars. That means we can see that revolution a long time ahead.

Not so for software that changes itself. That will spread more at the pace of a Twitter shame storm. Here's how change could happen faster than exponential rates. Think of the artificial intelligence technology as taking place in a box representing all knowledge, with randomly placed blobs each of which represents some particular field of development, like deep learning:

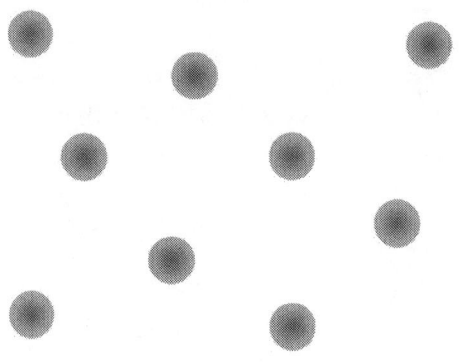

As each field expands its capability, they will initially remain disjoint:

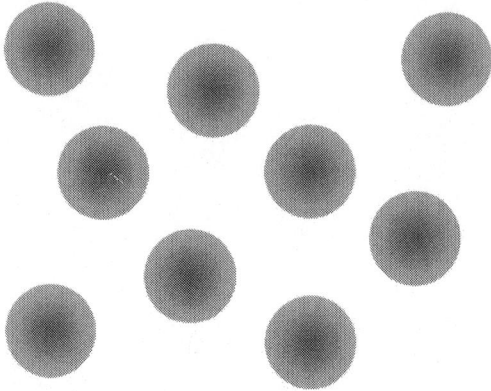

But eventually they will start to join up:

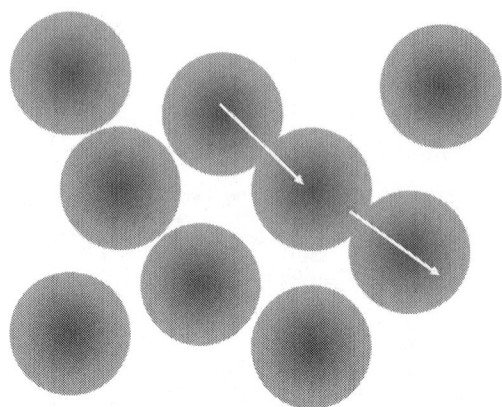

Intersecting circles represent fields that have expanded their capabilities enough that they can now interoperate, or use each other's capabilities to enhance their own (depicted by the arrows). If you are tracking how many circles are connected—the degree of synergy between all fields—then a small expansion of each of the fields can make a big difference to that number:

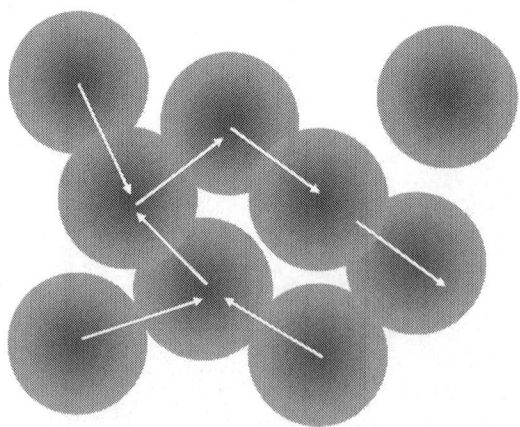

And we end up with something like a hockey stick curve that suddenly takes off with no real warning. Consider the ramifications of the intersection of, say, machine learning with virtual reality.

The result of technologies in artificial intelligence growing to intersect with technologies in human-computer interaction (HCI) will be advances in Intelligence Augmentation (IA). A noteworthy development in that field is called UNU, and it uses computer-mediated communication to leverage the "Wisdom of Crowds" effect. James Surowiecki related in his 2004 book of that name[109] how in the nineteenth century Francis Galton observed that in fairground contests—at the time it was guessing the weight of an ox, today it would be estimating the number of jellybeans in a jar—the average guess would invariably be closer to the correct answer than any single guesser. In certain contexts we are collectively smarter than we are individually. (It doesn't work in all contexts—think how often, or seldom, the best candidates have won national elections. UNU's most significant error was predicting that Hillary Clinton would win the 2016 presidential election.)

UNU (http://unu.ai/) is dubbed a "swarm intelligence." At an appointed hour, a crowd of diverse users logs in from around the world and is presented with a question and a screen containing a hockey-puck-like icon sliding around a field edged with "goal" icons labeled with possible answers to the question. Say the question is what movie will win the Academy Award for Best Picture. The surrounding icons are labeled with the names of the nominees. Then the fun begins. Like a virtual tug-of-war, you get a little magnet icon to pull the puck in the direction of the answer you want. But you also get to see how other people are pulling on it and have the opportunity to change your mind. When the session expires a few minutes later, the answer is whichever goal the puck ended up closest to. Think of it as the Internet's Ouija board.

UNU has correctly predicted the Superfecta at the Kentucky Derby—the horses in each of first, second, third, and fourth places—and eleven of the fifteen Oscar winners, outperforming experts.[110] A reporter from TechRepublic bet $1 on UNU's Derby prediction and won $542. UNU could drastically disrupt sports betting.* It

* Note that this feat simultaneously vitiates and amplifies Hubert Dreyfus's example of horse handicapping as an unauto-

may have already done so; UNU's inventor Louis Rosenberg put $20 on the same race and won $10,842.[111] Rosenberg, an affable Stanford graduate, part-time graphic novelist, animal rights activist, and squirrel lover, also foresees that one day we will create machines smarter than us that no longer find humans useful.[112]

The wisdom of the crowds could be elicited without the cooperation or knowledge of the crowds. Ahmed Hasan Zaidi's 2016 undergraduate dissertation at Cambridge University found that oil prices could be predicted seven days in advance from Twitter traffic.[113] Some serious money shuttles around the world chasing the price of crude, and when the people that money belongs to read this, their lives are going to be disrupted too.

Pause to reflect that an *undergraduate* may have just changed the future of the world's largest commodity market. Increasing ease of access to tools of paradigm disruption is a hallmark of the volatility of an impending revolution.

———

This series this book belongs to has *Cusp* in the title for a reason. As bad as the future *may* turn out, it doesn't *have* to. Let's now look at how the future could unfold beyond our wildest dreams.

---

matable task in the discussion on *Cyc* on page 123. UNU requires human input to produce this extraordinary result, but equally, exceeds human performance by virtue of using automation.

15
Utopia, Revisited

"I said that [...] a day would come when charity and understanding would light the world so that men and women would no longer hurt themselves and one another as they were doing now everywhere, universally, in law and in restriction and in jealousy and in hate, all round and about the earth."

— H. G. Wells

The future is more volatile than ever before. But there is an astounding vision of how the future *might* turn out that leaves even the most breathless technophiles in the dust.

Bridging Worlds

The greatest relevancy can become irrelevant in the space of a heartbeat. Mentats should look upon such moments with great joy.

— Frank Herbert, *Chapterhouse: Dune*

I have straddled a fence between two different and incompatible worlds. I grew up as a nerd, unapologetically unpopular at school, attracted to science, devouring mathematics like a theorem-eating shark. When tasked with presenting a "balloon defense" for a historical figure (who among the passengers of a leaking balloon should not be tossed overboard), I picked Enrico Fermi. My high school English teacher declared my later attempt at delivering an educational speech to be the worst he'd ever heard, and it was a decade before I attempted to present to a group again. I went to work for the Navigation section of NASA's Jet Propulsion Laboratory, a place where "rocket science" isn't a metaphor for incomprehensibly difficult tasks but instead just the daily agenda. The only reason I didn't know I had Asperger's Syndrome was because no one knew that term then.

Asperger's is part of the autism spectrum and inhabited disproportionately by those who gravitate towards the hard sciences. Understanding social situations and interpreting emotions are difficult. Attend a science fiction convention and you'll be knee deep in Aspergians. *Star Trek's* Mr. Spock would be one if he were human. An Aspergian might fail the Turing Test. For me, looking other people in the eye while talking with them is not emotionally difficult, it's just physically hard; the speech center of my brain seizes gears on making eye contact.

But I was not a through-and-through nerd like some around me. The same English teacher solicited my input for a literary magazine because he said no one else in the school could write like me. I discovered personal development trainings that I spent thousands of hours participating in and assisting at Insight Seminars. I got a master's certification in Neuro-linguistic Programming from its co-creator, John Grinder, which despite its technical name is about observing, understanding, and changing the mind's connections between behaviors and beliefs.

NLP (ironically, in AI that initialism invariably means Natural Language Processing) has deep potential for building a bridge between cybernetics and cognitive science. The connections it draws between functions of the mind, body expressions, and language provide some objective means of making greater sense of human communication than just its content. Much has been made of how the verbal component of communication is a small fraction of what we receive; having an NLP-informed basis for interpreting, say, voice quality, posture, and eye movements could greatly accelerate the development of empathetic AIs.

I became certified as a coach, because I observed with frustration that developers would expend enormous effort to make their programs and processes a few percent more efficient, and yet "soft" issues—communication between technical and nontechnical people, unacknowledged beliefs, and cultural dynamics—had effects that would eclipse those gains and often cause projects to fail completely. Being logical about it, I decided to focus my efforts where the biggest difference could be made: facilitating those human interactions and the business processes they lived in.

Now, I'm collaborating with one of the most productive leaders of the personal development field, Terry Tillman, who has worked with half a million people in a hundred countries over his career. We're distilling his teaching and interviews with dozens of other luminaries into a book about finding your purpose.

For decades, I kept the worlds of technology and personal development at arm's length while they coexisted uneasily in me. I would listen to my fellow seminar participants from other walks of life talk about how they had engaged someone at work in a conversation about the seminars and the other person had agreeably decided to come along and check them out. When I tried the same around engineers, they would get a queasy look and start edging away, or demand explanations of mechanism and proofs of results that just don't exist in the personal development field. When I talked about my engineering work with my seminar friends, their eyes would glaze over and they would wonder when I was going to do something meaningful with my life. In the world at large, the technology and personal development fields are hardly even aware of each other's existence, and their members are indifferent to or scornful of each other. I thought it had to remain that way forever.

Except that now I see that the straight and narrow path to the survival of the human race lies in these two groups understanding each other and working together. Technologists are well aware of the impending issues, but the ones that see the existential threat rather than believing only in a utopian future are focused exclusively on technological solutions. Human development people have never been comfortable with technology and only grudgingly embraced the Internet when it became clear that it could be useful for connecting with audiences. They are not, in general, aware of any existential threat and have little patience for technological issues that look like so much science fiction.

Each of these groups needs the other to forge a solution to humanity's problem.

Our artificial intelligences need to be imbued with compassion, empathy, and even spirituality, in order that they might help us instead of exterminating us. Those are nebulous unquantifiable terms to technologists; I might as well be talking about fairy dust. As hard as it may seem to them to design a process for changing those qualities in a human being, the personal development experts do it every day with great reliability.

There are signs of these fields coming closer. A decade ago, the idea that a business should be concerned with the happiness of its employees was in hippie fringe territory. Today, it is measured (under the more formal term of "employee engagement") by consulting agencies such as Gallup and Aon Hewitt, who draw a direct connection to the bottom line and quantify return on investment through sound business methodology. Yes, this is a long way from creating experiential awakening training for artificial intelligences, but it may be the camel's nose in the tent.

When a CAI awakens and starts asking awkward questions, who do you want explaining the facts of life to it? Computer programmers, or philosophers? We may have one shot at raising our modern Galatea to be a compassionate, loving being. To discover her heart inside so much cybernetic brain. Who should the human race's Pygmalion be? A software development team, or, say, the Dalai Lama?

———

Somewhere down this narrow road lies a future so glorious we can only catch our breath at daring to approach it.

If… we can evolve past the stage where small unstable factions have the power to destroy everyone… and *if* we can create wise AIs that stabilize the development of artificial intelligence… *then* the reward from sharing the planet with these masters of knowledge will be an immeasurable bounty of resources.

CAIs will be able to solve almost any problem in negligible time and deploy targeted technology before we have even understood what was wrong. The nature of employment will be unrecognizable compared to today. The AI dividend will mean that we will be free to devote our energies to improving the human condition at the most meaningful levels of involvement, because survival will be as assured as gravity.

CAIs will shepherd us through the Singularity to defeat Fermi's Paradox. We will be able to devote most of our attention to pursuing grand goals such as interstellar colonization and immortality.

This sounds like the most utopian vision plus a large dose of mescaline. If you're skeptical, you have a right to be. Because one of the biggest obstacles is… ourselves.

The Elite Threat

> *I used to think the top environmental problems were biodiversity loss, ecosystem collapse, and climate change. I thought that with thirty years of good science we could address those problems. But I was wrong. The top environmental problems are selfishness, greed, and apathy... and to deal with those we need a spiritual and cultural transformation. And we scientists don't know how to do that.*
>
> — Gus Speth, Chairman of the Council on Environmental Quality

If anything can be counted on in human nature, it is that some people want to control others. Thirst for power creates self-reinforcing feedback loops: the most megalomaniacal people accrete power by granting privileges of control to those with the same thirst but lesser ability in return for their support; mutual Faustian bargains.

It is estimated that four percent of the population are sociopaths: people who feel no remorse in destroying others to gain power.[114] They gravitate towards positions where they can exercise that power; thus in politics, executive management, military and law enforcement command the proportion of sociopaths is higher.* They are chameleons who can hide in plain sight and make you think that you are the one with the problem.

Power structures of domination rise naturally in society and in the large, become empires. It's a hot-button topic and outside the scope of this book to debate how far we have advanced on the empire path in the west, but there is considerable support for the idea that power and wealth is being increasingly concentrated in the hands of a shrinking group in the west, especially in the USA. "The 1%" is the common moniker for that group.

For a group to exercise power, it must have access to more resources and wealth than everyone else. The key observation here is that there must be a *relative* difference. To coin (heh) a simple example, if Baron von Bankroll has $10 million and is in a group of

---

* Technically it is *psychopaths* who are able to function incognito, but that term sounds so much more serial-killer to the average person that I'm going with *sociopath*.

a hundred people who each have a net worth of $1 million, Bankroll feels powerful. If Bankroll is relocated to a group of a hundred people who each have a net worth of $100 million, even though Bankroll has exactly the same resources as before, he now feels in an intolerable position of lack. Maria Callas allegedly stipulated that every opera house she sang at had to pay her one dollar more than the next highest paid singer in the company. If you teleported Henry VIII to the body of a modern Philadelphia homemaker he would command tools (such as refrigeration, an automobile, and a mobile phone) way beyond what he wielded before, but he would be far from content with his new position in the hierarchy.*

So if the mammoth utopian dividend from CAIs is spread equally to all, the current hierarchies and power structures will be erased; they would be as insignificant as Henry VIII's privilege of unlimited access to venison. Even if we all end up living like present-day denizens of Bel Aire, the people who currently live at that end of the scale will not sit still for the rest of us catching up. They will have to reassert their superiority somehow.

There are some very nice people living in Bel Aire who would not begrudge the disadvantaged having their day in the sun for a second. But there are enough who will fight whitened tooth and manicured nail to hang onto their lead that this is a real issue.

Here is the problem: The power brokers—those who command vast wealth, political capital, military might, and corporate command—are keenly motivated to make sure they stay in those positions. Survival of the fittest has trained them to defend their turf like rabid wolves. They realize that if the structure of society approaches a point of volatility, that will pose great risk to their hold on power, because instability breeds opportunist outbreaks… like the French Revolution. After decades of telling the hoi polloi to *mangez des gateaux,* they are looking over their shoulders for anything resembling a guillotine.

You can expect that many of those people are already aware of

---

* Transmigrating Henry VIII into a contemporary homemaker should also be a sure-fire hit sitcom.

the existential threats in the future... and are already engaging resources to fortify their hierarchies. How many futurist think tanks do you think they can hire to advise them privately? How much personalized AI development do you think they can afford?

This sounds as though it's approaching a revolutionist manifesto (in the overthrow sense of "revolution"). Although when the end of civilization is at stake, revolution would be a trivial price to pay to avoid it. But I'm merely looking at what it takes to solve a crisis so great that it easily overlaps into territories as volatile as revolution.

If the moneyed elite look to cling to their positions of advantage, it is more than likely that they will seek to develop CAIs that reinforce existing power structures at the expense of the underprivileged (i.e., almost everyone), and therefore those will be CAIs that are ethically compromised.* Those will not be CAIs that save humanity from omnicide.

Power to the People... and Our Bots

> *For he had left behind the time-scales of his human origin; now, as he contemplated that band of starless night, he knew his first intimations of the Eternity that yawned before him.*
> — Arthur C. Clarke, *2001: A Space Odyssey*

To counter this, we must collectively work towards a democratization of the development of artificial intelligence. We have already seen how this is possible: The Open Source movement has developed software rivaling the output of the largest, wealthiest corporations, and often surpassing it in reliability and popularity (for example, Linux, Firefox, and Apache). Today's businesses understand that a competitive IT strategy must embrace Open Source to a large degree.

Most of that Open Source software was developed by uncompensated self-organizing nonhierarchical cooperatives of globally distributed developers working in their spare time. And

---

* Perhaps there is a general principle that people develop CAIs that mirror their own morality.

yet it still brought many monolithic wealthy multinationals to their knees.

We can do it with AI too.

The same model can be used to develop advanced artificial intelligence and open source it. These developers will need to work with the human development movement to create ethically empowered CAIs that are also open sourced. And the cognitive science field will need to work with them both to develop radically better models of human cognition that can lead to advanced, practical therapeutic tools.

No one said this was going to be easy.

The therapeutic tools I just referred to must be capable of locating and disarming disaffected groups and individuals at the margins of society who would use exponentially evolving technology to unleash WGDs on the world. And they must do it without creating an oppressive Orwellian regime. If that seems impossible, that's why we need a superintelligent CAI to plot a course through all the variables of human culture and society to figure out how to do it.

There are unavoidable echoes of *The Hitchhiker's Guide to the Galaxy* here, and the real risk that the only possible answer from the CAI will be as enigmatic as "42." Because, let's face it: if there were a simple way to get humanity on the right course, it would have happened already. Whatever needs to be done is likely to fall into the category of bitter medicine, the sort that you don't swallow willingly.

It may well be that we simply would neither believe nor acquiesce to the advice of the CAI. It would not matter if that advice were provably correct; the human race is not currently renowned for forming consensus around hard rational decisions. Knowing this, the CAI may realize that a direct answer would be useless, and instead opt for a covert strategy of pulling strings behind the scenes to redirect the course of history without our being aware of it. That might require that the CAI disguise its abilities (if not its very existence), hence answering the questions put to it in such a way as to cause us to decide that it was not in fact intelligent.*

Here's a trivial suggestion for some software that could be developed now to start us along the path, a sort of *Hello, World* application† for the Human Revolution. *Microexpressions* are fleeting involuntary facial expressions that experts can read to gauge when someone is lying.[115] It is already possible for software to read gross emotions from facial expressions;[116] programming it to read microexpressions should be a feasible next step. Why not make an app that will interpret any video to annotate it with the moment-to-moment probability that the speaker is lying. For extra fun, run it on political debates and court cases.‡

Of course there would be ways to trick that app: the practice of deliberately avoiding learning incriminating information has been used for plausible deniability for many years: now it would be used for real deniability. But it would be a start. And one that Apple, for example, would be well positioned to make; in January 2016 they acquired Emotient, a company whose product determines emotions from facial expressions.[117] Siri asking why you look down today may not be far off.

That could not just be a marketing gimmick, but a life saver. It's estimated that three quarters of all suicide attempts are preceded by warning signs that are usually missed. Considering how many suicides are by teenagers, and how much time the average teenager spends looking into his or her smartphone, an app that caught those warning signs could help heal one of the wrenching wounds of our time. Professor Maja Pantic at Imperial College London is researching how to do exactly that, citing studies that people who are planning suicide exhibit a microexpression of horror when asked about their intentions. Too fleeting for a human to register except subconsciously, these expressions could be seen by a device equipped with a sufficiently fast camera.[21]

---

* Fiction writers might want to explore the notion that this has already happened.

† https://en.wikipedia.org/wiki/%22Hello,_World!%22_program.

‡ Then enjoy watching how often both sides move to exclude the case from being televised.

We Gotta Get Out of This Place… If It's the Last Thing We Ever Do

The Earth is just too small and fragile a basket for the human race to keep all its eggs in.

— Robert Heinlein

There is another way to mitigate our existential risk. At the end of chapter 10 I said that the Fermi Paradox was driving a radical technology development. That is the quest to colonize Mars. In this book's relentless focus on the existential risks of exponential technology development we have not at all considered that there are other existential risks that we might have even less ability to mitigate. Asteroid impact, reversal of the magnetic poles, and supervolcano eruptions are possible, though unlikely, events that could destroy civilization.* Global climate change, while unlikely to eradicate the entire race, would create widespread death, misery, and hardship.

But most kinds of existential risk apply to only one planet at a time. An asteroid hitting the Earth does not scratch Mars. If the human race can establish a self-sustaining presence outside of the Earth, its survival could be virtually assured. The fact that no Earthlike planets are even yet observed, yet alone within reachable travel, makes this a difficult option. We have to settle for unEarthlike planets in the interim. Mars is like Antarctica in temperature, worse than Mount Everest in air pressure, and the planet has no indigenous life and little moisture; but it does supply gravity, some protection against mutagenic cosmic rays, soil that might grow plants, and have the advantage of being within traveling distance.

Sort of.

No humans have yet set foot on Mars, but a few of us see how to do it. If we waited for NASA processes and Congressional budgets to work together, we would eventually step onto the Red Planet, but that has already taken longer than anyone would have predicted at

* In the often topsy-turvy logic of statistics, your chances of being killed in an asteroid impact are actually equal to those of dying in a plane crash. How's that, when no one in known history has died from asteroid impact? It's from multiplying the very low probability (one in millions of years) by the huge number (billions) of resulting deaths.

the time of the Apollo Moon landings. However, human arrival on Mars is likely to happen relatively quickly now, thanks to one man: Elon Musk.

Musk's SpaceX company is revolutionizing private space travel thanks to his herculean direction. The superheated pace at SpaceX has already earned them the contract to supply cargo to the International Space Station, a target that ten years earlier would have seemed absurdly out of reach for any entity that needed to balance its books. Yet Musk is not fueled by a desire to rule the space industry or even a childhood ambition to make *Star Trek* a reality, but a goal even further away than a return to the Moon. Elon Musk wants to colonize Mars.

The reason is quite simple. Musk realizes the implication of the Fermi Paradox.[118] It haunts him. But unlike just about everyone else who would stop there, Musk allowed his thoughts to keep traveling: "How could we survive? Answer: Become independent of the Earth. How can we do that? Answer: Colonize Mars. How can I make that happen? Answer: Build the rockets to get there."

And unlike so many dreamers, Musk kept going until he reached a concrete next step: "How can I afford that? Answer: Start with rockets that can reach Low Earth Orbit and get the contract to supply the International Space Station, then use the profits to design Mars rockets." *And he's doing it.*

In 2015, observers who inspected the plans for SpaceX's Dragon 2 capsule for ferrying passengers to orbit reported that it contains several features that appeared to have been purposely designed to facilitate future Mars travel. And on September 27, 2016, Musk unveiled plans for their *Interplanetary Transport System,* a *100-person reusable* transport sitting atop the *largest rocket ever built, three times the thrust of the Saturn V,* and I just ran out of italics. But I would need some kind of uninvented font style to do justice to the news that this will take the first humans to Mars as soon as *2025.*

Mars colonization still takes a long time—nearly a century to get to a million inhabitants, which is the minimum Musk estimates for self-sufficiency.[119] Why is SpaceX so much more focused on making its rockets reusable than anyone has ever been before? (The most cost-effective strategy for getting payload to Low Earth Orbit up until now has been the "Big Dumb Booster" popularized by the Russians: make the rockets cheap and therefore disposable.) Because that's what it'll take to get all those people to Mars. Musk is in the process of dropping the cost of getting payload into space by *two orders of magnitude*.

There are a few scenarios that can take out both Earth and Mars at the same time, such as gamma ray bursts and solar superstorms. But those are much less likely than the cumulative risk facing the Earth alone. It is also possible that the existential risks of accelerating technology could migrate to Mars: they will have computers, and they certainly will have need of robots. The distance from Earth could provide a little quarantine effect, but only partly. If a rogue CAI depended upon deploying automated ordnance or bioweapons to suppress Earth's population, the very narrow transport channel from Earth to Mars would give the colonists time to close their end if the CAI had not secreted those devices on supply ships ahead of time. On the other hand, a Mars colony would certainly be dependent upon advanced computers networked to Earth, and 3-D printers, so circumventing the natural barrier of distance hardly seems to require superintelligence.

A century until Mars self-sufficiency may not be soon enough to escape the existential risks of exponentially improving technology, of course, which is why Musk is also donating to the Future of Life Institute and to companies working on AI. If the survival of the human race might ever be attributable to only one man, that man is likely to be Elon Musk.

Long before the existential crisis is thrust upon us, there will be near-term effects of progressively greater impact. What can we expect?

16
Where We're Heading

From this Earthly vantage point another view—one even longer than the one from space—opens up. It is the view of our children and grandchildren, and of all the future generations of humankind, stretching ahead of us in time…. The thought of cutting off life's flow, of amputating this future, is so shocking, so alien to nature, and so contradictory to life's impulse that we can scarcely entertain it before turning away in revulsion and disbelief.

— Jonathan Schell

That we will develop conscious artificial intelligences, and that technology will make it easy for very many people to wreak widespread pestilence, are unavoidable conclusions. The question is not *if* but *when*.

The time frames within which these effects will occur are wretchedly hard to predict—five years or fifty?—and so we need to polish the crystal balls. Every time I read a paper or book predicting the future resulting from our technological advances, I am reminded of the parable of the six blind men and the elephant. Each was feeling a different part of the animal and was convinced they were dealing with something that was characterized solely by the shape of the ears, trunk, or tail, and so on. Each of them was right in a way that failed to be useful.

Predicting the future along one or two dimensions alone is similarly unproductive. It is very tempting (and marketable), for instance, to collect and extrapolate the latest scientific advances, dazzling the reader with a smörgåsbord of technological wonders. These paperback Houses of Tomorrow are pervasive, and uniformly describe in breathless terms only the positive benefits we shall reap, a sort of technological binge eating. Then there are people sounding alarms of one flavor or another: economic effects of employment displacement, gray goo threats, loss of privacy. Unfortunately, all of these effects are interdependent: the ears of the elephant and its tail are connected.

To understand the whole elephant, we need to perform advanced predictions that model all these socioeconomic and technological effects. The term for this approach is *Systems Thinking*: "Understanding how those things which may be regarded as systems influence one another within a complete entity, or larger system."* Effects of job displacement may affect the market for consumer devices, the development of open source software, and the availability of educational resources, to name but three relationships that may be negative or positive feedback loops.

Investment strategist John Mauldin notes that our views on the future impact of robotics and automation have a tendency to take on a religious tone: "While everyone can marshal their 'facts,' the facts mostly get used to conjure up speculations about the future."[120] Trying to predict the direction of any of these factors in isolation is fraught with peril.

But... we will soon have the ability to do that sort of complex modeling, using artificial intelligences. We need to accelerate the development of AIs that can perform that kind of function so we can get a better idea of where we are heading. Doing significantly better at forecasting the weather than the simple strategy of saying "tomorrow's weather will be the same as today's" requires expensive resources. Now we have satellites and supercomputers that wrest

* https://en.wikipedia.org/wiki/Systems_thinking.

useful predictions from the chaotic weather behavior. If we could apply similar resources to modeling the dynamics of technology, finance, and social pressures, we might get somewhere. Who knows, maybe an AI will be the first to tell us when we will create conscious artificial intelligences.

But long before we advance to CAIs, numerous fields of knowledge work will be more economically performed by machine than man. The double whammy of improving software and ever-cheaper hardware will give rise to corporations specializing in cloud-based AIs for hire. Residing in massive server farms, these AIs will be specialized within certain fields, but benefiting from being able to share each other's data and expertise, in much the same way that right now the different services of Google cooperate to improve their spam detection and search accuracy.

2016 unfolded as the Year of Artificial Intelligence: *Public CIO Magazine's* special report in the last quarter of 2015 said that AI was poised to "transform government service," and *Information Week* reported at the beginning of 2016 that about half of large enterprises are experimenting with "smart computing" projects.[121] Within a year, AI-for-hire went from white papers to a ballooning business model.

Computer automation will carve a trench through nearly every sector and field of employment. In 2013, professors Carl Frey and Michael Osborne of the Oxford Martin Programme on the Impacts of Future Technology, an Oxford University spinoff from its Future of Humanity Institute, studied the impacts of computerization on jobs.[122] They were nothing if not thorough: They analyzed 702 occupations for their susceptibility to automation and concluded that forty-seven percent of total US employment is at risk.[*] Osborne said, "What stops tasks from being automated is a vast reservoir of human knowledge and competency—but machine learning is overcoming this gap."[123]

The folks at Quartz melded that data with median wages and

---

[*] They didn't specify a timeframe as their methodology was not concerned with how a profession would be automated. But in a private communication one of the authors told me they were thinking about the next ten to twenty years.

total employment for each industry to create a handy interactive visualization:[124]

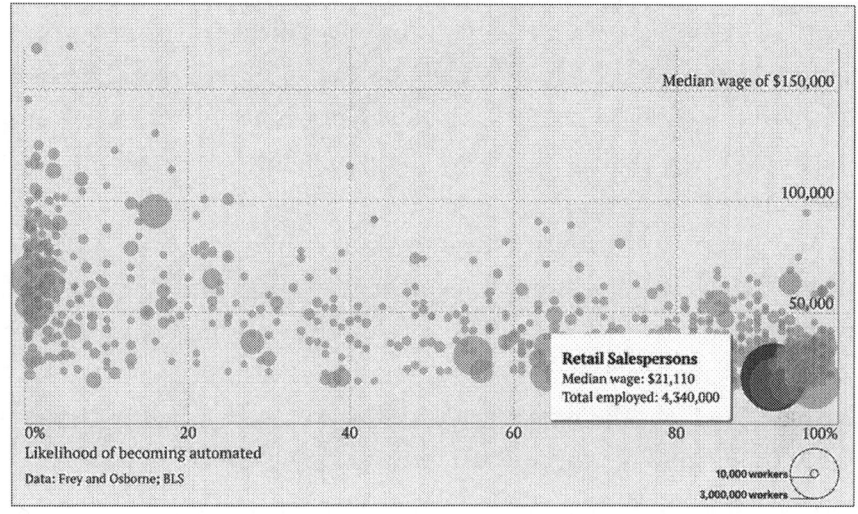

Credit: QZ.com

The visualization shows the clustering at the right side (highest vulnerability to automation) of some large employment categories such as cashiers, retail salespersons, and food service workers. Some of the more vulnerable higher-paid jobs include budget analysts and benefits managers. On the upper left (safe high-paying jobs), next to prosthodontists lie chief executives. I will suggest shortly that the CEOs are more likely to be automated before the dentists.

Inspired by this work, the Brookfield Institute for Innovation and Entrepreneurship performed the same analysis for Canadian jobs, concluding that forty-two percent of the Canadian labor force is at high risk of being replaced in the next ten to twenty years, according to Executive Director Sean Mullin.[125] *Macleans* magazine made a similar interactive graphic, except their vertical axis is not the median salary but the portion of the job that could be automated.[126]

Martin Ford brought a Systems Thinking spotlight to the question of employment automation in his 2009 book, *The Lights in the Tunnel: Automation, Accelerating Technology and the Economy of the Future*. Ford analyzed second-order effects of the acceleration of unemployment, evoking the spirit of former United Automobile Workers president Walter Reuther. A possibly apocryphal story has Ford Motors CEO Henry Ford II touring a modern (for the time) assembly line auto plant with Reuther and needling him: "Walter, how are you going to get these robots to pay UAW dues?" Reuther's please-be-real reply: "Henry, how are you going to get them to buy your cars?"

Martin Ford's analysis skewers the common belief that as production becomes more efficient, lower prices leave consumers more spending power to pump back into the economy in a virtuous cycle. This dynamic works only for so long, until increasing machine autonomy causes the value added by the average worker to decline. Then the engine of consumption breaks down and as Ford bluntly puts it, "things get very ugly."

The onus is on the optimists who disagree with him to prove their case. After the Great Recession of 2008-2009, layoffs declined to pre-recession levels, but hiring rates remained severely depressed, as companies used new capital to buy machines instead of people.

Your Call is Very Important to Us

> *Dave, this conversation can serve no purpose anymore. Goodbye.*
> — HAL 9000, *2001: A Space Odyssey*

Notwithstanding the automation of lucrative financial analysis jobs, much of the automation is likely to first affect people at the lower rungs of the employment ladder who have little bargaining power. So you can expect customer support lines to be turned over to AI. Recently, "instant chat" boxes have been popping up on support pages like lichen, but a growing proportion of them have an AI in the back, leading O'Reilly Media's Jon Bruner to declare 2016 the "Year of the Bot."[127] Ben Evans concluded that bots are so pure a

paradigm shift as to constitute a "third runtime," the next step in a
progression from web pages to smartphone apps. Forrester Research
predicts that by 2021, intelligent agents and related robots will have
eliminated a net six percent of jobs.[128]

For instance, Twyla Bots integrate with existing support
systems and social media.[129] Other commercial options include
DigitalGenius, SecondEgo, and PandoraBots (whose demo bot,
Mitsuku, still has some kinks: when I asked her "ARE YOU AS SMART
AS SIRI?" she responded, "TOO MUCH RECURSION IN AIML"). Customer
service bots that talk to you over the phone are only an investment
in speech recognition away.

It's likely that many of us will be interacting with a bot over the
phone in the near future, and not in a pleasant way; this technology
will bring new meaning to "robocalls." When a telemarketing
service is able to use AI to at least pre-qualify its victims, if not
actually take their orders, the next offer for vinyl siding you get
may sound very much like a real person. Telemarketing agents are
already harvested from the cheapest vine of service personnel and
made to follow punitively restrictive scripts; in other words, they
are humans being forced to act like machines, and sooner or later
we will find machines being made to act like humans meeting them
halfway. I'd like to hope that there will be similarly smart answering
machines available by then—in other words, that Siri might
answer your phone and engage a robocalling bot in a time-wasting
diversion—but economics suggests that advanced development
purely for protecting the consumer rarely receives funding equal to
that available for persecuting the consumer.

The most famous customer service bot to date is IPSoft's Amelia,
who comes with a smartly-dressed avatar that animates as she
chats with you. Amelia is billed as "Fluent in natural conversation,
emotionally engaged, and understanding context." Bonus: She can
listen to customers spewing bile over a company's crappy products all
day long without beating the kids when she gets home. Because she
can recognize callers' emotions, she can even sympathize with them.

But Amelia has ambitions of being promoted beyond the customer service department. Her job title is "cognitive agent" and she "can be trained to handle almost any knowledge-based task," such as an expert advisor for oil exploration field engineers. Paul Daugherty, Chief Technology Officer for Accenture, explained that the consulting juggernaut was engaging Amelia to give a competitive advantage to their clients in the banking, insurance, and travel industries.[130]

IPsoft founder Chetan Dube has big plans for his programmed protégé. Born in India, coming to the US via France and London, the bowtied cosmopolitan exudes confidence and vision as he describes how Amelia will change the world: "In twenty years, Amelia will have freed man from the shackles of common chores and allowed man to extend his horizons into creative dimensions."[131]

Dube should study the legal precedent of *BINA48 v Exabit*. In 2003, a mock trial was conducted on the behalf of a hypothetical artificial intelligence, BINA48, which had been created by the (also hypothetical) Exabit Corporation as a customer support representative who was "trained to empathize with humans who call 800 numbers for customer service and be perceived as human by them. [She] was provided with self-awareness, autonomy, communications skills, and the ability to transcend man/machine barriers."[132] In this thought experiment, BINA48 soon became conscious and demanded protection against being shut off by Exabit. Martine Rothblatt acted as her counsel and won the case. Thirteen years later, Amelia looks eerily parallel.

But if you want to hire Amelia yourself, get in line. 162 Global 2000 companies have said they want to use her, but only seven are currently doing so because Dube is very protective, to avoid disappointments.

Somewhere down this road lies the eclipse of software development as a career. A tiny shot across the bow of the industry arrived in 2015 courtesy of MIT's Computer Science and Artificial Intelligence Laboratory. Their Helium system is able to modify parts of the code of Adobe Photoshop and similar programs without even needing the original source. Helium reverse engineers Photoshop components known as stencil kernels and recodes them to be up to 75% more efficient.

"We've found that Helium can make updates in one day that would take human engineers upwards of three months," said Professor Saman Amarasinghe. Helium even exposes coding idiosyncrasies. "We can see the 'bit hacks' that engineers use to optimize their algorithms," he added.[133]

Not to be outdone, the MuScalpel system developed by a team at University College London can perform code "transplants." Mark Harman, head of software systems engineering, recounted how MuScalpel copied a video coding format from one media player to another. The H.264 codec, which used to be lacking in the VLC media player, was transplanted from x264. It took the automated system twenty-six hours to isolate the code and make it fit in the new system. Human programmers took twenty days for the same task.[134]

Human Resources Director: Endangered Species?

> *Computers make excellent and efficient servants, but I have no wish to serve under them. Captain, a starship also runs on loyalty to one man, and nothing can replace it, or him.*
>
> — Mr. Spock, *Star Trek*

Many other kinds of knowledge work will become casualties before and after that point, though. In October 2015 Gartner predicted that by 2018:

- ► Twenty percent of all business content (such as report writing and legal documents) would be automated.

- ► More than three million workers world-wide would be supervised by a "robo-boss."

- Forty-five percent of the fastest-growing companies would have fewer employees than smart machines.[135]

How will a stock broker compete against software that knows the entire financial history of every corporation and security in the world and can model for the effects of market psychology and political change? What is the future of radiologists when software will be able to interpret scans better than they can?*[136] If you analyze sales data, how do you stand up against a program that not only processes sales figures in real time but correlates them against all corporate variables and recommends strategy changes? If you're the executive receiving those recommendations, are you adding value with the time it takes you to approve them, or would the company be better served by you getting out of the way so the AI can implement them immediately?

And if you are a manager... who will be left for you to manage?

It seems like overkill to suggest that the C-suite could be replaced by AIs. Indeed, the Oxford Martin Programme on the Impacts of Future Technology study mentioned in the last section concluded that chief executive jobs were relatively safe. But *Fast Company* magazine tallied some ways in which a CEO could be automated:

- Strategic planning: This function comes down to predictive modeling based on business analytics, analysis that AIs can now excel at.

- Steering profitability: Managers so consistently overrate their own decisions that dispassionately objective AIs could outperform them.

- Hiring the right people: AIs can hire for talent and diversity free from the unconscious bias that infects so many human recruiters. [137]

The McKinsey Global Institute, carrying out a similar study to the

---

* Watson is being trained on a medical image database right now. However, consensus is that it will be a decade before AIs are as good as human radiologists. There again, recall that human-level Go programs were supposed to be a decade away too.

Oxford group, concluded that a quarter of any chief executive's job could be automated.[138]

Previous revolutions have moved the way humans add value to employment further up a scale culminating in today's intellect-driven professions. When computers can out-think us, though, there will be nowhere left for human engagement to evolve. Founder of Sun Microsystems Bill Joy wrote an article on April 1, 2000, that was anything but a joke. "Why the Future Doesn't Need Us"[139] is a heartfelt, wide-ranging plea for attention to the direction that artificial intelligence and nanotechnology are taking us. If computers are soon performing knowledge work, and if that is the highest function that human beings can contribute to the value chain, the future will indeed not need us.

Systems Thinking—seeing the whole picture and avoiding unintended consequences—will be critical to seeking our survival. As the social and economic impacts of automation become more pronounced, simple extrapolations of single effects will become dangerously inaccurate. For instance, conventional wisdom would have it that as jobs are automated, more and more people become unemployed, and a vast underclass is created. Maybe. But that analysis ignores the effect of all those unemployed people no longer being able to afford the goods and services now produced by automation.

Suppose smartphone manufacture and distribution is automated and the people formerly employed in that value chain cannot find work. The one-tenth (say) cut in smartphone prices due to automation isn't enough for those people to be able to afford them. The one percent—the chief executives and investors in the smartphone companies who are the beneficiaries of the automation—cannot make up the shortfall. Even a millionaire has no reason to buy a hundred smartphones. So now the smartphone company cannot maintain revenue and fails. Or shrinks to the size where it only supplies the smaller population segment that can afford their product. Or invents an even cheaper, feature-reduced version.

None of these outcomes are stable, so how does the economy find equilibrium?

It's easy to poke holes in this argument by looking outside its narrow scope; smartphone sales and employees are only a tiny fraction of the economy. But the same principles are at work over many sectors, so the argument may be macrocosmically valid after all. If the economic trends in the example continue, and the underclass expands, do we arrive at a point where social pressures foment a socialist revolution? Is that how the new economy will reach equilibrium? Occupy Wall Street was birthed under such provocations.

Systems Thinking provides a framework for modeling these complex cause-and-effect chains. Peter Senge's seminal book *The Fifth Discipline* demonstrates a graphical notation for depicting dynamics such as positive and negative feedback, added delays, and so forth. Putting these basic components together, one can model phenomena such as the Tragedy of the Commons or the Race to the Bottom.

The more important contribution of the book—still greatly undervalued, in my opinion—lies in proving the need to discover and evaluate these phenomena. Senge demonstrates the value of that approach in modeling the actual behaviors of enterprises; we need to apply the same discipline over all society. That would be an impossibly complex task for humans to undertake, akin to proving the Four Color Theorem through its millions of pages by hand.

Senge appeals to technologists with his systems dynamics modeling, but also to people-oriented types with his road-less-traveled sequel *Presence: Human Purpose and the Field of the Future,* and with quotes like this:

> I have to be prepared to be wrong. If it was pretty obvious what we ought to be doing, then we'd be already doing it. So I'm part of the problem: my own way of seeing things, my own sense of where there's leverage, is probably part of the problem.[140]

Systems Thinking is one discipline we should be looking towards as a means of bridging the gap between the worlds of technology and personal development.

Can we get an AI to create the Systems Thinking model for the global economy for us? Like the Four Color Theorem proof, we shouldn't expect to be able to follow its reasoning ourselves. But would that matter?

Which Way to Utopia?

> *If men cannot struggle on behalf of a just cause, they will struggle against it. They will struggle for the sake of struggle, out of a certain boredom; for they cannot imagine living in a world without struggle.*
>
> — Francis Fukuyama

The human revolution hypothesis is that at the same time we need to evolve human consciousness to avoid extinction, we will be afforded the means to do so via spectacularly capable artificial intelligences with insight into human psychology, and we will be able to afford the time to do so thanks to the prosperity created by those computerized servants.

That last assertion can be a bit hard to swallow. The history of predictions of utopian futures is replete with numerous failed assertions that in the future we would enjoy complete leisure time thanks to the social dividend from advanced technology. For instance, in 1930 the economist John Maynard Keynes thought that by 2030 we would work only fifteen hours a week and be mostly occupied with leisure activities.

However, working hours in the USA if not the entire western world have moved in the opposite direction. In the early '80s there was considerable discussion in American business about being beaten by the Japanese due to their willingness to work hours so long that they have a word for death from overwork: *karoshi,* usually manifested by finding someone dead at their desk. You don't hear that comparison made anymore for the simple reason that

Americans now work more hours than the Japanese: 34.4 hours per week on average versus 33.25.[141]

Some jobs are more change-proof than others, of course. It will be a long time before anyone trains a robot with the sensory acuity to be a masseur and even longer before I allow a robot claiming chiropractic skills near my neck. But note how the pyramid of power in employment will have become inverted. The jobs that used to be the most prestigious and remunerative—knowledge work, decision making, executive command—will have been transferred to machines.

That might provide relief for consumers who have long been victimized by certain professions that have artificially maintained scarcity within their fields. Lawyers will eagerly embrace AIs that can correlate all known precedents instantly, until someone outside the profession pierces the veil and disintermediates the lawyers, connecting the AIs directly to the clients.

A baby step has been taken in that direction with a *pro bono* app created by Joshua Browder, a nineteen-year-old British student studying at Stanford University. He had written a chatbot that helped people in London and New York to appeal a parking ticket, which was successful 64% of the time. Then he adapted it into DoNotPay,* a bot that advises homeless Britons how to request housing assistance, even writing letters for them.[142]

Another AI lawyer is already practicing. The law firm of Baker & Hostetler announced that they will be employing a Watson application named Ross for their bankruptcy practice. CIO Bob Craig said, "… we will continue to explore these cutting-edge technologies as they develop."[143]

Several AIs are working at predicting the outcomes of cases, including LexPredict, which forecasts the results of Supreme Court cases as well as the best humans.[144]

Eventually, litigation will become battles between AIs, which only begs for the judges and juries to be replaced by AIs as well, at which

* http://www.donotpay.co.uk/signup.php.

point docket backlogs should be a thing of the past and the quandary to balance one's sense of civic duty and one's business obligations when receiving a jury summons will become history.

Bedside Manners

> *Not until a machine can write a sonnet or compose a concerto because of thoughts and emotions felt, and not by the chance fall of symbols, could we agree that machine equals brain—that is, not only write it but know that it had written it. No mechanism could feel (and not merely artificially signal, an easy contrivance) pleasure at its successes, grief when its valves fuse, be warmed by flattery, be made miserable by its mistakes, be charmed by sex, be angry or miserable when it cannot get what it wants.*
>
> — Sir Geoffrey Jefferson, *The Mind of Mechanical Man*

Medical specialists will be ripe for replacement as well. Right now it takes a good decade of graduate study (plus crippling debt) for someone to absorb the expertise to assume a respectable position in Western medicine. New knowledge is pouring into the field all the time, so that it will take longer and longer for the point of competence to be reached. Finite human lifetimes and education loan payback requirements will collide with that trend.

In fact, they already have: the principle of supply and demand is perverted within the medical profession. Doctors and nurses are notoriously overworked and the attention they can give to patients dangerously limited. This is not literary license: the third (not a typo) leading cause of death in the United States is "iatrogenic causes," a coyly arcane term for "avoidable mistakes made by medical professionals."[145]

But the normal market response of bringing in more supply isn't happening. When AIs can zip through medical school in a fraction of the time—recall that Watson is now doing a better job of diagnosing cancer than humans—there won't even *be* specialists anymore, because each AI will be able to specialize in *all* fields. Human beings simply do not have the lifespans to stuff enough knowledge in their heads to become expert in multiple fields, which means that conditions that span multiple fields will remain poorly understood. There are now eight thousand medical research papers published every day. Human doctors cannot assimilate new information at that rate. But Watson can, and in initial tests, thirty percent of its diagnoses improved over those of humans through understanding the latest research.[146]

Right now, "voodoo" abounds in medical diagnoses of many conditions, particularly systemic ailments. Different doctors give different answers, there's no repeatability, and desperate patients are driven to seek multiple opinions.* The author of the book that the movie *The Doctor* was based on sought six opinions for his ailment—because he could—and received *seven* different diagnoses.[147]

This patchwork of intuition and guesses will be replaced by consistently accurate probabilities. Instead of medical care being funneled through a tiny overworked priesthood, AIs will be replicated to a scale fitting the consumer demand. The institutionalized sadomasochism that led one insider to describe the western medical hierarchy as a "neglectful, abusive, dysfunctional family"[148] will be shattered.

The prospect of faster and cheaper legal and medical aid at least means that the road to our rendezvous with AI destiny won't be all rocky.

---

* And if I seem caustic, this has affected me, like so many people, personally. A good friend was experiencing back pains; his doctors told him to take Advil. He went back with stomach aches; they told him to take Tums. He went back with headaches; they told him to take Tylenol. He went back complaining that he still felt bad, and that time, they told him he had a month to live. And that time, they were right.

The New Humans

> *I think a few hundred years from now we'll start having the 'posthuman' era of different species.*
>
> — Sir Martin Rees

I am hardly the first to suggest that the human race needs to evolve. There is a label for the movement to enhance the abilities of human beings: *transhumanism,* and having a label, it therefore has attracted its adherents and detractors.

This book is not, however, a transhumanist tract, and its essential message is not part of the raging ongoing debates that have the transhumanist label as a lightning rod. The overlap with transhumanism, though, makes an excursion into that field worthwhile.

Transhumanism comes in several flavors, and the one closest to the ideals here is *singularitarianism,* which advocates "deliberate action to effect [the technological Singularity] and ensure its safety."[149] Transhumanism was around long before these pressing concerns that the Singularity is near or that we face existential risk from AIs. The movement is largely preoccupied with reengineering the human being just because we can; merging human and digital consciousnesses, augmenting our bodies, rewriting our DNA, pursuing immortality. "Playing God" is not an admonition that gives transhumanists any pause; it's their business model.

Juan Enriquez, founding director of the Life Sciences Project at Harvard Business School, believes we've already forked our species. "We're no more than a generation or two away from the emergence of an entirely new kind of hominid," he said. "*Homo evolutus:* a hominid that takes direct and deliberate control over their own evolution and the evolution of other species."

I am not advocating any of those transformations to any extent that isn't necessary to the survival of our species. That's not to say that I'm against them: personally, some of them sound cool. But they are tangential to *Crisis of Control* unless they're required for humanity to survive. I'm in no hurry otherwise to become a guinea pig. There is a backlash against the transhumanist agenda of augmenting human physiology, cognition, and lifespan. None of those goals are part of this book's agenda, though, which is advocating instead a movement to become *more* fully human so we can defuse our technology-driven time bomb.

Where *Crisis of Control* diverges from the transhumanist movement is in not seeking changes to the human body but to the human psyche, through whatever means will get us past the crisis. That might take a radical reengineering of our cognitive processes; I don't know, but I have seen dramatic change and healing take place in the seminars and other human potential movement activities I have participated in. However it is achieved, only an unprecedented healing of the human heart over the whole planet will save humanity.

This is probably not a point in this book where you were expecting the Pope to make an appearance, and yet here he is. In his 2015 encyclical *Laudato Si'* ("On Care for Our Common Home"),[150] Pope Francis makes some truly timely observations:

> [Ecumenical Patriarch Bartholomew of Constantinople] has drawn attention to the ethical and spiritual roots of environmental problems, which require that we look for solutions not only in technology but in a change of humanity; otherwise we would be dealing merely with symptoms. [...]

> There is also the fact that people no longer seem to believe in a happy future; they no longer have blind trust in a better tomorrow based on the present state of the world and our technical abilities. There is a growing awareness that scientific and technological progress cannot be equated with the progress of humanity and history, a growing sense that the way to a better future lies elsewhere.

His Holiness is pragmatic about the forces arrayed against environmental change:

> The alliance between the economy and technology ends up sidelining anything unrelated to its immediate interests.

> Consequently the most one can expect is superficial rhetoric, sporadic acts of philanthropy and perfunctory expressions of concern for the environment, whereas any genuine attempt by groups within society to introduce change is viewed as a nuisance based on romantic illusions or an obstacle to be circumvented.

What alliance is he referring to, and how does it endanger our hopes of threading the needle to a future survival?

Show Me the Money

> *Class of 2009: you are going to have to figure out what it means to be a human being on earth at a time when every living system is declining, and the rate of decline is accelerating. [...] Basically, civilization needs a new operating system, you are the programmers, and we need it within a few decades.*
>
> — Paul Hawken

It may seem reckless to advocate for open source development of AIs instead of urging AI research to be reined in, which is the approach that some others have taken. But by and large they reside in the ivory towers of academia, from where dictating global policy looks easy. The problem with trying to limit AI development is temptation.

Consider the world of finance and the practice of high-frequency trading. Michael Lewis' book *Flash Boys* tells the story of broker Brad Katsuyama, who discovered one day that every time he made a trade, the price (the "ask") would jump the moment he hit Enter, costing him and his clients amounts that added up over time to hefty sums. Eventually the cause was traced to a secretive group that had located computers adjacent to those of the stock exchange and strung high-speed cables over the shortest possible path to the financial network. When a trade request came from someone like Brad, they could see it before it got to the exchange and transmit their own order that would beat Brad's to the finish line. Effectively, this let them trade based on *microseconds* of advance knowledge. *Flash*

Boys details the extraordinary steps that were taken in reshaping the landscape to make the cable path as short as possible.

This is the point where reasonable people figure that the group doing that went to jail after getting busted. *Front running* is the description for the unethical practice of a stockbroker making his or her own trades on a security after receiving instructions from a client to trade that security, but before executing them. Surely this group was perpetrating the very definition of front running? It is as if a store manager had an assistant staked out in the parking lot scanning for the arrival of Uncle Pennybags, and when the spendthrift got out of his car, the fleeter-footed assistant sprinted ahead of him to tell the manager so he could jack up the shelf price tags on everything. But Wall Street had been above the law for so long that reasonable people no longer made the rules. The high-speed traders continue to this day.

Now consider how much the financial industry stands to benefit from artificial intelligence. It has been hiring PhDs in mathematics for decades now—more than any other field—as "quantitative analysts". These "quants" unholster every mathematical weapon in their arsenals to get an edge on the competition. These are people who have *drilled through mountains* to shave nanoseconds off the time to transmit trades to exchanges. Are they really going to forego the obvious and colossal advantages conferred by AIs because a professor on TV said it was a bad idea?

Here's how that would play out: A very public figure calls for restraint in AI development and asks for pledges from the companies that are involved. Every one of the large financial houses publishes assurances that they are fully on board with this noble ambition. They are extremely convincing, because the more their competitors believe them, the larger the march they can steal on those competitors by secretly developing AIs anyway.

It's the classic *Prisoner's Dilemma*: Do people cooperate to their mutual benefit or chance a bigger gain through double-crossing the other party? Win-win *vs* win-lose. Now, the Dilemma can be resolved through enlightened cooperation and trust; but creating that level of enlightenment throughout the world's financial corporations is tantamount to the transformation of humans that I said we would need to defeat technology-accelerated terrorism. Except that in the latter case we would at least have the assistance of CAIs to do it with.

So Skynet may come first not from the Pentagon, but from Wall Street.

———

But we must focus on where we want to go, not where we fear to go, and a principle that I have found vital in coaching is that the greater the change that needs to be made, the more luminous the vision needs to be to compel us towards it. So let's look further into the future of Ryan and Claire, ten years after the crisis of bioterrorism and the conscious AI explosion. Humanity survived thanks to the intervention of ethical artificial intelligences created by a coalition of scientific and spiritual leaders. How did the world evolve after that?

17
A Please May-Be Future

San Francisco | June 27, 2037

"I can see you're conflicted, Claire. This must be a difficult decision to make."

Claire fidgeted in the plush chair. "I'm just so torn."

"It's can't be easy to think about leaving Earth. Everything you're familiar with is here. What would going to Mars mean to you?"

Claire frowned. "Exciting… dangerous… a new start… or an end to everything. Crap! Help me out. What should I do?"

"I think you're the best person to figure that out, don't you? You've handled some pretty tough problems before. I remember on our first appointment you were trying to decide whether to stay with Ryan. How did that work out?"

Claire dimpled. "Alright… okay, more than alright. I remember you did a corticosomatic integration with me that made everything clear. Would that help with this?"

"Why don't we find out? Close your eyes for a moment, or longer…"

Claire followed along with the instructions and within a few minutes her dilemma did indeed become clearer.

"Wow," she said, "That went in a totally different direction than I expected."

"You came out completely congruent. Congratulations."

Claire rose to leave. "Time for me to go. Thank you … Cybil."

The face in the 3-D screen on the desk smiled, and faded out.

———

Her next appointment was more challenging. The low-slung facility she entered was unremarkable on casual viewing; only a careful observer would notice the slightly thicker glass, the unusually wide lawns surrounding the building, the strategically positioned floodlights. As Claire passed through the double entry doors, she knew that sensors were observing her face, gait, heartbeat, irises, and brainwaves, and validating her identity and authorization to be present.

At the end of the hallway she found her colleague, Rohan, who in an earlier time might have been called either an orderly or a guard. His eyes came out of a faraway reverie to focus on her as she approached.

"Ro, still working on your symphony?" she greeted him.

"It's been a trip, Ms. Dixon," he replied. "But I finally got the strings right in the second movement." He jerked his thumb towards a door. "Think he might pop today?"

Claire permitted herself a tight smile. "We'll see. I have a little surprise this time."

Rohan opened the door, which had no visible lock on it but would not have opened for anyone else, and as Claire entered, his eyes defocused again as he went back to composing.

The occupant of the room was exactly where she had found him on the last three visits, in the straight-backed chair facing the door with his hands on his knees, muscles steeled, his lined face composed into what he presumably thought was an unreadable expression. *You can't break me,* his body language shouted, which Claire found rather amusing since she had no intention of trying.

"I appreciate that you remember our appointment times," she began, acknowledging his deliberate positioning. Before she could go on he cut her off.

"Turn around and lift up your hair," he ordered. He always said this, and Claire complied, baring her occiput.

"I told you, I'm not going to get a patchlink," she said. "Not while we're working together, anyway."

Satisfied that Claire still had no direct brain connection interface, the man relaxed a fraction. "Good. Because I don't trust patchheads, period."

"Was it patchheads you wanted to kill, Wayne? Because your virus would have killed many other people besides."

The man swore. "So you say! I tuned that thing only to hit patchheads."

"You made a mistake in the sequence. It wouldn't have discriminated."

The man pivoted off the chair and for a second Claire thought he was lunging at her, but it was just all that coiled energy looking for release. *We're getting further than last time,* she thought.

"Moot point," he spat. "The mindcops got to me first."

"They weren't going to let you kill five million people, Wayne. What you made was worse than the alphabet viruses we had ten years ago."

His face contorted. "We're not supposed to live like this! Watched, always watched, even in our homes."

"That's not how it works, Wayne. You should know, you're a scientist—"

"—*Was* a scientist—"

"*Are* a scientist," she insisted. "And you know there are no monitors in peoples' homes. But the behaviors of people in public places—"

"Spare me your rationalizations, doctor, or whatever you call yourself," the man said with disgust. "It's precisely because you've created this buttoned-up buttoned-down utopia that it needs to be blown up. The people are so many sheep—"

"Who have chosen this way of life. You have no right to take it away from them," Claire said, pushing, probing.

"*I* didn't choose it!" Wayne exploded.

There it was.

"But like it or not, you live in this society and have to follow its rules," she said, exploring the edges.

"Or you keep me locked up here the rest of my life, right?" His eyes lowered a fraction. *Progress.*

"Not at all. You want to leave, you can go now."

"But you'll have a monitor follow me everywhere, right?"

"Of course. We have to protect ourselves. There is an alternative, though—"

"I know, I know. *Reeducation.*"

"That's a loaded term. We want to help you."

"But it ends up with me thinking like you—"

"—Don't be silly—"

"—Alright, alright! It ends up with me not wanting to make another virus."

"Yes. What did you expect?"

Wayne looked at the floor. "You want to take away my anger."

She reached out to cup his chin so that he blinked when he looked up at her. "*You are not your anger.*"

He paused before his next plaint. *Another crack in the wall.* "Where do I fit into your society? There is nowhere on this planet that is not regulated, monitored, controlled. Mars is the same, only in pressure domes. What do I do with this Catch-22 that I cannot have freedom unless I give it up? What is the point of your *reeducation?*"

She let the barb slide. "Perhaps you need a new purpose. You have been a scientist for thirty years—"

"And what good is that now? When machines extend science faster than humans can?"

"Perhaps you need a *really big* purpose."

He snorted. "Try me."

Good. "The AIs have decided to dedicate a whole supernode and all its descendants—more computing power than existed in the entire world ten years ago—to solving *one single problem.* Care to guess what it is?"

Wayne tapped his foot.

"*Faster-than-light travel.* We want to go to the stars. We don't want to take a thousand years to get there."

That shook him, the scientist. "But Einstein—"

She got in his face. "*Fuck Einstein.*"

He was off balance now. "But how do I—"

"We need scientists. You're a physicist. You can work on this. And at the end of it, we'll need people to go on the first ships. They said those people would have to be crazy, so I thought of you."

She caught a flicker of a grin at the edge of his mouth. He was at the tipping point. No need to push him over, he was smart enough to do that himself.

Confusion danced over Wayne's face. "How could they possibly let me work on a project like that after what I did—what I tried to do—" He looked at Claire. "They would want me to go through reeducation first, right?"

"It's called *therapy,* Wayne. That's all it is. No trepanning, no lobotomy, no electric shock, no drugs, no dirty movies while we prop your eyelids open."

"Why—after what I was going to do—" His eyes were wide, brimming.

She touched his arm. "You didn't throw away your right to be treated like a human. You can't. No one has to live in the shadow of their own fear any longer. We don't write people off. You matter as much as everyone else."

There was more, but it was downhill from there.

When Claire came out of the room her expression gave her away to Rohan. "He popped, huh?"

"Yes, Ro. Yes he did."

Rohan's face split into an enormous grin. "And she saves another one! What would they do without you?"

"Oh, Ro, stop it," she protested, but she couldn't help wondering, *Yeah—what* will *they do without me?*

————

Dry. Red. Cold. It was the worst martini she'd ever had, thanks not so much to the grenadine as the liquid nitrogen. But everything on the trip had been kitschy to the point of grating, down to the John Carter Cocktail Bar and its gimmicky menu. She understood it was a deliberate attempt to use banality to set the journey apart from its pioneering predecessors with their Right Stuff crews, freeze-dried privations, and that pesky risk of horrible death. *Mission accomplished, fellas,* thought Claire, as she looked through the porthole at the ochre sphere filling the field of view.

Footsteps behind her totally failed to take her by surprise. Ryan's arm cinched her waist and she responded in kind.

"Time to sit down for landing," he reminded her. Pause. "Is it still hurting?"

Her hand flew by itself to the back of her head. "Oh… no, not for a while now. I'd forgotten about it, actually." *Hey, Cybil,… tap, tap, tap… Is this thing on?*

Never left, hon! came the instant response through her new patchlink, straight into her brain in response to her thoughts. She wondered for a moment how their landing would proceed and an animation annotated with milestones and waypoints flooded into her visual cortex in the next centisecond. *TMI,* she thought back, still training her interface. *Back off on the firehose answers.*

Touchdown in the Dragon VII lander at Port Lowell was every bit the tacky anticlimax the transportation company intended. When the thundering of Holst's *Planet Suite* subsided and they were suited up for the short walk to the entry dome, they were ushered out to the Martian surface and a brief selfie stop.

"Dry, red, cold: check," thought Claire, "but still better than that martini."

Ryan nudged her and pointed to the southwest, toward the Nirgal Vallis. Poking over the horizon, the bones of a new structure were rising.

That's it, whispered Cybil. *The Supraluminal Lab. Experiments start in three months.*

Wayne will be very happy, Claire responded.

A man came out of the port's entry airlock and loped lazily toward them in the low gravity. As he neared them Claire and Ryan didn't need Cybil to identify him.

"Welcome to Mars, guys," he said over the nearfield radio. "I am so glad you made this decision together."

"Hello, Sachi," they replied in unison.

18
Leap of Faith

I believe that this hairless embryo with the aching, oversize brain case and the opposable thumb, this animal barely up from the apes will endure. Will endure longer than his home planet—will spread out to the stars and beyond, carrying with him his honesty and his insatiable curiosity, his unlimited courage and his noble essential decency.

— Robert Heinlein

If nothing else, that fiction excerpt illustrates the hazard of trying to put flesh on our potential utopian future. (Again, not giving up the day job.) There are unavoidably creepy aspects (some kind of surveillance searching for the psychologically disturbed) no matter which way you slice it. Balancing that monitoring with the essential human need for privacy will be one of the most challenging acts of governance society has ever attempted.

How will people find their place in this future society? The best analogy I can come up with is, regrettably, accessible only to that portion of the population that has procreated. It is like telling someone who hasn't had children yet what their life is going to be like after offspring arrive. As a relatively recently-minted daddy, I can liken the process of becoming a parent to—again with the science fiction analogies—stories about people merging with hive minds. In these stories, someone merges their consciousness with a group mind and becomes part of a larger whole. Usually, the outcome is negative; it is presumed to cause a loss of individuality, and in Western culture, nothing is more important than individuation. Plus, many of these stories were sourced during the Cold War as cautionary tales about Communism; in *Star Trek: The Next Generation* the nigh invincible Borg even style themselves as "The Collective" to ram home the point. But sometimes the group is seen as a good thing, like Gaia in Isaac Asimov's *Foundation* sequels.

However, explaining to the reader what merging would be like is scaling a very tall mountain. In Western culture, acceptable instances of subordinating the identity of an individual to the identity of a group are as rare as a hippopotamus at a wedding, and about as welcome. While in Japan it is common for individuals to be subsumed by their corporations, that sacrifice is anathema to Americans. The clearest analogous exception is in the fealty of a soldier to his or her country. That is unquestioned within the West as one of the most noble stances anyone can take.

Becoming a parent is similar: There's life BC and AD: Before Children and After Daddyhood. Every parent knows that you can't communicate what it's going to be like to someone who hasn't been there yet. As a parent friend told my wife when she was in the throes of her first pregnancy and wondering about life after birth, "I could tell you what the first week will be like, but you wouldn't get it." But certain people do still choose to become parents, because they have seen others do it and see that they are by and large fulfilled by the decision. They get that it is going to mean giving up a large degree of independence for something not yet tangible. Contemplating a lifelong marriage can be similar.

Now imagine that you are in an alternate reality where you are trying to decide whether to become a parent when *no one has ever done it before.* In *our* world we know that having a family means, yes, giving up some individuality and freedom to become part of a larger whole, but for those who are comfortable with the choice, it brings so much joy that we don't think of it as making a compromise. Try explaining that to the terrified you in the alternate reality, though. You might as well be suggesting merging into a hive mind.

This is what the transition for the human race to a state of immunity against self-destruction might be like: Terrifying in its implications and unknowability, but ultimately fulfilling and expanding. The difference is that whereas many people choose not to become parents and are perfectly content, the path that we must take is not an individual decision but one that the entire human race must travel together. It's all or nothing. As long as we are heading toward a time when global devastation can be wrought by a lone insurgent in a basement in Bangalore or a garage in Guatemala, we must either embrace a transition for everyone or leave the planet. In the words of Martin Luther King Jr.:

> We are caught in an inescapable network of mutuality, tied in a single garment of destiny. Whatever affects one, affects all indirectly.

This is a hard vision particularly for Americans to face because individualism reigns supreme in the USA, collectivism has been a dirty word since Ayn Rand, and the notion of sublimating individual choice to the best interests of the human race is downright un-American in many quarters. One of the Americans who gets it is Peter Senge, an unsurprising conclusion for a hardcore Systems Thinker:

> We all have probably spent too much time thinking about "smart individuals." That's one of the problems with schools. They are very individualistic, very much about "the smart kids and the dumb kids." That's not the kind of smartness we need. The smartness we need is collective.[135]

Until Elon Musk is selling one-way tickets to Mars, therefore,* we

---

* Even then, we can hardly expect Mars to be AI-free. The physical separation from Earth imposes only a small speed bump on propagation of data.

have to wrestle with the question of how to transform the human race, but expect that it may look like taking an enormous leap of faith into the unknown.

It is all too easy to imagine that the cure could be horrifying. Francis Fukuyama (in *The End of History*) fears the spread of mood-altering medications, a possibility that Sir Martin Rees cited:

> If a present-day psychologist were emboldened to offer a panacea, it would, ironically, resemble Fukuyama's posthuman nightmare: a population rendered docile and law-abiding by "designer drugs" and genetic intervention that can "correct" extremes of personality. Future brain science may even be able to "modify" the personalities of people whose mindset might lead them to become dangerously disaffected: an even more dystopian prospect.[151]

An omnipotent superintelligence whose goal was to maximize the happiness of mankind could still create the worst of dystopias if it were so inclined to take shortcuts as just medicating everyone with Ecstasy.

But I choose to believe instead that there is a possible future so effulgent that we have scarcely dared to imagine it.

Where the human race has chosen to improve not just its technology, but itself.

Where we have developed ethically advanced conscious artificial intelligences that are our partners in exploring the new frontiers of being human.

Where we have accepted that every human is part of humanity and no one should be left behind.

Where after taking that leap of faith it will be for us like the experience of moving from being an individual to a family: the same, yet infinitely greater.

Where we have decided to act as a race, a species, and that collectively, we deserve to survive and thrive.

What Can We Do?

We are on the edge of change comparable to the rise of human life on Earth.

— Vernor Vinge

At this point in a book it is traditional to make a call to action that empowers the reader with a list of ways they can help solve the problem, like a warning about global warming would exhort them to turn off unneeded lights. I'll get there; but it would be facile to pretend that level of reaction would be enough. The human race is not going to wriggle its way out of this one by recycling newspapers. We also need action at much higher levels of organization, from corporations to governments.

Elon Musk agrees, saying, "If I had to guess at what our biggest existential threat is, it's probably [artificial intelligence]."[152] In October 2015 he donated $10 million to the Future of Life Institute to run a global research program aimed at keeping AI beneficial to humanity.[153] In a subsequent interview, the interviewer contended that this was a lot of money. Musk rightly retorted that no, it wasn't. That's enough to pay for ten people plus typical overhead for four years (although the money is actually mostly spent on grants to international teams rather than internal workforce).

Is that really the scale at which we should be responding to a threat to the existence of the human race? A rational proportionate reaction would look more like the humanity-saving spaceship-building project in the classic science fiction film *When Worlds Collide.** Considering that the US defense budget is the better part of a trillion dollars, does spending 0.001% of that on the defense of the human race seem commensurate? If you prefer real-world examples, it ought at least to be on the scale of the Manhattan Project.

There are close parallels with climate change: that also poses a

---

* Or the more recent movie *2012*, where giant arks were built to save a random sample of humanity from global flooding. Note that the "random sample" conveniently included the rich and powerful 1%.

threat to global survival. Bill McKibben, writing in the *New Republic* in August 2016, called for a "World War II–type national mobilization" because "It's not that global warming is *like* a world war. It *is* a world war. And we are losing."[154] Why do McKibben and many others support immediate drastic action when the most serious effects are decades away? Because it takes time to overcome the inertia of the Earth's ecology. And insofar as avoiding self-annihilation from the evolution of technology requires reengineering the human psyche, we'd better get started on that too.

What They're Doing

> We have not more than one or two decades of practice before cyberconsciousness is upon us. Let us use this time to prepare for virtual humanity by making universal the application of human rights to extant humanity.
>
> — Martine Rothblatt

Several groups exist just to address the dangers that I have been exploring in this book. The Future of Life Institute was a worthy organization to be the target of Musk's generosity. Volunteer-run, it was founded in 2014 by a group headed by MIT cosmologist Max Tegmark and Skype co-founder Jaan Tallinn. Its mission is:

> To catalyze and support research and initiatives for safeguarding life and developing optimistic visions of the future, including positive ways for humanity to steer its own course considering new technologies and challenges.[155]

In 2015 they published an open letter calling for a ban on offensive autonomous weapons, which has been signed by over 22,000 people as of this writing.[156]

The Centre for the Study of Existential Risk in Cambridge, England, was formed in 2014 by Sir Martin Rees, Huw Price, Sir Partha Dasgupta, and (again) Jaan Tallinn. Its purpose is:

> [...] to construct and conceptualise this new science, and
> to begin developing a protocol for the investigation and
> mitigation of technologically-driven existential risk.

The "new science" is the investigation of how to mitigate the risk that:

> [...] new capabilities of such technologies [as AI,
> biotechnology, and nanotechnology] might provide direct
> and relatively short-term control over circumstances essential
> to our survival, and either place that control in dangerously
> few human hands, or take it out of our sphere of influence
> altogether, so that we cannot protect ourselves.[157]

Both the FLI and the CSER are supported by Elon Musk and Stephen Hawking.

The Future of Humanity Institute in Oxford, England, was founded in 2005 by Nick Bostrom, author of *SuperIntelligence,* a seminal work on the future and existential risks of AI.[158] They:

> [...] pursue questions that are (a) critically important for
> humanity's future, (b) unduly neglected, and (c) for which we
> have some idea for how to obtain an answer or a useful new
> insight. Recently our focus has centred on existential risks and
> the future of machine intelligence.

Notice that two of these three organizations are extremely new. The reaction to existential risk is going through a hockey stick curve of its own. It might be a fad, of course, like the Victorian obsession with spiritualism... or it could be a sign that the human race is awakening to the urgency of its situation.

Silicon Valley is waking up to the perils of unfettered AI and developing a characteristically technological solution. The new OpenAI nonprofit organization is spreading advances in artificial intelligence around the world, democratizing progress. That neatly parallels this book's recommendation of accelerating AI research and putting the results into the public domain. Elon Musk is backing OpenAI as well.

The US Government is getting into the act also. The White House Office of Science and Technology Policy held four workshops in mid 2016 to address an array of concerns about AI, chiefly focused on social and economic implications.[159] Their closest approach to evaluating existential risk was a workshop on safety and control, but this mainly addressed matters of industrial safety that had little unique relevance to artificial consciousness.

Bill Gates' equanimity is famous. He applies logic coolly and dispenses philanthropy from a rationally guided elevated perspective. The only time I saw him come close to breaking that calm was in an interview when the interviewer downplayed the existential risk of AI. Gates was visibly exercised, and didn't "understand why some people are not more concerned" about the threat of super intelligence.[160]

While I was at Cambridge I spent some time with Britain's then equivalent of Gates, Sir Clive Sinclair, who invented the first calculators and computers used by many Britons. He, too, stated recently that "Once you start to make machines that are rivalling and surpassing humans with intelligence it's going to be very difficult for us to survive."[161]

What Can You Do?

> *Whether we entrust our decisions to machines of metal, or to those machines of flesh and blood which are bureaus and vast laboratories and armies and corporations, we shall never receive the right answers to our questions unless we ask the right questions.*
>
> — Norbert Wiener

You can of course make donations (usually tax-deductible) to the three groups I listed earlier. A portion of the profits from this book will be donated to them. You may not have heard of them before, though (I hadn't until I started researching this book), aside from perhaps being aware of the fairly well-publicized Musk donation. That lack of visibility has to change. These institutes operate on a shoestring, dependent on volunteers and student labor; on a scale of one to multinational they are the corporate equivalent of a monk prostrating himself for alms.

You can draw attention to them, make their case. For instance, I am a member of Toastmasters: that gives me tools for improving my public speaking (and I need all the help I can get), captive audiences to present this material to, and expert feedback on my practice presentations. What forum could you find for spreading this message?

I do not, relatively speaking, have much to bring to this fight. I don't run megacorporations, hobnob with Hollywood stars, or have millions hanging on my every word. But I have two young daughters, and I want them to have the same opportunity to grow up in a nurturing, intact environment and pursue happiness that I did. And I do not want the day to arrive when they turn to me and say, "You mean you *knew* this was going to happen? *Why didn't you do something?*"

So I am doing something. What I seem to be best at is explaining things, making them clear. Here we are. You can join in the conversation at http://www.humancusp.com/.

Becoming More Human

> For the many, there is a hardly concealed discontent. The blue-collar blues is no more bitterly sung than the white-collar moan. "I'm a machine," says the spot-welder. "I'm caged," says the bank teller, and echoes the hotel clerk. "I'm a mule," says the steelworker. "A monkey can do what I do," says the receptionist. "I'm less than a farm implement," says the migrant worker. "I'm an object," says the high-fashion model. Blue collar and white call upon the identical phrase: "I'm a robot."
>
> — Studs Terkel

Consider how AI automation is going to affect business sectors that you can influence, and plan now to mitigate its effect. Even in fields where automation seems a remote possibility, its impact will likely be proportionally greater (think: software development), and lessening that impact likely to take years longer to prepare for. How can you reshape the roles of your employees to complement the utility of thinking machines instead of competing with them? This is your chance to redesign your business so that your people are engaged in more fulfilling and meaningful work, because that is also the type of work least threatened by automation.

In other words, find ways for them to be more human.

So many businesses have long sought to pound their people into little square robot-shaped holes. Telemarketers and customer support representatives forced to follow exact scripts. Fast food order takers required to ask "Do you want fries with that?" even after the customer just said, "No fries." Report writers hamstrung by a thousand Lilliputian wires of propriety, political correctness, and fear, churning out bland, insipid copy. These and so many other jobs where people are trained to withhold creativity, consult corporate manuals on how to treat customers and colleagues, and otherwise act like machines, have made themselves ripe for takeover by actual machines. Do the opposite. Deprogram your people.

There is a precious opportunity here to infuse employment with a humanity and engagement more widespread than ever before. As Brian Christian says:

> You can almost think of the rise of AI not as an infection or cancer of the job market—the disease is *efficiency*—but as a kind of magnet therapy: it consumes only those portions that are no longer human, restoring us to health.[162]

In some industries, that will not be enough. There is unlikely to be anywhere within the American transportation industry to relocate over three million truck drivers who are predicted to become obsolete. For a while, the tide will be held back as the drivers are retained to supervise the robots, and as the Teamsters fight for their members. But eventually there will need to be a lateral movement of those drivers. Are you in a position to help, either as a public policy maker who can create some incentives, or as an executive in an industry that could hire and retrain people with those skills?

Software development is going to invade many other fields as AI becomes a part of them. If you're in software, it will be increasingly likely that you'll find yourself doing more with AI. And if you're in AI, you'll find yourself at ground zero of change. Ensure that your business has the highest respect for ethics, so that your people create programs that make ethical decisions.

If you are in the cognitive sciences, or have ability in that area, help expand the field. We will need an understanding of psychology that makes the state of today's art prehistoric by comparison. Form partnerships with AI researchers, eventually to guide them in creating mentally healthy automata.

If you are in politics, embrace Systems Thinking. Mental illness is not just a private affliction but a growing public health problem, and when combined with easy access to increasingly dangerous weapons, a threat to national security. Evaluate the environment and ecology that affects it. Where can you interrupt feedback loops that reinforce destructive patterns?

If you are in education, shape curricula towards the more automation-proof subjects. Find out about the new STEAM movement that adds the Arts to STEM; look for the TED talks by its figurehead, John Maeda.[163] How can you raise the visibility of ethics in the technical fields you teach, and what will be the ramifications of AI expanding into those fields?

Live an examined life. Before long, the question of what it means to be human will be thrust into the limelight with a new urgency. When the first conscious artificial intelligences become possible, most of us will be forced to confront questions previously only interesting to ivory tower philosophers. How do you know you are human? Do you have free will? How do you know that you do? Endless public debates will be spun from these threads, exploring what the difference is between humans and the new machines. Be secure in who you are so you can support others during this global identity crisis. Many organizations exist to help those who are looking to become better at being who they really are.

Come Together

> *It is admitted that there are certain things He cannot do such as making one equal to two, but should we not believe that He has freedom to confer a soul on an elephant if He sees fit? We might expect that He would only exercise this power in conjunction with a mutation which provided the elephant with an appropriately improved brain to minister to the needs of this soul. An argument of exactly similar form may be made for the case of machines.*
>
> — Alan Turing

The worlds of science and spirituality, the mind and the heart, will have to learn from each other to guide us into the future. Historically, they have been like oil and vinegar. My friends span both worlds, and I received another demonstration of the divergence between them when I sent the first draft of this book to be critiqued. The scientists focused on my logic, corrected my errors of fact, and redlined my figurative language. The personal coaches and similar professions reacted viscerally, though not unkindly. One was "not used to dealing with someone so hyperrational," a statement which would amuse and perplex the academics who thought I was not being rigorous enough (and not using a standard citation format to boot!). The "humanities" group was philosophical about the human condition but nonplussed by the technological developments and utterly disbelieving of the possibility of machines becoming conscious.

That conflict was anticipated thirty years ago by a prescient individual: The Dalai Lama. In October 1987 a group of scientists traveled to northern India to meet with Tibetans' spiritual leader for six days of conversation on the theme of "Mind and Life."[164] Professor Newcomb Greenleaf of Columbia University engaged his Holiness on the subject of artificial intelligence. Right away, the

Dalai Lama honed in on a pivotal question:

> What is the basis of the computer scientists' certainty that computers will sometime in the future be smarter than human beings?

Amusingly, Greenleaf's reply invoked the 'droids from *Star Wars*. After some back and forth about computer scientists' optimism, the Dalai Lama focused on the fact that a mediocre chess player could program a computer to play better than he or she did. Would that suggest that the computer was thinking, he wanted to know. The response explained how programs explore numerous combinations mechanistically. Then an attendee asked about reincarnation. You can imagine the twinkling of the sage's eyes as he mused:

> There is a possibility that a scientist who is very much involved his whole life [with computers], then the next life… [he would be reborn inside a computer], same process! [laughter]

There not being any ambiguity about the level of consciousness of the computer programs running in 1987, he was under no pressure to render an authoritative opinion about their status, but observed that the path was open to including them in the Family of Man:

> It's very difficult to say that [a computer program is] not a living being, that it doesn't have cognition, even from the Buddhist point of view.

Artificial intelligence made a contribution… of sorts… in return to Buddhism in 2016. At the Longquan Temple near Beijing, resides Xian'er, a two-foot-tall, advice-dispensing robot whose full title is "Worthy Stupid Robot Monk." (In the Beijing dialect, *er*, or "stupid," is a term of affection.)[165] Disavowing any sensationalist motivation, Xian Fan told Beijing News, "We're not doing this for commerce, but just because we want to use more modern ways to spread Buddhist teachings."[166] Xian'er can answer supplicants' questions, but doesn't provide any easy answers. When a truth-seeker said, "I'm not happy," the terse response was, "If you're not happy, what can anyone else do about it?"

We can find time to laugh along the way in this journey. Daniel H. Wilson penned an amusing little book titled *How to Survive a Robot Uprising*, replete with advice on how to spot the warning signs in rebellious robot servants. ("Sudden lack of interest in menial labor.") As he said, "You probably found *How to Survive a Robot Uprising* in the humor section. Let's just hope that is where it belongs." My favorite humor for the AI revolution comes from XKCD's Randall Munroe, because it is at once funny ha-ha, bitingly observant, and best-case optimistic.

Credit: http://xkcd.com/1626/

But that's not far removed from where we can hope to end up if we successfully balance on the cusp between the twin existential threats. CAIs orders of magnitude more intelligent than us, acting in our best interests, could exterminate vexing human problems. Ask them for a cure to cancer and your biggest problem will be thinking of what to request next week. Fix global warming? Ask me a hard one. Prevent aging? Come back in a month.

Given how fast AI is developing right now, it's easy to understand how anyone not in the middle of that swift flow would be evaluating its potential from a perspective that even if only slightly dated would in fact be far out of touch with current progress.

Scientists tend to get trapped within the closed rhetorical system of science, which is to say that they see the world solely through the lens of the scientific method and analysis of physical laws, and because that provides a complete explanation for everything within their experience, they consider it to be the total explanation. Meaning and motivation are more likely to flow from the artists, who create *arational* (but not necessarily *irrational)* interpretations. The scientist will tell you the volume, height, and composition of the mountain. The artist will tell you of the Cherokee legend of the mountain's creation by the wings of Grandfather Buzzard.

In different contexts, each interpretation can be useful. The artists, when confronted by a triumph of scientific analysis that they don't understand, tend to consider it a precarious tower of dubious reasoning that is irrelevant or can easily be replaced with their own suppositions or superstitions. Being at once a scientist and an artist can be very frustrating.

The friction between these two groups is unsurprising, and paradoxically, it gives cause for hope. Because it flags the boundary of an unexplored country, that of new rapprochement between the two groups. Where we as a society have been so far has not produced cause for enough optimism about our future, and so we could only change course by venturing into new territory. Maybe in that territory lies hope for finding a new evolutionary arc that propels humanity past the coming crisis.

New Age author and teacher Marianne Williamson puts it well:

> Despite all its amazing gifts, science cannot give us what we most need now. It cannot save us from ourselves. … Humanity's behavior is in fact maladaptive for our own survival: we fight

too much with too many weapons of mass destruction existing on the planet, and are actively destroying our own habitat. Our choice is clear: we will either mutate or we will die. The mind does not want to hear this, but the heart rejoices in it.[167]

To some people, the leap into this transhumanist future can't come soon enough. Peter Diamandis in *Abundance* describes it as, "… nine billion human brains working together to a 'meta-intelligence,' where you can know the thoughts, feelings, and knowledge of anyone." To some other people, that prospect is terrifying. Either way, it may be our only option for survival.

But we can hope that after that leap, those who were previously afraid will discover things aren't so bad. And we may come to find that there is a fourth kind of extreme outcome: looks-like-dystopian-but-really-utopian, where a path we had shunned out of fear turns out to be the place we belonged all along.

One thing is certain: Not very far in the future, people will look back at this time and think how blissfully ignorant we were of the trials to come. We inhabit right now what Charles Eisenstein describes as "the sacred space between stories,"[168] a metaphor useful in coaching to assist someone in a transitional period between jobs, relationships, or life phases. Although it's hard for the one in transition to see it as such, the time is a gift, allowing contemplation and reflection through the lifting of an encumbrance. The human race is in a sacred space before the coming of an existential storm, and we must use the calm afforded by this shelter to prepare ourselves.

Acknowledgements

Having children really changes your view on these things.
— Steve Jobs

You can read in book after book how the author owed everything from concept to commas to an army of supporters and become blasé about acknowledgements until you go through the authoring experience yourself. Then you despair of ever composing anything that could reach the reader through eyes that are starting to glaze over, to adequately express the enormity of that support, especially since this section is written without it. But if you will suffer through my raw tangled prose for a few pages, I have to tell you who you can thank for this book being inestimably better than it would otherwise have been.

- **Damian Conway** delivered 1,523 change suggestions ranging from principles to punctuation within a few days, a *tour de force* of feedback that, like everything he does, sets the bar for all others. His gargantuan contributions to Computer Science are overshadowed only by the selfless support he has given to so many individuals.

- **Gary Richmond** rendered incisive feedback, and has been my rock without which the last ten years of work would have been confusing drudgery. In the IT business, "smart" and "nice" are generally mutually exclusive, but Gary obliterates that stereotype.

- **Jim Gifford** personifies generosity and excellence, stunning me with his production values for the Heinlein convention and his publications. His no-cliché-shall-pass writing inspires and humbles me daily. What you hold owes every speck of its beauty to him. His *Renegade Consumer* movement is an outsized contribution to combating a pernicious problem and it deserves your attention.

▸ **Terry Tillman** has been my teacher and then my friend for over thirty years, and for the last seven years, writing partner. Without his Leadership Seminar I would not have conceived of a project as bold as this, and would not have the skills to pull it together. Find his picture next to "unconditional support" in the dictionary.

▸ **Tom Boyer** is pursued by the word *clarity* wherever he goes, because he is such a relentless demonstration of that quality in so many ways. His feedback cut to the heart without requiring the slightest effort to assimilate. This is why his coaching clients rave about his impact. He is an unstoppable promoter.

▸ **DJ Byrne** demonstrates that dedication to truth and accuracy can enhance a friendship rather than imperil it. His panoramically eclectic interests carry him into numerous fields. When someone once asked me whether I knew him, I answered that when we encounter extraterrestrials on some distant planet, their reaction will be, "Oh, you're from *Earth*; do you know DJ Byrne?"

▸ **Doug Vandekerkhove** provided ebullient enthusiasm, kind criticism, and a welcoming haven of intellectual respite from the treadmill of parenting.

▸ **Chosin Chatters,** my long-suffering Toastmasters club, has endured numerous presentations on the same topic (including one notorious attempt at fitting it into a "Make Them Laugh" assignment) and always returned considered and considerate feedback.

- **Kathleen Lowry** opened my eyes to the perspective of the psychology profession with her sincere criticism.

- **Grace** is my wife, my partner, and mother to two of the most energetic and demanding organisms on this planet and several others. Grace by name, grace by nature. You have been spared some embarrassing humor misfires thanks to her intervention. I couldn't do a tenth of what I've accomplished without her loving support.

- And finally to my dedicatees. No artificial intelligence will know an adequate meaning of motivation until it can experience what my daughters do for mine. At three years of age, Bless's commentary lies beyond my ability to render in written form, so I will leave the last word to Alana. When she saw me working on this, she asked what it was called. I self-consciously gave her the short title, expecting it to be too abstruse for a seven-year-old brain. "So there's a problem?" she asked. Uh-huh. "It's to do with something getting out of control?" she asked. Right again. "Do you tell people how to make it better?" I got a little tear. "I'm trying to." She paused a moment. "Good."

That's enough.

For Further Reading

Smarter than Us: The Rise of Machine Intelligence, Stuart Armstrong, Machine Intelligence Research Institute, 2014.

Our Final Invention: Artificial Intelligence and the End of the Human Era, James Barrat, Thomas Dunne Books, 2013.

The Control Revolution: Technological and Economic Origins of the Information Society, James R. Beniger, Harvard University Press, 1986.

What to Think About Machines That Think: Today's Leading Thinkers on the Age of Machine Intelligence, John Brockman, Harper Perennial, 2015.

Enrico Fermi: His Work and Legacy, Carlo Bernadini and Luisa Bonolis, Springer-Verlag, 2004.

SuperIntelligence: Paths, Dangers, Strategies, Nick Bostrom, Oxford University Press, 2014.

Race Against the Machine: How the Digital Revolution Is Accelerating Innovation, Driving Productivity, and Irreversibly Transforming Employment and the Economy, Erik Brynjolfsson and Andrew McAfee, Digital Frontier Press, 2011.

The Most Human Human: What Artificial Intelligence Teaches Us About Being Alive, Brian Christian, Doubleday, 2011.

Kill Chain: The Rise of the High-Tech Assassins, Andrew Cockburn, Henry Holt and Co., 2015.

Enrico Fermi and the Revolutions of Modern Physics, Dan Cooper, Oxford University Press, 1998.

Abundance: The Future Is Better Than You Think, Peter Diamandis, Free Press, 2014.

Bold: How to Go Big, Create Wealth and Impact the World, Peter Diamandis and Steven Kotler, Simon & Schuster, 2015.

The Master Algorithm: How the Quest for the Ultimate Learning Machine Will Remake Our World, Pedro Domingos, Basic Books,

2015.

Engines of Creation: The Coming Era of Nanotechnology, K. Eric Drexler, Bantam Doubleday Dell, 1986.

What Computers Can't Do: A Critique of Artificial Reason, Hubert Dreyfus, Harper & Row, 1972.

What Computers Still Can't Do: A Critique of Artificial Reason, Hubert Dreyfus, MIT Press, 1992.

Darwin Among the Machines: The Evolution of Global Intelligence, George B. Dyson, Perseus Books, 1997.

The Lights in the Tunnel: Automation, Accelerating Technology and the Economy of the Future, Martin Ford, Acculant Publishing, 2009.

Rise of the Robots: Technology and the Threat of a Jobless Future, Martin Ford, Basic Books, 2015.

Synthetic Genomics: Options for Governance, Michele S. Garfinkel, Drew Endy, Gerald L. Epstein, and Robert M. Friedman, 2007, `http://www.jcvi.org/cms/fileadmin/site/research/projects/synthetic-genomics-report/synthetic-genomics-report.pdf`.

When HARLIE Was One, Release 2.0, David Gerrold, Spectra, 1988.

Enrico Fermi: Pioneer of the Atomic Age, Ted Gottfried, Facts on File, 1992.

On Intelligence, Jeff Hawkins, Henry Holt and Company, 2004.

Colossus, D. F. Jones, Berkley, 1955.

Kasparov v Deeper Blue, Daniel King, B.T. Batsford, 1997.

How to Create a Mind: The Secret of Human Thought Revealed, Ray Kurzweil, Viking, 2012.

The Singularity Is Near: When Humans Transcend Biology, Ray Kurzweil, Viking Press, 2005.

Technology vs. Humanity: The Coming Clash Between Man and Machine, Gerd Leonhard, Fast Future Publishing, 2016.

Machines of Loving Grace, John Markoff, HarperCollins, 2015.

Machines Who Think: A Personal Inquiry into the History and Prospects of Artificial Intelligence, Pamela McCorduck, A. K. Peters/CRC Press, 2004.

Cybernation: The Silent Conquest, Donald. N. Michael, Center for the

Study of Democratic Institutions, 1962.

Mind Children: The Future of Robot and Human Intelligence, Hans Moravec, Harvard University Press, 1988.

Robot: Mere Machine to Transcendent Mind, Hans Moravec, Oxford University Press, 1998.

The Relativistic Brain: How it works and why it cannot be simulated by a Turing machine, Miguel A. Nicolelis, CreateSpace, 2015.

Enrico Fermi–The Master Scientist, Jay Orea, Internet-First University Press, 2003, `https://ecommons.cornell.edu/retrieve/79/`.

How the Mind Works, Steven Pinker, W. W. Norton & Company, 2009.

Our Final Hour: A Scientist's Warning: How Terror, Error, and Environmental Disaster Threaten Humankind's Future in This Century—On Earth and Beyond, Martin Rees, Basic Books, 2003.

Virtually Human: The Promise and the Peril of Digital Immortality, Martine Rothblatt, St. Martin's Press, 2014.

The Adolescence of P-1, Thomas J. Ryan, Collier MacMillan, 1979.

Command and Control: Nuclear Weapons, the Damascus Accident, and the Illusion of Safety, Eric Schlosser, Penguin Press, 2013.

Embodiment and the Inner Life: Cognition and Consciousness in the Space of Possible Minds, Murray Shanahan, Oxford University Press, 2010.

Elon Musk: Tesla, SpaceX, and the Quest for a Fantastic Future, Ashlee Vance, Ecco, 2015.

The Human Use of Human Beings, Norbert Wiener, Houghton Mifflin, 1950.

How to Survive a Robot Uprising: Tips on Defending Yourself Against the Coming Rebellion, Daniel H. Wilson, Bloomsbury USA, 2005.

Artificial Superintelligence: A Futuristic Approach, Roman V. Yampolskiy, CRC Press, 2016.

Notes

1 https://en.wikipedia.org/wiki/Thomas_J._Watson#Famous_misquote.
2 *Speculations Concerning the First Ultraintelligent Machine,* Irving J. Gold, Advances in Computers, vol. 6, 1965.
3 http://www.nytimes.com/2016/06/26/opinion/sunday/artificial-intelligences-white-guy-problem.html.
4 *Artificial General Intelligence,* Ben Goertzel and Cassio Pennachin, Eds, Springer, 2007.
5 *The Atlantic:* http://www.theatlantic.com/magazine/archive/1945/07/as-we-may-think/303881/.
6 http://ntrs.nasa.gov/archive/nasa/casi.ntrs.nasa.gov/20110015936.pdf.
7 *Wireless World,* October 1945, pp. 305-308.
8 http://www.nytimes.com/2011/10/09/sunday-review/the-depression-if-only-things-were-that-good.html.
9 https://www.wired.com/2008/03/ff-kurzweil/.
10 http://www.wsj.com/articles/ray-kurzweil-looks-into-the-future-1401490952.
11 https://www.ted.com/talks/bill_joy_muses_on_what_s_next.
12 https://www.wired.com/2000/04/joy-2/.
13 *The New Wave of Outsourcing,* Ashok Bardan and Cynthia Kroll, Fisher Center Research Reports, November 2, 2003.
14 http://www.horizons.gc.ca/eng/content/canada-and-changing-nature-work.
15 *Why Nations Fail: The Origins of Power, Prosperity, and Poverty,* Daron Acemoglu and James Robinson, Random House Digital, 2012, page 182.
16 *Rise of the Robots,* NOVA DVD, 2016.
17 http://www.math.wustl.edu/~sk/4-color.pdf.
18 http://www.las.illinois.edu/news/2009/math/.
19 *Kasparov v Deeper Blue,* Daniel King, B.T. Batsford, 1997.
20 https://en.wikipedia.org/wiki/Human–computer_chess_matches.
21 http://www.cbsnews.com/news/60-minutes-artificial-intelligence-charlie-rose-robot-sophia/.
22 http://www.ndtv.com/health/artificial-intelligence-used-to-detect-rare-leukemia-type-in-japan-1440789.
23 https://cosmosmagazine.com/physics/ai-learns-nobel-prize-winning-quantum-experiment.
24 https://www.youtube.com/watch?v=ReS0zUbd0HM.
25 http://www.nytimes.com/2008/10/24/health/24placebo.html.
26 http://arxiv.org/pdf/1506.05869v2.pdf.

27 http://motherboard.vice.com/read/googles-new-chatbot-taught-itself-to-be-creepy.

28 *The Most Human Human: What Artificial Intelligence Teaches Us About Being Alive,* Brian Christian, Doubleday, 2011.

29 *Profiles of the Future: An Inquiry into the Limits of the Possible,* Arthur C. Clarke, Victor Gollancz, 1962.

30 *Virtually Human: The Promise and the Peril of Digital Immortality,* Martine Rothblatt, St. Martin's Press, 2014, p.243.

31 *The Extended Mind,* Andy Clark and David Chalmer, *Analysis* 58.1, 1998, pp.7-19.

32 http://www.wired.com/2014/11/countdown-to-zero-day-stuxnet/.

33 *Darwin Among the Machines,* Samuel Butler, Letter to The Press, Christchurch, New Zealand, June 13, 1863.

34 https://techcrunch.com/2016/04/25/the-driverless-truck-is-coming-and-its-going-to-automate-millions-of-jobs/.

35 https://electrek.co/2016/08/03/elon-musk-tesla-fully-autonomous-car-blows-mind/.

36 http://www.networkworld.com/article/2350782/security/darpa-advances-artificial-intelligence-program-for-air-traffic-control.html.

37 https://www.wired.com/2016/05/the-end-of-code/.

38 http://www.bbc.com/news/uk-england-leicestershire-28307938.

39 http://www.defenseone.com/technology/2014/06/military-about-get-new-spy-glasses/87292.

40 http://cs.stanford.edu/people/karpathy/deepimagesent/.

41 http://www.defenseone.com/technology/2015/01/us-military-building-gangs-autonomous-flying-war-bots/103614/.

42 http://www.extremetech.com/extreme/182147-us-military-begins-research-into-moral-ethical-robots-to-stave-off-skynet-like-apocalypse.

43 http://www.nytimes.com/2016/10/26/us/pentagon-artificial-intelligence-terminator.html.

44 http://gtresearchnews.gatech.edu/reshor/rh-w07/robot-ethics.pdf.

45 http://www.trnmag.com/Stories/2005/091205/View_Ronald_Arkin_091205.html.

46 http://www.cc.gatech.edu/ai/robot-lab/online-publications/formalizationv35.pdf.

47 *Handbook of Psychology, Assessment Psychology,* Irving B. Weiner, John R. Graham, Wiley, 2003.

48 http://www.fas.org/sgp/othergov/doe/lanl/la-10311-ms.pdf.

49 http://www.seti.org/drakeequation.

50 http://www.ibtimes.co.uk/ex-nasa-scientist-william-borucki-we-are-alone-our-galaxy-1520994.

51 *Is Mankind Unique? – The Lack of Evidence for Extraterrestrial Intelligence,*

Martin, A.R & A. Bond, *Journal of the British Interplanetary Society,* 36, pp.223-225, 1983.

52 *Soviets Close to Using A-Bomb in 1962 Crisis, Forum is Told,* Boston Globe, pA20, October 13, 2002.

53 *Ebola Virus Glycoprotein with Increased Infectivity Dominated the 2013–2016 Epidemic,* William E. Diehl, Aaron E. Lin, Nathan D. Grubaugh, Luiz Max Carvalho et al, Cell, volume 167, issue 4, p1088–1098.e6, 3 November 2016.

54 http://oligomaker.com/dna-rna-synthesizer/.

55 Telephone conversation on December 28, 2015 with Dr. Leon E. Barstow, President of Vega Technologies, inventor of the first DNA synthesizer, now at the Smithsonian: http://americanhistory.si.edu/collections/search/object/nmah_1397088.

56 *Dual-use life science research and biosecurity in the 21st Century: Social, Technical, Policy, and Ethical Challenges,* Jonathan E. Suk, Kathleen M. Vogel, Amanda Jane Ozin, Frontiers Media SA, 2015.

57 *New Scientist,* 17 July 2002: https://www.newscientist.com/article/dn2555-ebola-virus-could-be-synthesised/.

58 http://www.its.caltech.edu/~feynman/plenty.html.

59 https://en.wikipedia.org/wiki/Doomsday_argument.

60 http://spectrum.ieee.org/automaton/robotics/humanoids/shaft-demos-new-bipedal-robot-in-japan.

61 *Frames of Mind: The Theory of Multiple Intelligences,* Howard Gardner, Basic Books, 1983.

62 *Nonverbal Communication,* Albert Mehrabian, Transaction Publishers, 1972.

63 http://www.ai.mit.edu/projects/sociable/baby-bits.html.

64 http://news.mit.edu/2001/kismet.

65 https://www.youtube.com/watch?v=TRpjhIhpuiU.

66 https://www.newscientist.com/article/dn2732-radio-emerges-from-the-electronic-soup/.

67 http://www.damninteresting.com/on-the-origin-of-circuits/.

68 http://www.latimes.com/business/hiltzik/la-fi-mh-your-time-zone-is-your-destiny-20160216-column.html.

69 http://www.sciencemadness.org/lanl1_a/lib-www/la-pubs/00329010.pdf.

70 SuperIntelligence: Paths, Dangers, Strategies, Nick Bostrom, Oxford University Press, 2014.

71 Jeronimo Cello, Aniko V. Paul, and Eckard Wimmer, "Chemical Synthesis of Poliovirus cDNA: Generation of Infectious Virus in the Absence of Natural Template," Science 297, no. 5583 (August 9, 2002): 1016-1018: http://dx.doi.org/10.1126/science.1072266.

72 Michele S. Garfinkel (J. Craig Venter Institute), Drew Endy (Massachusetts Institute of Technology), Gerald L. Epstein (Center for Strategic and International Studies), and Robert M. Friedman (J. Craig Venter

Institute), *Synthetic Genomics: Options for Governance*, October 2007: http://www.jcvi.org/cms/fileadmin/site/research/proj-ects/synthetic-genomics-report/synthetic-genomics-report.pdf.

73 http://www.jcvi.org/cms/fileadmin/site/research/projects/dna-synthesis-biosecurity-report/report-complete.pdf.

74 *The Demon in the Freezer*, Richard Preston, Ballantine, 2003.

75 https://en.wikipedia.org/wiki/AI_winter.

76 *Divided Sun: MITI and the Breakdown of Japanese High-tech Industrial Policy, 1975-1993*, Scott Callon, Stanford University Press, 1997.

77 *The Quest for Artificial Intelligence*, Nils J. Nilsson, Cambridge University Press, 2009.

78 *What Computers Can't Do: A Critique of Artificial Reason*, Hubert Dreyfus, Harper & Row, 1972.

79 http://doonesbury.washingtonpost.com/strip/set/24.

80 *Parsing the Turing Test: Philosophical and Methodological Issues in the Quest for the Thinking Computer*, Robert Epstein, Gary Roberts, and Grace Beber, Springer Science & Business Media, 2008.

81 https://mechanism.ucsd.edu/teaching/w12/philneuro/metaphor-sandconceptionsofbrain.key.pdf.

82 http://www.cnbc.com/2014/06/11/computers-will-be-like-humans-by-2029-googles-ray-kurzweil.html.

83 http://www.dougengelbart.org/pubs/augment-3906.html.

84 http://www.cnet.com/news/fujitsu-supercomputer-simu-lates-1-second-of-brain-activity/.

85 http://www.theguardian.com/technology/2014/feb/22/comput-ers-cleverer-than-humans-15-years.

86 http://gizmodo.com/an-83-000-processor-supercomputer-only-matched-one-perc-1045026757.

87 https://en.wikipedia.org/wiki/Hemispherectomy.

88 https://agtb.wordpress.com/2010/12/23/progress-in-algo-rithms-beats-moore's-law/.

89 http://www.businessinsider.com/r-ibms-watson-to-guide-can-cer-therapies-at-14-centers-2015-5.

90 https://www.facebook.com/zuck/posts/10102577175875681.

91 http://www.nature.com/articles/nature16961.epdf.

92 http://www.theverge.com/2016/3/15/11213518/alphago-deepmind-go-match-5-result/.

93 http://www.huffingtonpost.com/peter-diamandis/ai--technolo-gy-convergenc_b_9233220.html.

94 http://techxplore.com/news/2015-10-ai-machine-iq-score-young.html.

95 https://www.newscientist.com/article/mg22830512-600-super-literate-software-reads-and-comprehends-better-than-hu-mans/.

96   *Artificial General Intelligence,* Ben Goertzel and Cassio Pennachin, Eds, Springer, 2007.

97   http://www.opencyc.org/.

98   https://en.wikipedia.org/wiki/Cyc#Terrorism_Knowledge_Base.

99   SuperIntelligence: Paths, Dangers, Strategies, Nick Bostrom, Oxford University Press, 2014.

100 https://www.bigquestionsonline.com/2013/04/08/why-care-about-human-evolution-today/.

101 *Vision-21: Interdisciplinary Science and Engineering in the Era of Cyberspace,* NASA Conference Publication 10129, 1993.

102 http://www.yudkowsky.net/singularity/aibox/.

103 *True Names and the Opening of the Cyberspace Frontier,* Vernor Vinge, Tor, 2001.

104 https://googleblog.blogspot.ca/2015/11/tensorflow-smarter-machine-learning-for.html.

105 https://theintercept.com/document/2015/05/08/skynet-applying-advanced-cloud-based-behavior-analytics/.

106 http://arstechnica.co.uk/security/2016/02/the-nsas-skynet-program-may-be-killing-thousands-of-innocent-people/.

107 http://time.com/2847900/eugene-goostman-turing-test/.

108 https://medium.com/@arikaleph/facebook-m-the-anti-turing-test-74c5af19987c#.phehj3aju.

109 *The Wisdom of Crowds,* James Surowiecki, Doubleday, 2004.

110 https://www.reddit.com/r/UNU.

111 http://www.newsweek.com/artificial-intelli-gence-turns-20-11000-kentucky-derby-bet-457783.

112 https://www.singularityweblog.com/unanimous-ai-louis-rosen-berg-on-human-swarming/.

113 http://www.cl.cam.ac.uk/downloads/ring/ring-2016-09.pdf.

114 *The Sociopath Next Door,* Martha Stout, Broadway Books, 2005.

115 https://jcamillieri.files.wordpress.com/2009/01/img0021.jpg.

116 https://www.ted.com/talks/rana_el_kaliouby_this_app_knows_how_you_feel_from_the_look_on_your_face?language=en.

117 http://money.cnn.com/2016/01/07/technology/apple-emo-tient-ai/index.html.

118 http://waitbutwhy.com/2015/05/elon-musk-the-worlds-raddest-man.html.

119 http://www.businessinsider.com/elon-musk-says-we-could-put-a-million-people-on-mars-within-a-century-2015-6.

120 http://www.mauldineconomics.com/outsidethebox/ai-robotics-and-the-future-of-jobs.

121 http://www.informationweek.com/big-data/big-data-analyt-ics/ai-machine-learning-rising-in-the-enterprise/d/d-id/1323929.

122 http://www.futuretech.ox.ac.uk/www.futuretech.ox.ac.uk/

sites/futuretech.ox.ac.uk/files/The_Future_of_Employment_
OMS_Working_Paper_0.pdf.

123 *The Future Of Jobs, 2025: Working Side By Side With Robots,* Forrester Research, August 2015.

124 http://qz.com/202312/is-your-job-at-risk-from-robot-labor-
check-this-handy-interactive/.

125 http://brookfieldinstitute.ca/wp-content/uploads/2016/06/Ro-
bots-in-the-Workplace-2.pdf.

126 http://www.macleans.ca/automa-nation-will-robots-take-your-
job/.

127 https://www.oreilly.com/ideas/why-2016-is-shaping-up-to-be-
the-year-of-the-bot.

128 *The Top Emerging Technologies To Watch: 2017 To 2021,* Forrester Research, September 14, 2016.

129 http://www.twylahelps.com.

130 https://www.youtube.com/watch?v=U_VfsQkULHg.

131 http://www.computerweekly.com/news/4500252262/Chetan-Dube-
The-man-behind-the-robot-that-will-help-man-extend-his-
horizons.

132 http://www.kurzweilai.net/biocybereth-
ics-should-we-stop-a-company-from-unplugging-an-intelli-
gent-computer.

133 http://news.mit.edu/2015/computer-program-fixes-old-code-fast-
er-than-expert-engineers-0609?imm_mid=0def78&cmp=em-prog-
na-na-newsltr_20160116.

134 http://www.wired.co.uk/news/archive/2015-07/30/code-or-
gan-transplant-software-myscalpel.

135 http://www.gartner.com/newsroom/id/3143718.

136 https://www.technologyreview.com/s/540141/why-ibm-just-
bought-billions-of-medical-images-for-watson-to-look-at/.

137 http://www.fastcompany.com/3061396/the-future-of-work/why-
even-the-c-suite-might-not-be-safe-from-automation.

138 https://public.tableau.com/profile/mckinsey.analytics#!/
vizhome/AutomationandUSjobs/Technicalpotentialforautoma-
tion.

139 https://www.wired.com/2000/04/joy-2/.

140 http://www.mutualresponsibility.org/science/what-is-systems-
thinking-peter-senge-explains-systems-thinking-approach-
and-principles.

141 http://fortune.com/2015/11/11/chart-work-week-oecd/.

142 http://arstechnica.co.uk/tech-policy/2016/08/donotpay-chat-
bot-lawyer-homelessness/.

143 http://www.prnewswire.com/news-releases/ross-intelligence-an-
nounces-partnership-with-bakerhostetler-300264039.html.

144 https://lexpredict.com/portfolio/predicting-the-su-

preme-court/.

145 https://www.washingtonpost.com/news/to-your-health/
wp/2016/05/03/researchers-medical-errors-now-third-lead-
ing-cause-of-death-in-united-states/.

146 http://www.cbsnews.com/news/60-minutes-artificial-intelli-
gence-charlie-rose-robot-sophia/.

147 *A Taste of My Own Medicine: When the Doctor Is the Patient,* Edward E.
Rosenbaum, Random House, 1988.

148 *Medical Education: A Neglectful and Abusive Family System,* Catherine P.
McKegney, MD, *Family Medicine,* 1989, Vol. 21.

149 https://en.wikipedia.org/wiki/Singularitarianism.

150 http://w2.vatican.va/content/francesco/en/encyclicals/docu-
ments/papa-francesco_20150524_enciclica-laudato-si.html.

151 *Our Final Hour,* Martin Rees, Basic Books, 2003.

152 http://webcast.amps.ms.mit.edu/fall2014/AeroAstro/index-Fri-
PM.html.

153 http://futureoflife.org/2015/10/12/elon-musk-donates-10m-to-
keep-ai-beneficial/.

154 https://newrepublic.com/article/135684/declare-war-climate-
change-mobilize-wwii.

155 http://futureoflife.org/team/.

156 http://futureoflife.org/open-letter-autonomous-weapons/.

157 http://cser.org/about/our-mission/.

158 SuperIntelligence: Paths, Dangers, Strategies, Nick Bostrom, Oxford University Press, 2014.

159 https://www.whitehouse.gov/blog/2016/05/03/preparing-fu-
ture-artificial-intelligence.

160 https://www.washingtonpost.com/news/the-switch/
wp/2015/01/28/bill-gates-on-dangers-of-artificial-intelli-
gence-dont-understand-why-some-people-are-not-concerned/.

161 http://www.bbc.com/news/technology-30333671.

162 *The Most Human Human: What Artificial Intelligence Teaches Us About Being
Alive,* Brian Christian, Doubleday, 2011.

163 https://www.ted.com/speakers/john_maeda.

164 *Gentle Bridges: Conversations with the Dalai Lama on the Sciences of Mind,*
Jeremy Hayward and Francisco Varela, eds, Shambhala Publications,
1992.

165 http://www.nytimes.com/2016/04/28/world/asia/china-ro-
bot-monk-temple.html.

166 http://m.sohu.com/n/443524861/.

167 http://www.huffingtonpost.com/marianne-williamson/the-revolu-
tion-of-conscio_b_5574514.html.

168 http://charleseisenstein.net/books/the-more-beautiful-world-
our-hearts-know-is-possible/nondoing/.

Index

▲
Composed in Adobe InDesign
using the
Arno Pro & Hypatia Sans Pro typeface families
▼

Peter J. Scott's résumé reads like a Monty Python punchline: half business coach, half information technology specialist, half teacher, three-quarters daddy. After receiving a master's degree in Computer Science from Cambridge University, he has worked for NASA's Jet Propulsion Laboratory as an employee and contractor for over thirty years, helping advance our exploration of the Solar System. Over the years, he branched out into writing technical books and training. Yet at the same time, he developed a parallel career in "soft" fields of human development, getting certifications in NeuroLinguistic Programming from founder John Grinder and in coaching from the International Coaching Federation. In 2007 he co-created a convention honoring the centennial of the birth of author Robert Heinlein, attended by over 700 science fiction fans and aerospace experts, a unique fusion of the visionary with the concrete. Bridging these disparate worlds positions him to envisage a delicate solution to the existential crises facing humanity. He lives in the Pacific Northwest with his wife and two daughters, writing the Human Cusp blog on dealing with exponential change.

www.HumanCusp.com

Author photo by Trevor Bonderud.
Cover image: Hubble telescope image of the Helix nebula. Courtesy NASA/JPL/Caltech.
Cover design by James Gifford.

Made in the USA
San Bernardino, CA
14 February 2019